AF361626

THE CHINESE ATLANTIC

FRAMING THE GLOBAL SERIES

The Framing the Global project, an initiative of Indiana University Press
and the Indiana University Center for the Study of Global Change,
is funded by the Andrew W. Mellon Foundation.

HILARY E. KAHN AND DEBORAH PISTON-HATLEN,
SERIES EDITORS

Advisory Committee

Alfred C. Aman Jr.   Bruce L. Jaffee
Eduardo Brondizio   Patrick O'Meara
Maria Bucur   Radhika Parameswaran

Richard R. Wilk

THE CHINESE ATLANTIC

SEASCAPES AND THE THEATRICALITY OF GLOBALIZATION

SEAN METZGER

INDIANA UNIVERSITY PRESS

This book is a publication of

INDIANA UNIVERSITY PRESS
Office of Scholarly Publishing
Herman B Wells Library 350
1320 East 10th Street
Bloomington, Indiana 47405 USA

iupress.indiana.edu

© 2020 by Sean Metzger

All rights reserved
No part of this book may be reproduced
or utilized in any form or by any means,
electronic or mechanical, including photo-
copying and recording, or by any information storage and retrieval system, without
permission in writing from the publisher.
The paper used in this publication meets
the minimum requirements of the
American National Standard for
Information Sciences—Permanence
of Paper for Printed Library Materials,
ANSI Z39.48-1992.

Manufactured in the United States of
America

Cataloging information is available from the
Library of Congress.

ISBN 978-0-253-04736-6 (hardback)
ISBN 978-0-253-04751-9 (paperback)
ISBN 978-0-253-04753-3 (ebook)

1 2 3 4 5 25 24 23 22 21 20

For Marc Major,
who showed me how to navigate the global,
and our dog Cleo,
who insists on the production of locality.

CONTENTS

THE CHINESE ATLANTIC

PROLOGUE

AN IMPROMPTU CRABBING EXPEDITION IN TRINIDAD: NOT BEING much of a nature guy, I inspected a machete that I found, quite curiously, placed in my hand. So you spot a scurrying decapod and use the blade to scoop it into the basket? I neglected to vocalize my confusion, believing the answer would present itself in the appropriate situation. Into the twilight I marched with my hosts. A couple hours of chasing crustaceans left me with no understanding of the appropriate relationship between sword and crab. When we returned, machete still in hand, I asked after its purpose. "That's to fight off bandits," announced my evening guide.

"Bandits as in . . ."

"Mangroves . . . drugs . . . doh min' dat." My host shook his head and smiled. Clearly, I did not understand the potential perils of Mayaro, a community that includes many rental homes along the beach and those who might take advantage of properties left vacant for extended periods of time. As I stared at my blade, the leader of my shellfish expedition laid a pistol before me on the table.

The research for this book frequently immersed me in unexpected situations. In this particular case, I had arrived in Trinidad intending to do archival work on artist and writer Willi Chen before I learned that he kept most of his writings scattered across his very cluttered study. In fact, the plays I had hoped to access were, in Chen's estimation, not worthy of scrutiny. Instead, he expressed an eagerness to share with me his visual art, some of his short stories, and the company of his kin. Over the course of several days, I met his wife, his sister, most of his brothers, and several of his children, one of whom had taken me for an evening of crabbing. The artist's archive opened into the world he experienced as recounted in family reminiscing as well as in their current preoccupations, which included much discussion of the many pit bulls raised to protect household assets.

My research process began to alter; I became an observer of daily habits and also a houseguest cared for and scrutinized by what became the host family of me and my "friend." Having landed on the island with my partner, I expected to do my research during the day and to take the evenings for touristy activities. However, I found us whisked out of Port of Spain before I had a chance to explain our relationship. So I didn't. Nor did I answer directly the questions about marriage and girlfriends posed to me. I learned about the Chen clan, and they watched over us. As literary scholar and my former professor King-Kok Cheung has written, silence can articulate. And in this case, my queer hush enabled me to perform the role of an academic invested in Chinese flows through the Caribbean because of my own familial background, notwithstanding (or maybe because of?) the white guy at my side. The interest in my Chinese ancestors or lives that might have paralleled those of my forebears seemed to justify our presence, perhaps because of the primacy accorded to biological family units in stories concerning migration. Even though my own work renders suspect the ideas that race inheres in bloodlines and that households sustain ethnicity, I found it all too easy to claim to investigate Chinese roots in different parts of the world.

This claim may not be totally spurious. Sometime during the writing of this book, my mother asked me if her grandfather had influenced the direction of my research. A Chinese man who had moved from China to Cuba in the early twentieth century, my great-grandfather had left his family for opportunities overseas. He returned to China only once while my grandmother was living there. Indeed, his departure may have been the reason why my grandmother submitted, sight unseen, to an arranged marriage with a San Francisco-based Chinese man a dozen years her senior. The details of my great-grandfather's migrations interest me less than the lacuna they have generated in terms of family origin stories. To some extent, my mother was right: This book emerges from that gap in knowledge as speculation became the stuff of family legend. The missing patriarch served as a sort of breakwater that interrupted the flow of Chinese kin from one shore to another. My family's history, like those of many Asian American families, fits within complex models of US immigration but also seeps outside of such paradigms. My own family's journeys to seek economic opportunity reminded me of the Chens', but the paths that our respective families took also differed in many respects. However, pursuing inquiries in both cases required an archaeology of seaways that might surface journeys for which no tracks remain.

One of Willi Chen's brothers was, in fact, writing a family history during my first visit to Trinidad. Transoceanic migration had also split his people, some landing in Kingston and others in Port of Spain. The migrant groups evolved into different clans, separated by the sea that facilitated little interaction for them. That story resonated with me, as my ancestors had also drifted apart following marine currents to different fates, many of which remain unknown to me. In part, my mother was right. This book dives to certain depths to allow stories and images of people who have left, for the most part, only scant traces to bob up. In that manner, I follow scholars like Saidiya Hartman and Christina Sharpe, who work in the wake of the slave trade, although I am more focused on that system's replacement by coolie traffic. Furthermore, I am comparatively less interested than Chen, Hartman, or Sharpe in loss and fragmentation, my own ancestral story, or even narrative itself.

My shift of emphasis is one of degree rather than kind. The artistic works I analyze in the following pages frequently center on familial loss. However, my inquiries highlight what Hartman calls "making possibility out of dispossession."[1]

This book examines how artworks invent or otherwise help us to imagine ways of seeing the world and its interconnections that push against dominant paradigms. In this regard, Chinese families become one means of mapping a larger history of capitalism. Here, I am reminded of work such as that of anthropologist Aihwa Ong and her selective tracing of these currents. In contrast to Ong's work, which has emphasized movements across the Pacific Ocean, I am interested in how the histories of Chinese circulations might play out or be challenged in cultural production within the region often seen as the cradle of capitalism: the Atlantic world.

The unfinished stories about Trinidad and Cuba served as ports of departure for this project; another had to do with my interests in Caribbean art and intellectual history. My first book, which overlapped with work on this one, owes much to the writings of Martinique-born Frantz Fanon and his particular thoughts on processes of racialization. I thank those teachers with whom I first became acquainted with him, including Marie-Florine Bruneau, Marsha Kinder, Karen Shimakawa, and Teresa de Lauretis. Such study led me to explore Caribbean film, literature, and philosophy more broadly, and, in that reading, I encountered the work of Carlos Felipe, whose play *El Chino* stuck with me. The narrative of that play, which features a Chinese brothel owner in Cuba, is circular like an Ionesco piece; the theatrical repetition may well have prompted my continual return to this topic. The 2003 Asian American Studies conference gave me the first opportunity to think about the idea of what I called Chinese/Cuban cultural critique.

When I arrived at my first tenure track job at Duke University in 2004, I became submerged in conversations about the Atlantic. Recruited through an "Asian American literature and culture" line in an English department, I became the first Asian Americanist ever hired as such at the university. To support my work (and avoid loneliness), I sought allies on campus. Moving through various networks, I met an undergraduate student, Stephanie Crystal Fung, who asked me to do an independent study with her in 2005 on Chinese Caribbean and Latin American literature. That experience served as a catalyst. Engaging this body of literature pushed me to think about the compartmentalization of race in the United States into discrete categories: black, Asian American, Latinx, and Native American.

I had the opportunity to develop and expand my thinking when the Race, Space, Place (RSP) collective took shape at Duke in 2006–2007. For that first engaging year, I applaud our faculty and graduate student reading group: Michaeline Crichlow, Ishtar Govia, Alexis Pauline Gumbs, Patricia Northover, JoAnna Poblete, Matthew Jordan Smith, Maurice Wallace, and Ara Wilson, as well as the many participants at our final conference, particularly Francisco-J. Hernández Adrián, Saskia Sassen, and Rebecca J. Scott. RSP has morphed over the years, but Michaeline and Adrián became my sustained interlocutors from that first public event through the 2010 States of Freedom/Freedom of States conference in Jamaica (thanks to Deborah Jenson and, again, to Patricia Northover) to our Islands, Images, and Imaginaries working group, which convened throughout 2011–2012 and then again in the summer of 2013. Overlapping this last endeavor, the additional participants in the "Chinese in Africa" reading group from 2011–2012 planted the seeds for what has become chapter 5 of this book; my appreciation remains for the discussions I had with Michaeline Crichlow, Howard W. French, Margaret C. Lee, Ralph Litzinger, J. Lorand Matory, Charlie Piot, and Carlos Rojas.

During those years, this ongoing intellectual activity began to put pressure on how I constructed my principal research stream (which eventually produced my first book, *Chinese Looks*). In that first study, I followed Rey Chow and others in terms of reevaluating how *Chinese* and *Chineseness* signify, particularly as descriptions of culture, race, ethnicity, and nationality tended to become intermeshed. This line of questioning continues in this book, where I again scrutinize Chineseness in order to consider the contexts that activate it as a meaningful. Whereas the analysis in *Chinese Looks* examined dress through a Sino/American interface, my project here looks at the meanings of Chineseness across comparatively broader spatial coordinates.

Per my work more generally, I use the term *Chineseness* to indicate the forces that construct the term *Chinese*, which means very different things in different historical and spatial contexts. In other words, I do not assume that the word *Chinese* refers back to some stable referent, like the current nation-state of China (which, in its present form, has existed for less than one hundred years and which continues disputes with Taiwan and many other countries about its jurisdiction and boundaries). Given that my first book examined how certain material conditions in the United States produced particular understandings of China and Chineseness for mainstream audiences at different moments in Sino-American relations, I wondered about how Chineseness manifested in other areas of the globe.

The Chinese Atlantic follows this line of inquiry: Rather than assuming that *Chinese* designates or points back to a specific culture, geography or kinship relation, I examine in the following pages how Chinese and Chineseness are produced contingently in response to locations beyond the bounds of my first book. In choosing geographic locales largely outside of the United States, I attempt to decenter globalization, shifting to nodal points that highlight Chinese-inflected processes of cultural assertion, capital accumulation, and artistic invention. The shifts across space do not mean that the book aims to be infinitely expansive.

Instead, I began by thinking about an intervention in the conceptual geography of Atlantic, particularly black Atlantic, studies. My neologism, the Chinese Atlantic, therefore, started not as a name for a new empirical phenomenon; rather, I sought a method of revisiting some of the central issues of black Atlantic studies through a deconstructive lens. In some ways, I extend in very different directions Paul Gilroy's ruminations in his book *Darker than Blue: On the Moral Economies of Black Atlantic Culture*. His call for a more global and less provincial African American and African diasporic framework provided impetus for me to ponder the boundaries of Chinese diaspora and Asian American studies, each of which has been undergoing their own expansions through approaches like Sinophone studies and hemispheric analysis. Gilroy's emphasis on consumer culture inspires here an inquiry into the spread of capitalism, where I join other scholars like Lisa Lowe. His query on human rights inspires my own examination of human traffic.

The major propelling force for conceptualizing this project as a book was my participation in the Framing the Global fellowship program from 2011–2018. This opportunity afforded me conversations concerning how one conceives of and studies global processes. What methodologies might produce the sort of large-scale analyses appropriate for a global rubric? What evidence might sustain generalizations about global discourses? In contemplating these conundrums, Framing the Global functioned like a research team for me. Stephanie Smith and Jennika Baines arrived on the editorial team in time to provide a needed push to the finish line. To Cathy Kreyche, I owe a debt I can never repay, as she listened to me work through every idea and read every sentence in this text. In general, I am sure I learned more from than I contributed to the scholars in Framing the Global group. I am indebted to our conversations both in terms of substance and also in terms of learning how to talk across disciplines. Thanks to Tim Bartley, Manuela Ciotti, Deborah Cohen, Stephanie DeBoer, Lessie Jo Frazier, Zsuzsa Gille, Anne Griffiths, Rachel Harvey, Hilary Kahn, Prakash Kumar, Michael Mascarenhas, Deirdre McKay, Faranak Miraftab, Alex Perullo, Deborah Piston-Hatlen, Katerina Teiwa, and Rebecca Tolen (whose memory I hope this book will honor). The Framing the Global conferences held in 2012, 2013, and 2018 provided much stimulus for developing my ideas. In particular, meeting Gillian Hart not only changed the way I thought about South Africa in relation to Chinese flows of people and capital, but it also reinforced the importance of that nation-state in thinking through my topic. As one of the few arts and humanities scholars in the Framing the Global group, I contemplated how imagination and artistic production might reflect and mold processes of globalization. Pursuing these quandaries, the book began to take shape as an inquiry into method as much or even more than a study of the economic and cultural flows that might describe processes I ultimately gather under the Chinese Atlantic.

Opportunities through UCLA also forged this book. I am grateful for the students in my undergraduate class "Debating Globalization," taught through the UC Education Abroad Program at Fudan University in Shanghai during the fall of 2014; my intermittent meals with Shu-mei Shih during that time informed my thinking more than she could know. I also thank the graduate students in my Transnational Media and Performance seminars in fall 2012 and winter 2017, as well as in my seminar on "Performance and the Postcolonial," where I worked through some of the bibliography. Anurima Banerji, Andrea Goldman, Aparna Sharma, and R. Bin Wong invited me to a yearlong working group on ritual that fostered my thinking about chapter 3; the Urban Humanities Initiative faculty group (2016–2017) offered themselves as the trial audience for another portion of the tai chi material. David Kim helped me at a crucial time with a translation check. My friends and colleagues Michelle Liu Carriger, Yogita Goyal, Suk-Young Kim, Ellen Scott, Jasmine Trice, and Shane Vogel all read a draft of the manuscript; I am ever indebted to these fabulous folks. Linzi Juliano, Carla Neuss, and Gwyneth Shanks (who has read almost every page) served as my research assistants; without them, I might have given up.

Other current and former colleagues at UCLA and elsewhere have all supported me in important ways and sometimes unbeknownst to them. Thanks to Joseph Bristow, Alexandra Chang, Allyson Field, Grace Hong, Cathy Irwin, Jinqi Ling, Tavia Nyong'o, Leah Rosenberg, and Kim Welch. Across town, my queer of-color reading group also spurred my thinking. For food, companionship, and good talks, my appreciation goes to Lucas Hildebrand, Sarita See, Kyla Thompkins, Karen Tongson, and Hentyle Yapp. Of course, the book would not have been possible without the many artists who allowed me access to and frequently shared their thoughts about their work. I have given each due attention in the book, so I refrain from listing them here.

"In the field," I would like to thank the many people who made me feel at home when I was far away. The list also indicates the networks required to do a project like this one. I owe much gratitude to my Trinidad contacts during my visits in 2008, 2014, and 2016: Christopher Cozier, Willi Chen and his family, Geoffrey MacLean, and Nimah Muwakil-Zakuri. For his repeated attention to my visits every other year to Martinique from 2012–2016 (and for that emergency visit to the hospital), *merci* Michel Assouvie. I also thank Isabelle Dubost, who generously shared her research. In Amsterdam, Maaike Bleeker, Walter Melion, Sjoerd Oostrik, and Marike Splint prompted my thinking about the legacies of Dutch colonialism. My pals in Montreal have provided warmth and conversation over these last several years and many visits short and long; thank you to Alice Jim, Patrick Leroux, Greg Robinson, Tom Waugh, Mary SuiYee Wong, and Tracy Zhang. Another Canadian, Richard Fung, has been exceptionally generous with his time and his work. Finally, I thank the people who guided my research in South Africa (2008, 2012, 2015, 2018): Evelyn and Willi Bester, Sven Christian, Francis Chouler, the elusive DALeast (who virtually guided me to his remaining murals in Cape Town), Sakhisizwe Gcina, Sven Grimm, Jay Panther, Tina Steiner, and Wu Qianlong.

Over the last decade, I tested several ideas at various events and meetings. My fellow panelists and the audiences at the following conferences have helped rework this text: the IX Encuentro (2014), the American Comparative Literature Association (2014, 2016, and 2017), the American Society for Theatre Research (2012, 2013, 2015), the American Studies Association (2016), the Asian Experience in the Caribbean and the Guyanas (2007), the Association for Asian American Studies (2016), the Caribbean Studies Association (2012), the Modern Language Association (2014), and Performance Studies International (2016, 2017, 2018). I am especially grateful to Colleen Daniher, Esther Kim Lee, Christine Mok, Ju Yon Kim, Lok Siu, and Jack Tchen for feedback at various points.

Audiences at Brown University (special thanks to Patricia Ybarra and Rebecca Schneider), the Chinese American Museum, Columbia University, Duke University, Hong Kong University of Science and Technology (especially Daisy Du), Indiana University, Monash University (as ever, Olivia Khoo), USC (especially Dorinne Kondo, Viet Nguyen, and Nayan Shah), the University of Connecticut (thanks especially to Cathy Schlund-Vials and Margo Machida), the University of Melbourne (thanks to Sarah Balkin, Eddie Paterson, Paul Rae, and Robert Walton), the University of Washington (especially Scott Magelssen), and the Zeitz Museum of Contemporary Art Africa all provided nurturing environments for me to think through some of my arguments. I appreciate the receptivity to scholarship in progress.

As one might imagine, this book reflects a lot of research costs. In addition to Indiana University's Framing the Global project, funding at various stages came from my home university. At Duke, supporting units included the Center for African and African American Research, the Center for Latin American and Caribbean Studies, and the Visual Studies Initiative. At UCLA, I also benefited from a number of funding sources, including several faculty research grants and money from the Institute of American Cultures, the TFT Dean's Vision Fund, and the UCLA Urban Humanities Initiative. Michaeline Crichlow, David Eng, Brian Kite, Jo Lee, Fred Moten, Karen Shimakawa, and Priscilla Wald have all written supporting letters or performed other miracles to support my many funding applications, both successful and not. I thank them all for their exceptional efforts on my behalf.

I have written the genealogy of this book at some length to explain something about the methodology and interdisciplinary engagements that helped me to produce this text. Part of the process involved reading everything I could find in English or French on Chinese in the Caribbean, since that region served to anchor the study. I have far more limited linguistic skills in other languages, but I sought assistance with Mandarin and Spanish when my own abilities frequently faltered. I asked for a lot of help when encountering work framed in Afrikaans, Antillean Creole, Dutch, German, or Xhosa. I have dispersed my archival research throughout the book, where it most pertains to my arguments. These engagements, as I have endeavored to illustrate in this prologue, have been shaped by numerous live encounters, including structured interviews as well as hundreds of informal conversations I have had over the years of researching and writing. Chinese Caribbean scholarship is largely emergent, and I view my own contributions as enlarging a critical dialogue. The book is less an account of a singular phenomenon than a series of ongoing engagements with global processes, the outcomes of which are often not yet clear. I invite the reader to think with me as opposed to expecting an airtight analysis. To understand globalization requires, in my view, a dialogic and inductive approach that works against top-down views that produce generalizations rarely sustainable when applied across particular localities.

In the spirit of a developing scholarly dialogue, I published several earlier iterations of specific sections during the course of the last several years. My initial thoughts for the introduction and chapter 3 appeared in a book collection as part of my work with the Framing the Global Fellowship. This work, "Seascape: The Chinese Atlantic," in *Framing the Global: Entry Points for Research*, ed. Hilary Kahn (Bloomington: Indiana University Press, 2014), 276–295, has been substantially revised and extended to elaborate the key terms of my argument and situate my analysis in a longer genealogy of seascapes (to balance the more personal intellectual journey I relate in the prologue).

Chapter 1 draws some material from and reassembles pieces of writing I have done for different purposes, often with different examples. See "Caribbean Art and Chinese Imaginaries" (Los Angeles: Chinese American Museum, 2018), 196–213, and a short, but for me generative, piece, "Chineseness in Caribbean Cinema," *sx salon* 17 (October 2014), http://smallaxe.net /wordpress3/discussions/2014/10/22/chineseness-in-caribbean-cinema/. The Rigoberto Lopez discussion was part of an essay that explored an early chapter I considered including. For various reasons, I eliminated most of this line of research here. See "Unsettling: Towards a Chinese/Cuban Cultural Critique," *Cultural Dynamics* 21, no. 3 (November 2009): 317–338. This chapter submerges the reader in various examples as an analogue to being immersed in a seascape and in globalization.

Chapter 2 significantly elaborates my earlier journal publication, "Incorporating: Chineseness in Chen's Trinidad," *The Global South* 6, no. 1 (2012), 98–113. I have emphasized the visual culture elements of this earlier work. I have also reframed the argument based on additional artistic works and ethnographic and historical research.

Part of chapter 4 appears as "Isaac Julien's Ten Thousand Waves: Screening Human Traffic and the Logic of Ebbing," in *The Routledge Handbook of New Media in Asia*, eds. Larissa Hjorth and Olivia Khoo (New York: Routledge, 2015), 285–295.

All of these pieces have been recontextualized and, in some cases, radically altered. They constitute part of a long process of research, thinking, reconsidering, and rewriting that has ultimately produced *The Chinese Atlantic*. The book immerses the reader in my contingent conclusions and the journeys to them to offer new modes of analysis in our increasingly global world.

Before embarking on this intellectual voyage, I offer one more story about this project's launch. Although this particular tale does not involve Chineseness and only references potential seascapes obliquely if at all, it reminds me why studies of globalization matter. My partner worked for a consulting firm hired by Walmart to develop its environmental sustainability strategy. I would hear the echoes of conference calls about pushing this corporate monolith to act more responsibly in regard to the environment, especially since its founder had located the company in a remote corner of Arkansas in part in order to take advantage of disparate pheasant hunting seasons in three states. From humble beginnings, Walmart's rapid growth had led to impacts at an unforeseen scale. One overheard conversation involved testing the market with a set of clothes made from organic cotton. Eventually, Walmart executives realized this attempt would not immediately be possible, in spite of their desires, because the order for that much organic cotton would deplete the world's supply, given the years required to transform a traditional cotton field into an organic one. I heard this living in the American South, where the cotton plantation is overdetermined. That a single proposed shift in product would have this effect stunned me and left me considering available strategies of representation for this sort of phenomenon. Moreover, it forced me to scrutinize the ways individuals live awash in global flows of which most people remain unaware. I wrote this book with such a sense of overflow in mind. How do we see processes in which we are always already immersed?

The first drafts of this book attempted to replicate that sensation of immersion by generating a prose analogue to being adrift at sea. I had wanted the argument to surface here and there as the reader floated through a series of images and my analyses of them. Ultimately, that structure seemed to leave my audience too disoriented to follow my lead. I have in this published version corrected course a bit, offering a somewhat more linear trajectory with buoys in the forms of subheadings and the like to assist the reader in catching a view of the overall constellation guiding the argument. Notwithstanding these efforts, I value the frequent opacity of the sea and the discombobulation of tempestuous waves. We need not dive in, for we are already submerged.

NOTE

1. Saidiya Hartman, *Lose Your Mother: A Journey Along the Atlantic Slave Route* (New York: Farrar, Straus and Giroux, 2007), 7.

INTRODUCTION

THE FLYING DUTCHMAN INTRODUCED ME TO THEATRICAL SEASCAPES. As my family could not afford expensive seats, I sat surrounded by strangers in the balcony of the San Francisco Opera in an uncomfortable suit for the duration of the performance, which lasted well over two hours sans intermission. The first opera I had ever seen staged left an indelible impression on me; it would be several years before I would willingly listen to Wagner. I can still see the spectral ship and hear the spinning chorus. Thirty years later, I thought about the *Dutchman* again, but in a very different context. Purportedly, the *Dutchman* sank off the Cape of Good Hope while under contract by the Dutch East India Company (or the Vereenigde Oost-Indische Compagnie, or VOC). That transnational corporation founded in the seventeenth century serves as a historical mooring for contemporary discourses of globalization, and it provided the vessels to transport Chinese goods and people from Asia to the Atlantic. Dutch colonialism forms a background for this book, and so the *Dutchman* looms, with its indeterminate cargo, to haunt the pages that follow.

Sightings of the *Flying Dutchman* as a ghost ship have continued well past the decline of the Dutch Golden Age, and here, legends from the Netherlands intersect the lexicon of several other European colonial powers. A mirage on the horizon is called a fata morgana. The Italian variant of famed enchantress

"

Morgan Le Fay, the name continues to denote an optical phenomenon produced by light refracting due to air temperature variations particularly present near the ocean's surface. Fata morgana denotes a phenomenological engagement in which humans perceive an empirical phenomenon as a vision partially produced by the sea. A fata morgana thus raises questions about how we see and what we interpret in the visual field.

These qualities may explain why the French surrealist André Breton decided to call his 1940 poem *Fata Morgana*. Breton asked a young protégé of Picasso to illustrate the book. The artist undertook this task before returning to the Caribbean; that man was Wifredo Lam, a Cuban of African and Chinese descent and now perhaps the most famous painter from the region. Lam's images also haunt my imagination. Although I have not chosen to include discussion of his work in what follows because of limitations of scope and expertise, the trajectory I have outlined raises some of the questions I pursue hereafter.[1] Like the *Flying Dutchman* and its unexpected connection to Lam, how and under what conditions do we perceive networks of cultural exchange?

The Chinese Atlantic: Seascapes and the Theatricality of Globalization complicates and reworks theories of aesthetic, financial, and human movement by examining the experiences of and fantasies about people of Chinese descent (*huayi*) and overseas Chinese (*huaqiao*)—both categories that link the disparate geographies of the Pacific and the Atlantic and thereby destabilize epistemological frameworks such as the "Black Atlantic" or the "Pacific Rim." I focus on small islands, often seen as inconsequential in discussions of transnational art and finance.[2] To some degree, this emphasis recognizes an empirical reality of China's expansion around the world; foreign policy enacted through soft power as well as more traditional instruments of trade and military deployment (the Spratly Islands being a relevant recent example).[3] The changing material conditions of these ostensibly bounded spaces facilitate the frequently stark visualization of Chinese circulations in sometimes surprising places. However, they do not, or at least do not only, reflect the spread of Chinese hegemony. Indeed, insular sites render perceptible the morass of anxiety and aspiration through which Chinese speculation might be adjudicated. My project insists that globalization registers in but is also enacted through Chinese cultural investments, and centers on Chineseness in the Caribbean (with comparative studies of other sites from Canada to England to South Africa) to provide a genealogy for our current era, when Chinese capital seems suddenly everywhere.

The book is a multisited endeavor that interrogates theories of race in relation to notions of space. *The Chinese Atlantic* focuses on seascapes that depict islands to explore how globalization is often experienced, mediated, and institutionalized through national formations (here, I mean not only nation-states but also subnational political entities such as France's overseas departments). In other words, while globalization is often thought to occur at a level or scale beyond the nation-state, it is at the national level that we often witness the dramatic transformations of globalization—as once national institutions (including many banks and national performing arts centers) participate in and help to invent new forms of economic transaction and political procedure that move beyond the reach of regulations and other traditional instruments of nation-state power.

CHINESE-INFLECTED GLOBALIZATION

Popular Western news media describe China's industrial practices and its waste as an indicator of globalization today.[4] This argument casts globalization as the diffusion of capitalism and assumes that this mode of production organizes the larger social and political world. In western Europe and the United States, globalization has often been taken to reduce the juridical power of nation-states, particularly as multinational corporations evade regulation by moving selected functions "offshore." The handmaiden to these processes is neoliberalism: economic and political discourses and material processes that espouse individualist enterprise as the path to human well-being and freedom.[5] However, China raises serious challenges to such assertions, since regulation has proliferated along with the autocratic rule of the Chinese communist party, even as China's role in the global marketplace has rapidly expanded.

To understand this paradox, scholars have argued quite convincingly that the increasing interdependence of a capitalist world economy not only produces contradictory effects, but is itself produced by power dynamics, some of which weaken and others of which strengthen the authority of nation-states.[6] Although a narrative of neoliberalism might seem to celebrate the ineluctable spread of capitalism to every part of the globe, one might better explain China's current situation as the most recent of several large-scale, and, importantly, state-led modernization projects that China undertook during the twentieth century.[7] A model of progressive development that posits a more or less linear trajectory—from socialist isolation to the policies of reform and opening (*gaige kaifeng*) initiated by Deng Xiaoping to China's joining the WTO in 2001, followed by its successful hosting of the Olympic Games in 2008 and the Shanghai World Expo in 2010—fails to acknowledge that China has been and continues to be an active agent in the development of an increasingly globalized economy.[8]

Transoceanic cultural and economic contacts have helped to shape China at least as early as the Ming Dynasty (1368–1644). In this period, Jesuit missionaries' influence in the Middle Kingdom peaked, as evidenced through figures like Matteo Ricci (1552–1610). If religious conversion and intellectual exchange characterized the Jesuit presence through the sixteenth and into the seventeenth centuries as much as commercial interests, this situation would certainly change by the mid-seventeenth century as the Dutch East India Company expanded its overseas networks throughout Asia.

Scholar Giovanni Arrighi further reminds us that the period just prior to this age of European imperialism marked the apex of China's early modern nautical explorations.[9] The theorist of global capitalism notes that seafaring expanded China's economy from the Southern Song (1127–1279) through the early Ming dynasties, after which such ventures proved too costly to continue, thereby fostering China's turn inward. Yet, during the later Qing Dynasty (1644–1911), the Middle Kingdom constituted the largest market in the eighteenth-century world. This development is in many ways distinct from European expansion through overseas acquisitions and trade. First, the Chinese state did not generally yield authority to merchants and entrepreneurs, so the Chinese economic example should be considered a market economy within a noncapitalist state. This situation differs from that produced by a large firm like the British East India Company acting as a sovereign power, albeit nominally under the control of a European government.[10] Second, the Qing Dynasty pushed terrestrial expansion toward the current landmass over which the People's Republic of China now claims sovereignty. The contested claims to so much territory would, of course, cause the Qing government (and those that followed) many problems, but these situations arose in part as a response to the Qing's imperialist practices even as this last dynasty ceded some of its autonomy to American, European, and Japanese powers. Third, protocapitalist activity continued outside of the empire's immediate oversight among *huaqiao* populations.

These histories assist in explaining and complicating a narrative that centers the Atlantic as the cradle of global capitalism. Early Chinese–European connections, such as those in the Ming period, potentially shift the conventional view of China's rapid industrialization and sudden rise to dominance in the global economy.[11] Reframing such narratives can draw attention to, for example, overseas Chinese actors that receive little attention in major world news outlets, but that nevertheless might contribute to a richer understanding of global processes and the ways in which Chinese elements influence and are constructed by them.

Early transnational corporations (the Dutch East India Company, as well as the Dutch West India Company and British East India Company) initiated and sustained relationships among far-flung locales.[12] It bears remembering that the Dutch Empire dominated its European rivals in overseas trade during the second half of the seventeenth century, often called the Dutch Golden Age. Both the Dutch and the British repeatedly attempted to gain greater access to China's markets in the eighteenth century.[13] The British, who eventually displaced their competitors as the hegemonic force of European imperialism in China, would finally push the Manchus into the Opium Wars during the mid-nineteenth century in order to secure a dominant financial position. The import of such a background for this book is twofold. The Dutch Golden Age saw the development of artistic conventions that historically define the seascape as an artistic genre. And the British East India Company as a "Company-State questions any fast bifurcation between an early modern Atlantic, defined by colonial plantation and European imperial rivalry, and a 'trading world' of Asia and the Indian Ocean."[14]

Examining some of these enduring connections raises a salient question: How are processes of globalization understood now in ways that diverge from earlier historical moments? Certainly, the multiplication of Chinese people and things indicates a diffusion of Chineseness around the world. This diffusion seems to result from an increased speed of economic, migratory, and cultural flows along with the spread of goods, technologies, and information when compared to previous centuries. This rapidity results in a perceived and, in some cases, actual condensation of space (I can take out "my" money at ATMs around the world; communication and surveillance systems have a nearly planetary reach). Globalization, then, might be defined as a material and affective interconnectedness often associated with an increase in speed and dominance of a capitalist world order. However, the processes of globalization are complicated and contradictory, and interconnectedness does not always yield interdependence. The act of quickly erecting office buildings and malls in Shanghai frequently dispossessed former residents of both their homes and their livelihoods. What the anthropologist Anna Tsing observed in Indonesia has certainly been true elsewhere: As some things speed up, others slow down.[15]

SEASCAPE AS METHODOLOGY

The Chinese Atlantic investigates specific artworks (all seascapes of different sorts) through archival, ethnographic, and formal means as well as dominant discourses and counterdiscourses that articulate the significance of Chineseness in places where Chineseness often creates contestation rather than unification. By moving through a series of works situated in different places—all of which have recently received significant streams of Chinese capital and/or migrants and all of which have relationships to historical streams of Chinese money, goods, and people—I demonstrate how understandings of Chineseness have shifted over time, contingent on local conditions. Such conditions produce different logics for us to apprehend what may at first appear as a monolithic Chinese-inflected globalization.

The seascape is the principal tool for this endeavor. I define *seascape* as (1) a watery equivalent of a landscape, (2) an epistemological frame, and (3) an event, insofar as the seascapes that interest me involve some sort of action, either as part of the visual representation itself or as part of the process of spectatorship. Seascape is, thus, both a concept and a practice. In this regard, my use of the term overlaps to a degree with its use in Karin Amimoto Ingersoll's recent book, *Waves of Knowing: A Seascape Epistemology.* However, Ingersoll concentrates on Hawaii and discusses the seascape not as an artistic genre (indeed, that genealogy of representation does not factor into her work at all) but as a specifically embodied orientation evoked but also constructed through the traditions of *Kānaka Maoli* and the surf tourism industry.[16] Although I too highlight corporeal engagements in various sections of this book, my emphasis falls on how the circulation of certain cultural forms invents and iterates, rather than reveals, particular meanings of Chineseness. The seascapes included in this book reference and further genealogies of traffic between Pacific and Atlantic spaces that resulted in the conditions that foster globalization as we witness it today. I use *seascape* to articulate and, more importantly, to *envision* an emergent episteme that describes new waves of Chinese investment—fiscal and cultural—in the Atlantic world.

The sea has long provided a principal mechanism by which commerce moved beyond the boundaries of individual states and regions, and such movements can be and have been tracked. Drawings of nautical trade routes, usually called sea charts, have existed since antiquity. These documents reveal something about how their users saw the world in terms of their orientation and scale, the language and graphics used to indicate geographic features, and the miscellany that decorated the maps. Hydrography provides a window onto marine science and larger cosmologies, and it also provides a practical navigational guide. In this latter sense, the recent excitement over the rediscovery of the Selden Map showing East Asia as viewed (scholars suppose) by Ming traders led historians to see new ways China and England have been connected, often through material exchanges.[17]

What are often less emphasized in such studies are the aesthetic traditions in which representations of the ocean might participate and the fantasies such representations engage. The formal, the affective, the performative, and the theatrical as categories of expression and analysis might bring into focus and revise the "cultural dimensions of globalization" outlined by the anthropologist Arjun Appadurai. His proposal to look at culture through five scapes—ethnoscape, financescape, technoscape, mediascape, and ideoscape—can be productively reimagined and recombined through the elaboration of the seascape offered in the following pages. Much of the canonical literature of Europe and the United States' eras of imperialism concerns the sea. Works like Samuel Taylor Coleridge's *The Rime of the Ancient Mariner* (1798), Herman Melville's *Moby Dick* (1851), and Stéphane Mallarmé's "Brise Marine" (1865) demonstrate to different degrees how Appadurai's five categories might intersect in the imaginary worlds constituted by fiction and poetry. Moreover, topics somewhat elided in Appadurai's discourse, such as gender and sexuality, surge with force in the pages of these writers. Although literature is not the primary focus here, I gesture to these celebrated works because they indicate the importance of marine art in general as a creative practice that not only frames empirical knowledge of the oceans and the landmasses connected through them but also invents new perspectives. Such worldviews might be dystopian or utopian, and they may have very little to do with any kind of verifiable facts.

As a visual medium, the seascape became codified and popular during the seventeenth century. Given the lineages of paintings on religious and mythological subjects in which the sea features (*The Odyssey* from ancient Greece and the flood from *Genesis* being some of the earliest references in the Western tradition), the depictions of individual boats on some of the earliest surviving pottery in the world, and numerous artistic renderings of naval battles across many historical traditions, the claim that seascapes as an artistic genre emerged coeval with European imperialism may elicit surprise. Yet even if Dutch masters do not pioneer the visualization of the ocean (who could do that?), they did codify particular ways of seeing the sea. Figures like Willem Van de Velde the Younger are often credited with shifting the painter's focus to the marine scenes perceived by artists and their contemporaries.[18] Moreover, patronage by the Stuarts when the Van de Velde studio moved to England, as well as several commissions by the navy, enabled the family and their chosen genre of the seascape to flourish.[19] These images do not yet turn to the sublime, as later Romantics would do. However, they do draw on an increasingly well-developed formal vocabulary at a time when thousands of Flemish and Dutch men earned their livelihoods at sea as part of merchant capitalism.[20]

Maritime trade has, of course, shifted with the ascendance of a capitalist system that continues to accelerate and expand along with the "denser and more extensive communicational networks" that both propel and are fueled by it.[21] On the one hand, overseas trade may seem increasingly antiquated; globalization would seem to name a new feature of capitalism in which the market is unrooted, one in which the mode of production may seem unmoored and increasingly difficult to navigate. At the scale of that amorphous thing we might call culture, everyday life would seem to be in a state of hyperflux as unparalleled numbers of human migrants, together with ever faster and more sophisticated technologies, alter the ways in which people inhabit the world.[22] On the other hand, stories about and images of the oceans recurrently detail the perils that thousands of people experience in traditional, albeit precarious, modes of transoceanic crossing; witness the mass drownings of Syrian refugees in the Mediterranean, rendered infamous by the 2015 photograph of a deceased Syrian boy face down in the surf. As images that attempt to suggest, account for, or even briefly arrest movement, seascapes frame not only the fluidity of changes but also the imposition of stasis otherwise difficult to grasp.

The seascape provides one lens through which to look critically at processes of globalization. As a tool of analysis, seascapes isolate particular places, but with the accompanying sense that any one vision is necessarily incomplete: A sea flows beyond the boundaries of a given border, and an apparent surface floats on top of a deep history. For example, we might frame the Opium Wars through the seascape, demonstrating how important the ocean was to establishing and maintaining a position of international political and financial hegemony because China lost those conflicts at the hands of European naval powers.[23] Images of the sea and its inhabitants point to the complicated relations of geopolitics and the flows of power that render some states dominant in particular historical moments.

For purposes of this book, Chinese-inflected globalization emphasizes things in process more than an established world order. The seascape is a particularly useful tool in this regard because it captures a moment—that is, it offers a particular perspective on the sea, which is understood to be dynamic and ever changing. As such, seascapes decenter claims to authority and territory grounded in particular places. Views from and of the ocean enable ways of seeing and knowing that emphasize not only forms that lie on surfaces but the processes that enable and sustain those forms as well as the ripple effects emanating from such constructions. Within existing scholarship, the perceptual shifts facilitated through seascapes have primarily been used to register commercial networks on a regional level (for example, Ottoman trade in the Indian Ocean, slave traffic in the Atlantic, and computer hardware in the Pacific Rim) or to reveal the precarious conditions of human connectivity on a global one (such as the threat of nuclear contamination suggested in images of the 2011 Japanese tsunami or the consequences of climate changes captured in the photos of drowned polar bears throughout the Arctic).[24] The circulations of these concepts, pictures, and materials demonstrate relationships between surface and depth; they indicate changes in both information and epistemology. From hand-painted canvases to satellite-generated imagery, the look of the aquatic world and the life sustained by it serves as a means to track processes swiftly transforming the world. Far from being anachronistic or irrelevant, the seascape remains a useful optic for thinking through the phenomena often cast under the rubric of globalization.

Thinking about a Chinese Atlantic seascape requires an orientation toward the movement of forms and recognition of China's role as a major player on the global scene. Academic work in Chinese studies and Chinese diaspora studies has considered the question of global flows in terms of subjects linked through kinship to China, and a more recent turn has considered networks facilitated through Sinitic languages.[25] If ontological questions have organized the former oeuvre—what might it mean "to be" Chinese under different conditions of migration—the latter has favored epistemological queries: How is Chineseness produced through local contexts around the world? The Chinese Atlantic seascape, however, interrogates the visuality of Chineseness without a primary emphasis on language. It provides an aperture through which Chineseness in the Atlantic may be seen and linked to a dominant power on the edge of the Pacific, thousands of miles away.

As a heuristic for global studies, seascapes demonstrate the interconnectedness of oceanic zones as physical waterways and as paradigms of knowledge. To illustrate these elements of analysis, the next section constructs a genealogy in which China has entered or might enter this discourse. Because my own work uses *seascape* to designate an aesthetic vision and a theoretical framing, the methodologies here include formal and textual analysis as well as attention to what I call the theatricality of marine scenes. Affect moves spectators from the surface of the image to a state of feeling. I shift in scale and methodology to demonstrate the elasticity that is necessary to think and write about global flows and processes.

In a genealogy of seascapes, the most important examples, for my purposes, include Théodore Géricault's *The Raft of the Medusa* (1818–1819) and Joseph Mallord William Turner's *Slave Ship* (1840). Taken together, these seascapes produce ways of envisioning uneven encounters through which we might begin to understand globalization today. Here, I would also note that the seascape was not a genre in Chinese art history, although the landscape certainly was. Nevertheless, I would note that seascape and landscape both operate as kind of "cultural practice."[26] As Ann Jensen Adams has argued

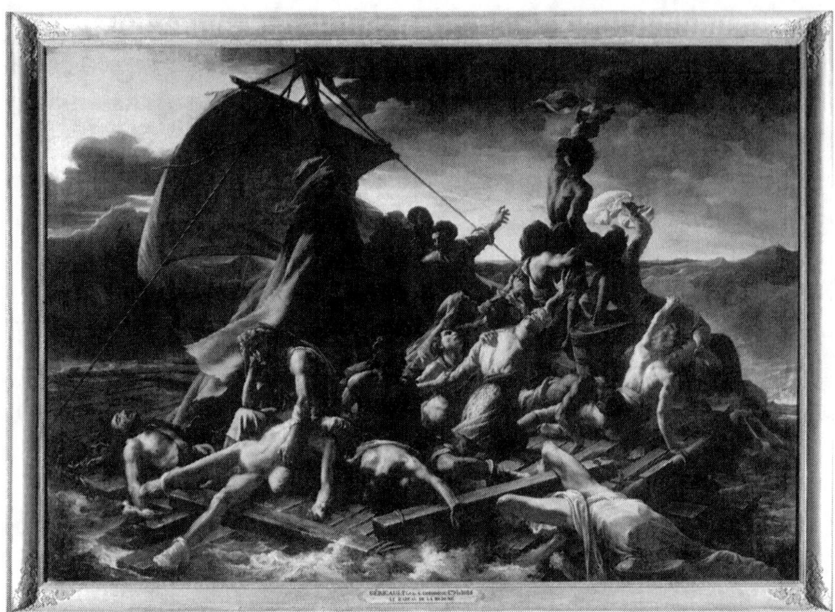

Fig. 0.1. Théodore Géricault (1791–1824), *The Raft of the* Medusa, 1819.
Musée du Louvre. Photo: Scala/ Art Resource, NY.

in relation to Dutch art, landscapes do not reflect the rural so much as they index urban concerns.[27] She follows Denis E. Cosgrove, seeing the landscape as ideological. Consonant with this view, seascapes also represent the class interests of certain parties and shape as much as they reflect historical narratives.

The Raft of the Medusa is perhaps the most famous seascape in the history of western European art. Over 16′ × 23′, the canvas is awe-inspiring. Its contemporary subject—the struggle for survival after the shipwreck of the vessel *Méduse*—depicts both the living and the dead, the latter having been based on meticulous studies of actual corpses and individuals in the process of dying. The dimensions exacerbate the gruesome quality of the scene depicted (fifteen survivors of the historical French frigate engaged in cannibalism, although this act does not appear). The dual pyramids of bodies in Géricault's masterpiece ultimately produce a sense of hope in the figure of a black man who hails rescuers and whom Géricault has positioned at the peak of stretched limbs and torsos.

The French painting brings certain colonial tensions into focus.[28] The *Méduse* met its end en route to witness the return of Senegal from the British to the French during the First Treaty of Paris, which began to shift the European balance of power as the Napoleonic Wars drew to a close. The defeat of France set the stage for the assertion of the British to control an empire on which the sun never sets. The cityscape of Shanghai to this day owes something to the international concessions established in the wake of the Opium Wars. *The Raft of the Medusa* aligns colonial infrastructure with mortality.

Slave Ship is the most provocative reference point for death on the high seas. Nowhere have the currents moving an emergent global economy been more crucial than in the Atlantic slave trade, which involved the transport of an estimated 12.5 million individuals through some 35,000 sailings over approximately three and a half centuries. The importation of low-cost human labor to particular sites for the production of goods later shipped through an extensive transnational distribution network anticipates many of the features associated with globalization today.[29] Yet the specificities of these movements, dictated as they were by "prevailing winds and ocean currents" that shaped the Atlantic system into two distinctive trade routes, is, in the end, mappable.[30] The Atlantic as a physical site vis-à-vis the transatlantic slave trade might thus seem only to serve as an antecedent for the flows that constitute the larger scale of the global.

The particular project of using the Atlantic as a heuristic has produced a productive focus on certain cultural streams while deemphasizing others; this constitutes part of the influential argument proposed by Paul Gilroy (1992) in *The Black Atlantic*. For Gilroy, "black Atlantic" names an assemblage of mobile elements that connect seemingly fixed places, sites from England to Africa to North America. His schema privileges the ship as a key term to mark mobility. The boats that motivate his discussion are not only literal ocean crafts, but also objects of discourse that surface in paintings, novels, and musical performances. Gilroy writes an intellectual trajectory to reshape British cultural studies that had, until that point, largely concerned itself with white working-class formations in England. The project shifts emphasis from these territories to a now familiar triangular model stretching from the United Kingdom through Africa to the United States. Below the sea surface (or the surface we can see) in Gilroy's work, another presence remains nascent that might complicate his admittedly fluid geography. This shadowy manifestation emerges in relation to *Slave Ship*, one of the best-known images associated with Atlantic studies. A reinterpretation of this painting facilitates a consideration of the ways in which Chineseness might drift into view and complicate rubrics like the black Atlantic.

For Gilroy, the canvas points toward transatlantic voyages through its subject matter and its own circulation. Originally titled *Slavers Throwing Overboard the Dead and Dying, Typhoon Coming On*, the painting has been much discussed for the ways in which it demands a changing sympathy for the plight of slaves. Ian Baucom has argued that Turner's depiction is most notable for evoking an "image of what we do not see," both literally beneath the deck and the waves, and more figuratively in terms of the capital investment black bodies represent and the affective responses they elicit.[31] The immediate reference for the work is the 1781 incident aboard the merchant ship *Zong*, in which the British captain ordered his slave cargo pitched overboard. The canvas itself works as something of a translation device, shifting the discourse around the ostensible subject matter from a question of inductive reasoning (such as the costs of slave traffic) to one that queries the spectator's emotive response. To gaze at the canvas is to generate feeling, sparked through formal composition: bold, clashing hues of pigment rendered through rapid brush strokes. The people in the image can be glimpsed only in fragments, most often a hand briefly escaping from the watery tomb engulfing it. This vision plays on the ways in which the seascape forecasts human fortune not only in terms of the horrific fate of the imprisoned Africans left to drown, but also of the brokers who would file an insurance claim based on cargo lost.

Baucom considers the canvas's depiction of loss (in terms of monetary capital and human life, inexorably linked) as constitutive of the modern epoch. For Baucom, the image almost threatens to flow out from the canvas to the spectator, to immerse the onlooker in the material contradictions of a system of slavery perpetuated by the British Empire. However, the border of the painting finally contains the horror depicted. This distance between viewer and object changes the potential effects of the image. Rather than a call to action, *Slave Ship* elicits a detached interest not so much in the specific scene depicted but in an aesthetic approximation of something horrible. The sentiment created is repeatable. It relies less on the particular content of the historical events involving the *Zong* and its cargo and more on a generalized

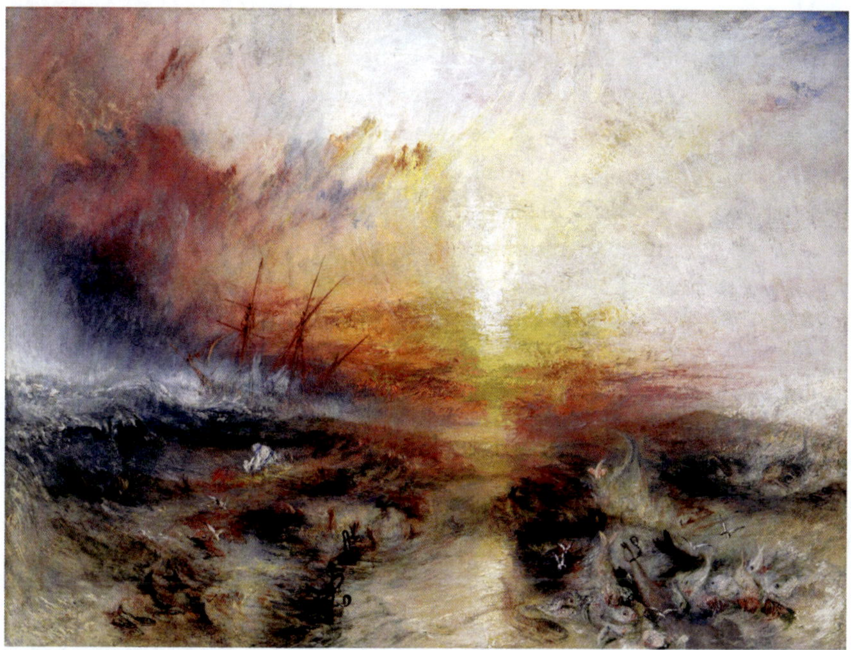

Fig. 0.2. Joseph Mallord William Turner (1775–1851), *Slave Ship (Slavers Throwing Overboard the Dead and Dying, Typhoon Coming On)*, 1840. Oil on canvas. 90.8 × 122.6 cm (35¾ × 48¼ in.). Museum of Fine Arts, Boston. Henry Lillie Pierce Fund. 99.22.

notion of slavery. The "real" event of slavery becomes a subject not so much of historical inquiry but of feelings about the past and those who have passed in the development of an industrial world (remember that Turner's lifetime witnessed the deployment of the steam engine for commercial purposes, including the shipping industry). Although not within the purview of Baucom's critical eye, this analysis of the painting as setting up a way of seeing the past within the present, of seeing a generalized notion of something horrible in relation to sea traffic and eliciting an affective response, helps to bring into relief a different laboring population also borne across the Atlantic.

From this perspective, the original title of the work allows for a geographically more expansive interpretation of Turner's *Slave Ship*. What is connoted by the phrase "Typhoon Coming On," the often forgotten subtitle? The present participle renders the scene in process but not yet fully realized. The word *typhoon* derives from weather patterns around East and South Asia; it appears in English via translation as early as 1588.[32] In the early 1600s, English clergyman Samuel Purchas described hearing *typhoon* during his travels to denote what Englishmen of the day would likely have called by the venerable label *tempest* (in use as early as the thirteenth century) or perhaps *hurricane*, a term that apparently originated from the transliteration of a Carib word that found its way into English during the sixteenth century. Given its appropriation from indigenous inhabitants of the Caribbean islands, *hurricane* would seem most appropriate, since it signifies the Atlantic passages that were Turner's subject. *Typhoon*, like its mid-nineteenth-century counterpart *cyclone*, emerged from locations far overseas from England and the principal waterways of slave trafficking, *typhoon* being linked to the Cantonese words for "big wind."

Sites like China became increasingly relevant to England and other European powers as the so-called coolie trade increased throughout the Atlantic following moves to abolish slavery during the mid-nineteenth century. As early as 1806, English merchants had experimented with obtaining labor from Asia rather than Africa to energize the plantation system. To augment the decreased (slave) workforce, planters exploited new recruits through the coolie trade, which procured field hands from various regions, primarily in India and China.[33] While Turner's work appeared too early to register the scalar expansion of coolie importation, the painting's earlier title nevertheless opens up a history of oceanic commerce until recently occluded from narratives that would historicize globalization and intersecting discourses of capitalism, liberalism, and race. This reorientation does not simply supplement existing knowledge with a recovery narrative: colonialism supplanted by ostensibly free trade. As Lisa Lowe has eloquently argued, primarily in relation to British archives from the eighteenth and nineteenth centuries, "an accommodation of both residual practices of enclosure and usurpation with new innovations of governed movement and expansion" marks new forms of imperial sovereignty that emerge in the nineteenth century in relation to Asia.[34] These emergent formations register across media not only in archival documentation, as Lowe has so ably demonstrated, but also in visual culture, like Turner's *Slave Ship*.

Given the number of masterpieces of maritime art, it is surprising that *seascape* itself is of relatively recent coinage from a historical perspective. In Dutch, "by 1718–1721, Arnold Houbraken in his *Grote Schouburgh*, an art theoretical text, uses '*zeegezicht*' (seaview) . . . and this suggests that the term was in use before then, certainly by the mid-seventeenth century, when several painters specialized in this category of picture."[35] In English, *seascape* dates to the cusp of the eighteenth and nineteenth centuries, when imperialist ventures brought visions of new expanses of oceans back to European metropoles. According to the *Oxford English Dictionary*, the earliest documented uses of the word are in 1799 and 1806 (the latter being the year that witnessed the first experimental shipment to the New World of Chinese coolie labor). Tracing the seascape particularly within English-language discourse suggests the sorts of emergence that Hester Blum has traced to oceanic studies in general—that is, the seascape "provides a new epistemology—a new dimension—for thinking about surfaces, depths, and the extra-terrestrial dimensions of planetary resources and relations."[36] Such a comment builds on studies that have situated the sea in relation to capitalism and cultural production.[37]

My work here is both less and more ambitious. I look at relatively recent visualizations of what might be called Chinese seascapes, but these provide a means of linking specific cultural flows across disparate ocean spaces. I use the term *Chinese Atlantic* to interrupt some of the logics that animate Atlantic studies writ large. Rather than the kind of generalized overarching structure that Gilroy and others have provided, I turn to particular case studies that seek to complicate notions of a totalizing configuration. My individual examples, taken together, create a different sort of assemblage, one that puts pressure on existing epistemes in order to encourage a renarration of the Atlantic and its assumed inhabitants. Although this assemblage draws on empirical shifts in the region, my goal in calling attention to the Chinese Atlantic is less to illuminate changing quotidian realities (I am neither an ethnographer nor a historian) than to point to certain fantasies about China and Chineseness evoked through the imaginative work of recent art, cinema, and performance (broadly defined), or art that functions in some ways like theater.

THEATRICALITY

In many respects, globalization is a theatrical discourse. This statement does not negate its specifically performative aspects in the sense that, for example, claims of global surveillance might produce certain legislation or behaviors.

Nor does theatricality undo the empirical realities of planetary phenomena like climate change or "nuclearization" that has resulted in all human bodies absorbing radioactive isotopes.[38] However, it does point to the ways in which people act *as if* globalization were a fait accompli. The fact that so much of the population chooses to ignore the system of undersea cables that create the Worldwide Web or that fluctuations in financial markets might result from particular actions reveals this dynamic.[39]

Samuel Weber's inquiries into the ways in which Western philosophical texts variously describe theatricality further illustrate the enmeshment of globalization and theatricality. Following Bertolt Brecht, Weber uses Beijing opera (*jingju*) to explain his ideas about theatricality as medium. Gesture and other elements of the performance create a kind of channel (medium) that "redefines activity as reactivity"; this notion shares something with Richard Schechner's views of performance as "restored behavior" or twice-behaved behavior.[40] However, Weber emphasizes the action of spectatorship more than Schechner does. His theatrical world-making is dependent on the viewer unleashing the potentiality of what could otherwise be a closed system. It is in this sense that Weber reveals the theatricality of globalization.

> *Globalization* names not so much an object as the conditions for all objectification, the conditions of cognition and action . . . [it] is a *process* by which the world of possibilities is at the same time *totalized* and *restricted*. This is why it serves as an appropriate figure to name a certain *vision* of the *world* in the post-Cold War period. The term *globalization* does not merely emphasize the transnational interdependence of different parts of the world: it implies that there is no longer any alternative to the not so new world order of "late" capitalism and to the relations of power and hierarchies of subjugation that this order entails (original emphasis).[41]

For Weber, globalization works something like certain kinds of theater in that both present a totality, a self-contained world in which actions produce reactions because there is no capacity to imagine outside this realm. Moreover, theatricality's emphasis on spectacles and audiences as well as bodies and their engagements both with each other and various forms of technology further suggests the ways in which globalization might productively be understood through theatricality. If globalization suggests a form of immersion, then theatricality renders the processes of world-making apparent by rendering immersive processes visible. In this regard, the coupling of theatricality and globalization calls attention to the fact that globalization is always about representation even when used to discuss material connections. This point, I think, is sometimes lost in the social science literature on this topic. To articulate the global is perhaps first and foremost to imagine, as Weber has emphasized, a totality, even when such articulation stresses processes as opposed to a product. Put otherwise, globalization names and stands in for specific processes of connection across vast distances and scales. Moreover, claiming the global often engages hyperbole. For example, one might say climate change is everywhere from the Artic to the Sahara, but McDonald's is certainly not.

The seascape provides a medium to see and perhaps experience globalization in relation to theatricality. Theatricality implies a frequently hyperbolic narrative and affect as well as a live event that mines the relationships among embodied action, places, and spectators. To return to a previous example, Géricault painted a dramatic tableau that pictures a moment of desperate action. Although an oil painting is a static work of art, the image nevertheless conveys dynamism through contrasts of light and color as well as the composition and arrangement of human subjects relative to their aqueous surroundings. It produces pathos and may elicit hope. The scale of Géricault's piece means that a spectator must walk away from the canvas to see the image in its entirety and then move closer to study the details.

My use of theatricality differs from that of Michael Fried, the critic and scholar who has perhaps most influentially elaborated this concept in relation to art history. Frequently cited by performance studies scholars, Fried's writing "Art and Objecthood" (1967) deals with minimalist art, or what Fried calls "literalist art." That essay, perhaps in spite of itself, helped to inaugurate a discussion of aesthetics that placed emphasis on human perception and phenomenology. Curiously, given the intense emphasis on theatricality in his text, Fried never precisely defines that term. However, he does suggest that theater and theatricality in the late 1960s had reached a crisis in which the central issue is the relationship between performer and audience. As evidence for his claims, he lists Bertolt Brecht and Antonin Artaud, although he does not explain exactly what these writers attempted in relation to theater.[42] Fried would seem to disparage a theatrical encounter in which players enact some narrative for an interested audience but one whose commitment to watching and thinking lasted only to the final curtain, when applause would signal a return to the nondiegetic world. The players thus work to engage the audience for a brief period as a distraction or escape from the spectator's everyday experience. In a later reflection on the 1967 essay and his later art historical text, *Absorption and Theatricality: Painting and Beholder in the Age of Diderot,* he succinctly sums up theatricality as "playing to an audience."[43]

In attempting to move away from the theatrical, Fried calls attention to "the actual circumstances in which the beholder encounters."[44] Contrary to Fried's evaluative remarks in 1967 and as his own writing suggests, the United States and Europe accelerated "experimental" theater-making that tried to rethink passive audience-performer relations. Various companies initiated new forms of theatrical engagement, but they also appropriated and cited conventions that insisted on audience interaction and immersion across a wide spectrum of performance traditions, from ritual to didactic theater to a host of non-Western dramatic forms. Fried, therefore, remains quite useful in bridging art history and theater by detailing how beholders do and do not engage with artworks, even if his own assessment remains inconsistent with, if not completely contradictory to, my own understandings of theatricality in relation to seascapes. Therefore, the chapters that follow revisit some of Fried's assertions, although they often extend that work in directions he did not intend and might likely oppose.

As one salient example, Fried briefly discusses *The Raft of the Medusa* in *Absorption and Theatricality.* For Fried, Géricault's display of bodies enacts "not simply . . . a desire for rescue from the appalling circumstances depicted in the painting but also by the need to escape our gaze, to put an end to being beheld by us, to be rescued from the ineluctable fact of a presence that threatens to theatricalize even their sufferings."[45] In this text, Fried is more specific in terms of his understanding of theater, arguing that his idea borrows from Diderot. Diderot, of course, would have seen his own and his contemporaries' works on stage, including plays by Pierre de Marivaux, Voltaire, and, later, Beaumarchais. Fried reads Diderot as favoring artworks that, through various mechanisms, ignore the presence of the beholder. I divagate from Fried's interpretation of Géricault's masterpiece, because I see it as staged. The raft is literally the space of human action against the tumultuous waves and nimbus clouds that threaten to overwhelm them. The particular details of the painting (based on research to produce a cadaverous likeness between the image and actual corpses) is theatrical in the most fundamental manner: One thing substitutes for something else. Although the people in the painting seem absorbed in the business of signaling for rescue or dying, the painting demands an active engagement of the spectator. To reiterate, its sheer size means that the spectator will engage the work by moving to enable different perspectives.

Such demands on the beholder elicit questions that move beyond the ethics of gazing at spectacles of human precarity (although I do not deny the painting also evokes such queries). Most obviously, the Romantic valence raises issues of the relationship between human and environment. Furthermore, for those who know the historical events that inspired its creation, the artwork implicitly queries the costs of colonial transactions in a shift of the European balance of power that affected significant portions of the globe. The raft, therefore, becomes a literal platform through which painterly subjects and spectators in front of the canvas are positioned in relation to events that exceed the scene depicted.

In my view, Géricault's seascape conjures theatricality in relation to an incipient moment of globalization. Anticipating Weber's thoughts on the matter, Géricault conceives a scene connoting a world in transition, one in which French imperial ways of seeing will become subordinate to those of a stronger empire. The artist subjects his human images to a vast ecosystem represented through the ocean and atmosphere. He substitutes realistic images (themselves born out of painstaking study) for real people to create an affective charge that the viewer nonetheless acknowledges is a construction. That construction also uses, for its representation of hope, a body whose very status as human was in question at the time. The spectator, in turn, must decide how to move in relation to the canvas. What is the spectator's position in relation to the event and issues depicted? Unlike Fried, then, I see theatricality as a term connoting a productive immersion in, or at least in relation to, the seascape. Theatricality involves recognition of layers of mediation, approximation, substitution, and fakery (if not artifice). Nonetheless, I take seriously Fried's invitation to think through the relation of art and beholder even if I understand the theatricality of such encounters quite differently than he.[46]

BRIDGING OCEANIC FRAMES

If the Atlantic provides a major node for tracing an ascendant global capitalism, particularly during the nineteenth century, the Pacific has garnered increasing attention during the twentieth and twenty-first centuries as the region of capitalist acceleration. As Bruce Cumings has pointed out, Pacific Rim discourse is often apprehended by "academic pundits and government policymakers" engaged in what Cumings has called "rimspeak."[47] For Cumings, who gave the first version of his article as a keynote during the early 1990s (significantly, before the 1997 Asian financial crisis), *Pacific Rim* describes the spread of emergent global cities that had experienced tremendous economic growth. The press and other institutions of public discourse used "miracle" and "dynamism" to characterize the robust economies of several Asian countries where these urban centers are located, from South Korea to Singapore. The celebratory tone of these reports after the Cold War marked a clear break in the Euro-American reception of Asia. The perceived threat of "Communist pan-Asianism" or an earlier "imperial Pan-Asianism" orchestrated by Japan had waned.[48]

However, fiscal proclamations celebrating growth in terms of business statistics eschew the realities that those numbers might conceal. Arif Dirlik's work reminds readers of the contradictions engendered by capitalism, highlighting new and continuing forms of disenfranchisement and exploitation endured by laborers throughout the Pacific Rim's constituent countries.[49] Along similar lines, Epeli Hauʻofa cautioned against the use of economic instruments as a measure of health, success, or development. Such evaluations privilege surface output, literally, because they tend to assess value in relation to a landmass (for example, gross national product). In this worldview, he argued, the smaller island nations of the Pacific tend to be seen as isolated units that hold little or no currency in the global marketplace.

Hauʻofa insisted that his theorization of island relations emerged after his initial commitment to dependency theory, which posited peripheral islands as repositories of unskilled labor for industrialized core nations.[50] His notion of Oceania responds to dissatisfaction with such explanatory models. Hauʻofa offers in its place a regional articulation to displace economic determinism. To execute this move, Hauʻofa endorses a structure that is, perhaps necessarily, older than capitalism, one that asserts time and space as nonteleological and nonlinear both in the imagination and in lived experience. While this theory remains a geography understood etymologically as a writing of the world, it implies an almost limitless horizon. As expansive as the seas and as old as the geological formations that produced and continually reshape archipelagos, Oceania counters capitalism through a totalizing move of a different order.[51] Economics may not shape this worldview, but a faith in ecology and its effects on human subjects does. Remembering the sight of Hawaii's Mauna Loa inspires Hau'ofa's initial shift away from the discourses of economic development. The "remote majesty" of the volcano motivates a reflection on the sovereignty of islands. This geothermal vent erupts, producing lava flows that materialize into the environments people inhabit. Far from a backwater, the Pacific site becomes an index of earthly creation. Hau'ofa's seascape—for what else is he seeing but the tip of a mountain, most of which extends under the ocean?—offers a framing of islands that renders them part and parcel of the energies that literally shape the world. The stakes of his analysis of Mauna Loa are high indeed!

Insofar as Hau'ofa reaches for a grandiose view of Oceania that exceeds the minor roles allotted to small islands in Pacific Rim discourse, he relies in part on metaphors of movement; flows of lava set up the flows of kin later in his essay. The passage of islanders across water and continents produces an Oceania that expands beyond shores to wherever migrants might find themselves. The agents of Oceania are, finally, its people, whose journeys continually rewrite the world in an ever-evolving geography. This is a broad vision, one in which the ostensible story of a region flips into that of the globe. Yet as a concept aimed at thwarting theories of capitalist circulation that marginalize smaller Pacific islands, Oceania might still overlap with rhetoric emphasizing *flow*.

Stuart Rockefeller has scrutinized the uses of this term in certain anthropological literature, but his findings have a broader significance. For Rockefeller, the increasing use of *flow* has favored large-scale analyses that lose sight of local specificity and individual agency.[52] Movement overcomes fixity. Theoretical abstraction triumphs over empirical data. Such displacements finally shift focus from the often small and remote communities that for decades constituted the privileged object of anthropology—from a certain perspective. Rockefeller's critique alerts readers to the ways in which attention to macro-level phenomena (including, perhaps, concepts such as globalization) can obscure the details of how processes unfold on the ground. But there remains an important difference between the writing of Hau'ofa and, for example, certain cooperative projects that seek to further capitalist development. Hau'ofa finds particularity in flow; specific places not often connected in studies of globalization come into relief as a network. This set of interconnections, in turn, provides new means of evaluating the quotidian activities that occur on little islands and their possible significance in discussions of the global.

Hau'ofa's changing scales of analysis from the small isle to the ocean would seem to constitute a sort of "tidalectics," as articulated by the Barbadian writer Kamau Brathwaite. Tidalectics is a riff on dialectics, but whereas the popularized notion of Hegelian dialectics posits a somewhat linear trajectory from thesis to antithesis to synthesis, Brathwaite proposes a more circular model attentive to the gravitational pull that moves tides in opposing directions. The aquatic currents produced by the elementary force of gravity is further complicated by the ripple, or the small waves that occur because of local conditions including the weather and the composition of the shoreline. As elaborations of such processes, Elizabeth DeLoughrey has studied roots and routes in relation to Atlantic and Pacific literatures.[53] As homonyms, the terms of her analysis enable a tracking of flip sides of island discourse. DeLoughrey investigates how transoceanic voyages, including those of diaspora, might be held in tension with specific territorial claims, such as those associated with nationalisms and indigeneity. In Brathwaite's case, we might think of what is at stake in claiming him as a Bajan writer, a Caribbean writer, an Anglophone writer, a postcolonial writer, and so on. The sort of flows at issue here suggest that often tiny territories far removed from one another and the cultural productions that seem localized within each of those places might share surprising commonalties that would in turn help reveal and potentially unsettle larger discourses of empire and other structures of governance, today and in the past. Both Hau'ofa and DeLoughrey insist that the island cannot be thought of in isolation but as an active part of the sea.

Baucom, Brathwaite, DeLoughrey, Gilroy, and Hau'ofa introduce various conditions of possibility for globalization through islands by attending to continually shifting scales and types and levels of relations; seascapes function as literal or metaphorical manifestations that animate their theories. This group of writers deploys seascapes to move from aesthetics and narrative to political economy. The often explicit but sometimes implicit production of affect serves as one bridge that supports this move. The art they discuss, whether in prose or in other forms, engages a socially produced emotional response rather than a purely subjective one. This framework suggests and can also reinforce claims of feeling black or islander even as it can complicate or undo such assertions.

Seascapes, as artistic inventions that depict marine scenes and as ways of knowing the globe, provide different epistemological framings of globalization and its histories. The typhoon haunting the title of *Slave Ship* connects the Atlantic to the Pacific as much as *The Flying Dutchman*, which has itself been materialized on both canvas and screen. Though the Pacific region has gained critical currency in the last three decades as a zone of expanding capitalism, it has also generated responses that refute the perception of the oceanic space solely in economic terms. While all of these discourses anticipate certain features of globalization, they retain a spatially bounded unit of analysis, even if those boundaries extend across vast distances. Recent scholarship attempts to move beyond the exploration of any region in isolation, demonstrating the interconnections of far-flung locales. This foray through several paradigms of thought demonstrates the potential utility of thinking through seascapes to imagine Chineseness in particular. Recognizing that Chineseness increasingly registers as a symptom, or even a feature, of globalization, I write this book to think through some particular Chinese seascapes in more detail.

Rather than place China or economic thought at the center of analysis as Arrighi has done, I examine cultural production in the Chinese Atlantic. This neologism expresses both the insular and interconnected qualities of islands marked by the ascent of global capitalism—with Chinese characteristics. The temporalities available through such a notion of the Chinese Atlantic tend toward the anticipatory and future-oriented because past Chinese investments tend to be forgotten or harnessed to a developmental logic (in contrast to, for example, some strains of black Atlantic studies, which work through retrospection). My emphasis on cultural production follows Fredric Jameson in recognizing that the cultural and economic shade into one another as mutually reinforcing justifications of the discourse of globalization.[54] On a less grand scale, the focus on a constellation of islands facilitates new ways of thinking about Chinese migration, or migrations of Chineseness, read through specific localities, usually held apart from studies concerned with Chinese circulations.

Arjun Appadurai ends *Modernity at Large: Cultural Dimensions of Globalization* with a reflection on the "production of locality," which he sees as "a phenomenological property of social life, a structure of feeling that is produced by particular forms of intentional activity and that yields particular sorts of material effects."[55] His analysis juxtaposes locality against the material lived experience of the neighborhood. And this work in general would seem to run in an oblique relationship to the work of Henri Lefebvre, who suggests that space generates its own rhythms that facilitate the production of meaning. In following Raymond Williams, Appadurai emphasizes what Williams called the "forming and formative processes" that orthodox Marxists had undervalued in social organization.[56] Rather than social institutions producing behavior (base determining superstructure), Williams emphasizes that lived experience in the present mediates social forms. For Appadurai, structures of feeling enable him to track the continually morphing structure of, and the shifting dispensations available through, the neighborhood. He predicates this continual reformation on diasporic movement, virtual and electronic communities, and nation-state power. Appadurai's provocations about the production of locality provide scaffolding for questions on which I expand in my own work. Indeed, Appadurai's discussion cries out to be elaborated in relation to islands.

> Forms of human movement are created by the reality or lure of economic opportunity.... In yet other communities, the logic of movement is provided by the leisure industries.... The challenge to producing a neighborhood in these settings derives from the inherent instability of social relationships, the powerful tendency for local subjectivity itself to be commoditized, and the tendencies for nation-states, which sometimes obtain significant revenues from such sites, to erase internal, local dynamics through externally imposed modes of regulation, credentialization, and image production.[57]

Chinese flows through the Atlantic have been steadily increasing for economic reasons, but this movement has accompanied a revaluation of existing Chinese populations throughout the region, who are now being recognized (validated, celebrated, denigrated, or otherwise complicated) because of these new currents of migration. The localization of Chineseness on individual islands throughout the Atlantic contrasts with the circulation of Chinese investment and products flowing into the region. Appadurai's work provides a set of tools for analyzing the synergies and disjunctures among different forms and iterations of Chineseness.

Given that scholars frequently posit the engine of modernity as the Atlantic, obtaining regional coherence because of the transatlantic slave trade and the plantation economy writ large, the particular inflection of Chineseness on the consolidation of what is now ostensibly global capitalism draws attention to a formation called the Chinese Atlantic. On the one hand, such a formulation might return us to the structures of feeling that Appadurai takes from Williams. Williams, we may remember, uses the example of language to illustrate his point.[58] Because we enter into language before we can cognitively process what we are doing, language is a structure that exists before we ourselves come into existence. The life of language in the present, he argues, reveals shifts that are difficult to categorize. So the term "structures of feeling" indicates that unformed sense of something happening anew. This move would seem to correlate with the recent turn to Sinophone studies, in which contingent communities emerge across national and ethnic lines based on Sinitic language use. Although my project does not foreground linguistic commonality, it overlaps with Shu-mei Shih's notion to "rethink the relationship between roots and routes by questioning the conception of roots as ancestral rather than place-based" in order to create "not a theory of mobile citizens who disidentify from the local nation-state and disengage from local politics, but the politicization of that mobility."[59] This politicization of mobility strikes me as useful. Moreover, since Shih turns to visuality in part to mark the increasing speed of image production as communication in a globalized world, her work returns me to the implications of visuality in Appadurai's notion of scape.

Shih herself cautions that the stress on language, particularly *putonghua* (Mandarin), easily collapses Chineseness with mainland China. Rather, to register Chineseness as local, I look at cultural productions where language may not register explicitly at all. My privileging of nonverbal performance and theatricality rather than Chinese language emphasizes the visuality of seascapes. We might think of Arif Dirlik's query posed in relation to another seaview—"Whose Pacific?"—in his exploration of the Asia-Pacific idea.[60] Dirlik and other theorists find in the seascape a perspective laden with power relations of looking. The word also has an etymological resonance of "scape," as in escape, conjuring the different forces that have motivated the displacement of populations from greater China. Such occluded histories emerge in some unusual constellations in Trinidad and other islands that form seascapes of images and meaning.

Pursuing answers to these questions offers a new way of apprehending processes of globalization. The *Chinese Atlantic* names a formation perhaps not yet here, not so unlike globalization. As an analytic, the Chinese Atlantic points to symptoms of some shift in the present, one for which there seems to be increasing evidence as investment capital and overseas workers flow through the oceanic region. But these movements also produce unexpected responses. An ostensibly Chinese image animated by non-Chinese bodies may denaturalize and complicate the stories of migration that we already know, of people leaving one locale for another in search of greater opportunity, of migrations imposed on the unfortunate. Seascapes demand that spectators scrutinize such pat visions in order to think differently about the framing of such narratives.

The Chinese Atlantic is an organizing rubric that collects various seascapes as ways of knowing. Seascapes offer a mode of visualization that surfaces unstable processes of lived experience, material networks, structures of memory, and inventive fantasies that constitute globalization. Indebted to Atlantic studies generally, especially black Atlantic thought, I emphasize in this book the theatrical aspects of such models. Figuring globalization requires multiscalar movements, an expansive tidalectics that marks empirical circulations of labor, migrants, products, money, and aesthetic forms. At the same time, the positivist terms that often render such phenomena visible require deconstruction because, as I have argued, globalization is a productive discourse of substitution and hyperbole. Like the term *Chinese Atlantic*, it has prognostic qualities even if it also emerges from historical and even quantifiable antecedents.

OVERVIEW

Each of the constituent chapters elaborates a different logic that emerges through a specific set of seascapes. Together, these logics constitute a set of principles that underlie the elements in a complex system that might be referred to as Chinese circulation in the Atlantic world. While I demonstrate overlaps among the particular areas I study to the extent that I delineate shared histories and strategies of representation, I also find that seascapes aid in picturing "the global through the ways in which different localities are constituted."[61] What one might call the global dispersion of Chinese people and things leads to quite diverse effects depending on the conditions (both formal and informal) that govern such movements. Looking through these different sites, stark differences emerge. For example, Trinidad serves as a regional (Caribbean) financial center, and it earns significant income from the energy industry. The island's economy and its population is about triple that of nearby Martinique. Martinique's approximately $10 billion economy is based primarily on trade, with the service sector, including the government, providing the lion's share of jobs. The entire island population numbers about four hundred thousand, with one quarter living in Fort-de-France. Such differences obviously factor into how Chineseness comes to matter. I do not intend to flatten these discrepant conditions but to ask how a Chinese-inflected globalization might manifest particularly in these sites, even when some of the rhetoric about China as a world power starts to seem remarkably similar.

In chapter 1, I focus attention on the Chinese Atlantic documentary—contemporary narratives that assemble evidence from the past to highlight family and cultural identifications through structures of domestic ethnographies and synaesthetic experiences. These works insistently visualize Chinese subjects. The examples usually center the Caribbean, but their images and stories radiate across hemispheres. The technologies of film—including montage, superimposition, and sound mixing—produce a particular logic of assemblage that I call reeling. I begin here to foreground the ostensibly real factors of family, history, labor, and migration that might condition understanding of the Chinese Atlantic. Reeling further conjures the cinematic apparatus even as the verb *to reel* suggests both fishing for something (or, more generally, winding something) and staggering as a result of some sort of stimuli. The visible evidence of the Chinese in the Atlantic highlighted by the documentary genre also raises questions about the affective responses such materials engender. This affective solicitation complicates a genre, or mode (as my examples demonstrate, this "genre" is hardly stable), often thought to show "real" events and relationships rather than constructed narratives. I analyze approximately a dozen documentaries by directors such as Peter Chin and Jeremy Mimnagh, Richard Fung, Jeanette Kong, Rigoberto Lopez, and Natalie Wei that speak to processes of archiving ostensibly Chinese experience. All of these works feature seascapes to help explain Asian migration to the region. The chapter investigates the specific representational strategies used to represent these movements. My analysis further demonstrates how film, as an often-privileged form to discuss the circulation of cultural products in relation to globalization, provides different phenomenological means of apprehending Chineseness across an antipodal imaginary. Reeling evokes representational form (cinematic seascapes) and affect in relation to migration, cultural articulation, and globalization.

From the purportedly real depictions in chapter 1, I transition in chapter 2 to more abstract representations in the realm of murals, prints, and sculpture, a variety of seemingly local seascapes produced in Trinidad that figure Chineseness as finance. Here, I develop the logic of incorporating. I use this gerund intentionally to depart from the more obvious watery discourse I employ through this book, although events such as the Deepwater Horizon oil spill in 2010 suggest how quickly the sea and marine life incorporate chemical substances. This process I have dubbed incorporating reflects the ways in which seascapes and understandings of Chinese goods and people relate to the specific processes of industrialization on the island. Offshore oil rigs dot the harbor of Port of Spain, which has developed its coast for commercial and industrial, as opposed to recreational, purposes. Visions of this seaside capital, therefore, tend to emphasize urban cultural experiences over the tropical picturesque. For its workforce, Port of Spain offers more spaces for what locals call liming than it does for relaxing. Incorporating, therefore, describes the dynamics of Chinese bodies situated in this particular city but also in relation to the island more generally (I eschew mention of Tobago, which serves frequently as a recreational site in the national imaginary; the demographics there also skew toward a higher percentage of African-descended individuals). Chineseness in this chapter informs artworks, most of which have been designated for public spaces. Either implicitly or explicitly, this suggests a construction of Chineseness as inextricable from capitalism.

Trinidad has the oldest history of Chinese contract labor in the Americas, with a deep tradition of national discourse about racial mixing. Different seascapes (two quite explicit and two more abstract), each by a different Trinidadian artist—respectively, Nicole Awai, Carlisle Chang, Willi Chen, and Christopher Cozier—animate this chapter. I argue that these artworks inexorably incorporate Chineseness as figures of finance within the national context. I use *figures* as a play on words to suggest an artistic figuration and a numerical accounting; in other words, I suggest that Chineseness is repeatedly depicted in each piece as labor (e.g., a coolie, an entrepreneur, a commodity). This process of incorporating the Chinese on the island also plays on the sense of the word *incorporate* (as a verb, meaning a kind of financial consolidation; as an adjective, meaning without a body) when Chinese subjects disappear but register their presence through other means. This logic of incorporating is currently in flux as new waves of fiscal investment from China (and laborers attached to that investment) have begun to shift how the term signifies.

Chapter 3 changes focus to specific corporeal practices and moves from an Anglophone island to the Francophone site of Martinique, where I parse the logic of flowing. My passage from a former English colony turned independent nation-state (Trinidad and Tobago) to a former French colony turned French overseas department (Martinique) highlights the distinct histories and structures of governance that help to condition patterns of Chinese migration in the Atlantic. Indeed, although streams of Chinese workers have played a role in shaping and continue to inform life on Martinique, these developments should not be seen as equivalent to those experienced on Trinidad (despite the fact that Chinese migrants inhabit the commercial sector in both places). Martinique often seems to serve as a way station for recent arrivals and facilitates subsequent migration to Europe. Perhaps because of these dynamics, Chinese subjects have somewhat receded to the background, running bazaars and food service establishments, at the same time that individuals of various racial and ethnic backgrounds have connected to Chinese flows through an embodied practice. I focus on performances of Chineseness through tai chi, on non-Asian people performing putative Chinese bodily exercises in Fort-de-France even as an increasing number of Chinese immigrant entrepreneurs have set up shop in this seaside capital. However, these business endeavors are often imagined to provide owners with enough money to enable a move to the metropole (broadly understood as France). The contrast between these types of movements—bodily performance and human migration—facilitates an interrogation of the idea of flowing in terms of aesthetics, calisthenics, and volitional human passage from one place to another.

Chapter 4 moves to an island often not conceived as one: England, and particularly Morecambe Bay, where I elaborate the logic of ebbing. This chapter examines an art installation and documentary film that address a specific event involving Fujianese migrants, whose lives were circumscribed by factors outside of their control. In fact, the group of immigrants of interest to me nearly all drowned; their story constitutes part of Isaac Julien's screen installation *Ten Thousand Waves*. This installation deals with death, but it also elicits a discussion of human traffic and subjectivity under conditions of globalization. I contrast Julien's work to Nick Broomfield's feature-length docudrama dealing with the same topic.

Ebbing describes literally how bodies were revealed and also the structures of memory that theatricalize the subjectivity of the deceased. The ethics of having one thing stand in for another becomes even more pronounced in the representations of human traffic at Morecambe Bay. The installation and documentary film that focalize this discussion draw on all the modes of representation analyzed in the first three chapters of the book, from cinematic reconstructions of lives to more abstracted representations of Chinese labor to corporeal substitutions of actors playing the departed. Spaces of exhibition matter in these contexts, and that issue led me to look at specific art installations in quite different locales.

Chapter 5 turns to a more speculative analysis through several public displays of Chineseness that deal with South Africa. This country is a pivot point between Atlantic and Indian Ocean commerce, and, as such, it revises some of the assumptions made in Atlantic studies and Pacific Rim discourse. South Africa serves as a countercurrent to the discussions that precede it because of the ways in which apartheid and its legacies reframe what the Chinese Atlantic might mean; I call this logic *eddying*. China is now one of South Africa's largest trading partners. Given its particular history, South Africa has also been islanded at various moments. To bring a focus to the current conversations about Chineseness there, I revisit Julien's *Ten Thousand Waves* in its installation at the Zeitz Museum of Contemporary Art Africa. I further my investigation of South African–Chinese relationships through another installation at the same museum by one of South Africa's best-known artists, William Kentridge. His *More Sweetly Play the Dance*, an eight-screen installation, depicts a procession of silhouettes that aligns certain visions of communist China with a more African cosmology; this installation I also saw at the EYE Film Institute in Amsterdam, and I attend to the material contexts of each viewing experience. In contrast to these works, I look at a play by one of South Africa's best-known satirists, the frequently gender-bending Pieter-Dirk Uys, who premiered *African Times* (2015), which offers a dystopic view of the New South Africa under black and Chinese control. I conclude with a focus on a number of works, including art by the Chinese street artist named DALeast, who currently resides in Cape Town. Eddying complicates the twining of Atlantic discourse and globalization.

The afterlife of Dutch colonialism that haunts chapter 5 leads me to the epilogue, where I reconnect the world of the Atlantic to China through the internationally renowned artist Cai Guo-Qiang. Cai lives in New York but his major installation, *The Ninth Wave*, in Shanghai concludes my book. A massive seascape (the title designates a maritime expression for a series of escalating waves and also references Ivan Aivazovsky's eponymous painting from 1850), the installation brings the study to an end by raising critical questions about a formation I have called the Chinese Atlantic.

The continual movement of ostensibly Chinese people, goods, finances, and practices around the globe can only lead to contingent conclusions and a spiraling series of questions. I hope my interrogative process ultimately encourages others to immerse themselves in the cultural currents I have outlined and others I have not yet seen in order to develop further critical analysis of the global stage that we inhabit. The Chinese Atlantic is, after all, a kind of fata morgana: a contingent vision predicated on certain material conditions and the interpretive apparatus we have for making sense of it.

NOTES

1. I have published on Wifredo Lam a bit in relation to other artists from the region in my essay "Caribbean Art and Chinese Imaginaries," in *Circles and Circuits: Chinese Caribbean Art*, ed. Alexandra Chang (Los Angeles: Chinese American Museum, 2018), 196–213. Lam's illustrations for Fata Morgana can be seen in Catherine David, *Wifredo Lam* (Paris: Centre Pompidou, 2015), 76–77.

2. I have elaborated the benefits of such a focus in my work with Francisco-J. Hernández Adrián and Michaeline Crichlow. See the introduction to our coedited volume on "Islands, Images, and Imaginaries," *Third Text* 28, nos. 4–5 (2014): 333–343.

3. Richard L. Bernal, "China and Small-Island Developing States," *African East-Asian Affairs* 1 (August 2012): 3–30.

4. "The Globalization of Pollution," *New York Times*, Jan. 24, 2014, http://www .nytimes.com/2014/01/25/opinion/the-globalization-of-pollution.html?_r=0.

5. For an overview of this intellectual trajectory, see David Harvey, *A Brief History of Neoliberalism* (Oxford: Oxford University Press, 2005).

6. See Aihwa Ong, *Flexible Citizenship: The Cultural Logics of Transnationality* (Durham: Duke University Press, 1999), and Anna Tsing, *Friction: An Ethnography of Global Connection* (Princeton: Princeton University Press, 2005).

7. Kang Liu, *Globalization and Cultural Trends in China* (Honolulu: University of Hawaii Press, 2004).

8. This was, of course, precisely the narrative given when Tom Brokaw introduced the opening night ceremonies during NBC Universal's coverage of the 2008 Olympics in Beijing that screened to an estimated 215 million American viewers.

9. Giovanni Arrighi, *Adam Smith in Beijing: Lineages of the 21st Century* (New York: Verso, 2007).

10. Philip J. Stern, *The Company-State: Corporate Sovereignty and the Early Modern Foundations of the British Empire in India* (Oxford: Oxford University Press, 2011).

11. See, for example, Timothy Brook, *Vermeer's Hat: The Seventeenth Century and the Dawn of the Global World* (New York: Bloomsbury, 2008).

12. The vehicles for these connections were fleets of ships, the types and itineraries of which have been detailed in Robert Parthesius, *Dutch Ships in Tropical Waters: The Development of the Dutch East India Company (VOC) Shipping Network in Asia 1595–1660* (Amsterdam: Amsterdam University Press, 2010).

13. Jurrien Van Goor, *Prelude to Colonialism: The Dutch in Asia* (Hilversum: Uitgeverij Veloren, 2004), 41–43.

14. Stern, *Company-State*, 6.

15. Tsing, *Friction*.

16. Karin Amimoto Ingersoll, *Waves of Knowing: A Seascape Epistemology* (Durham: Duke University Press, 2016).

17. Timothy Brook, *Mr. Selden's Map of China: Decoding the Secrets of a Vanished Cartographer* (New York: Bloomsbury Press, 2013), and Robert K. Batchelor, *London: The Selden Map and the Making of a Global City* (Chicago: University of Chicago Press, 2014).

18. My observations about the origin of the seascape are based on Jeremy Gaschke, *Turmoil and Tranquility: The Sea through the Eyes of Dutch and Flemish Masters, 1550–1700* (London: National Maritime Museum, 2008); Lawrence Otto Goedde, *Tempest and Shipwreck in Dutch and Flemish Art: Convention, Rhetoric, and Interpretation* (University Park: The Pennsylvania State University Press, 1989); and Roger B. Stein, *Seascape and the American Imagination* (New York: Whitney Museum of American Art, 1975).

19. Remmelt Daalder, *Van de Velde & Son Maritime Painters: The Firm of Willem van de Velde the Elder and Willem van de Velde the Younger, 1640–1707,* trans. Michael Hoyle (Leiden: Primavera, 2016), chapters 10–13.

20. See Goedde, *Tempest*.

21. Fredric Jameson, "Notes on Globalization as a Philosophical Issue," in *The Cultures of Globalization*, eds. Frederic Jameson and Masao Miyoshi (Durham: Duke University Press, 1998).

22. My definition of culture here borrows from Raymond Williams, *Keywords: A Vocabulary of Culture and Society* (Oxford: Oxford University Press, 1983) and is attentive to Arjun Appadurai's reminder that culture should be thought of as a series of processes rather than as a thing (1996).

23. Arrighi, *Adam Smith*, 321–50.

24. On seascapes generally, see Jerry H. Bentley, Renate Bridenthal, and Karen Wigen, eds., *Seascapes: Maritime Histories, Littoral Cultures, and Transoceanic Exchanges* (Honolulu: University of Hawaii Press, 2007). See Kristin Dow and Thomas E. Downing, *The Atlas of Climate Change: Mapping the World's Greatest Challenge* (Berkeley and Los Angeles: University of California Press, 2011) for an investigation of waterways and risk.

25. See Shu-mei Shih, Chien-hsin Tsai, and Brian Bernards, eds., *Sinophone Studies: A Critical Reader* (New York: Columbia University Press, 2013), particularly Shih's opening essay.

26. W. J. T. Mitchell, ed., *Landscape and Power* (Chicago: The University of Chicago Press, 2002), 1.

27. Ann Jensen Adams, "Competing Communities in the 'Great Bog of Europe': Identity and Seventeenth-Century Dutch Landscape Painting" in *Landscape and Power,* ed. W. J. T. Mitchel (Chicago: The University of Chicago Press, 2002), 66.

28. It is beyond the scope of this book to examine the influence of *The Raft of the Medusa* within the history of art. Nevertheless, I would mention that some homages to the painting work through very explicit citation of the visual form that shifts colonial contexts; in this regard, we might think of Samoan Greg Semu's *Raft of the Tagata Pasifika* (2016), which uses photography to restage the European painting in relation to Pacific Island concerns. As a contrasting example, Frank Stella's sculptural work, *Raft of the Medusa (Part I)* (1990) and its siblings, capture the clinging figures in Géricault's painting in a much more abstract fashion; the unequivocal commentary on colonial and postcolonial dynamics foregrounded in Semu's work is difficult, although not impossible, to see in the twisting metal constructions that constitute Stella's series.

29. David Brion Davis, "Foreword," in *Atlas of the Transatlantic Slave Trade,* David Eltis and David Richardson (New Haven: Yale University Press, 2010).

30. David Eltis and David Richardson, *Atlas of the Transatlantic Slave Trade* (New Haven: Yale University Press, 2010), 2.

31. Ian Baucom, *Specters of the Atlantic: Finance Capital, Slavery, and the Philosophy of History* (Durham: Duke University Press, 2005), 275.

32. The etymological discussion in this paragraph comes from a reading of the relevant entries in the *Oxford English Dictionary: cyclone, hurricane, tempest, and typhoon, OED Online,* accessed August 25, 2012.

33. I have discussed some of the similarities and differences between coolie and slave labor in Sean Metzger, "Ripples in the Seascape: The Cuba Commission Report and the Idea of Freedom," *Afro-Hispanic Review* 27, no. 1 (2008): 105–121. On the issue of the interconnectedness of labor systems, see Lisa Lowe, "The Intimacies of Four Continents," Ann Laura Stoler, *Haunted by Empire: Geographies of Intimacy in North American Empire* (Durham: Duke University Press, 2006), and Lowe's later book of the same title.

34. Lisa Lowe, *The Intimacies of Four Continents* (Durham: Duke University Press, 2015), 15.

35. Walter S. Melion, personal communication, July 10, 2015. Daalder says baldly that "Marine painting is a Dutch invention" (Daalder, *Van de Velde*, 11).

36. Hester Blum, "Introduction: Oceanic Studies," *Atlantic Studies* 10, no. 2 (2013): 151. See also her "The Prospect of Oceanic Studies," *PMLA* 125, no. 3 (2010): 670–677.

37. Bernard Bailyn, *Atlantic History: Concept and Contours* (Cambridge: Harvard University Press, 2005); Sugata Bose, *A Hundred Horizons: The Indian Ocean in the Age of Global Empire* (Cambridge: Harvard University Press, 2009); Paul Gilroy, *The Black Atlantic: Modernity and Double-Consciousness* (Cambridge: Harvard University Press, 1993); Philip E. Steinberg, *The Social Construction of the Ocean* (Cambridge: Cambridge University Press, 2001); and Rob Wilson and Arif Dirlik, eds., *Asia/Pacific as a Space of Cultural Production* (Durham: Duke University Press, 1995). This is not to ignore work that emphasizes oceanic exchanges prior to the advent of capitalism. See, for example, Fernand Braudel, *The Mediterranean and the Mediterranean World in the Age of Phillip II* (Berkeley and Los Angeles: University of California Press, 1996), and Enseng Ho, *The Graves of Tarim: Geneaology and Mobility Across the Indian Ocean* (Berkeley and Los Angeles: University of California Press, 2006).

38. On this issue, see Elizabeth DeLoughrey, "Radiation Ecologies and the Wars of Light," *Modern Fiction Studies* 55, no. 3 (2009): 486. Here, she cites Eileen Welsome's *The Plutonium Files: America's Secret Medical Experiments in the Cold War* (New York: Dial, 1999).

39. On the latter issue, see Rachel Harvey, "The Particular: The Persistence of the Particular in the Global," in *Framing the Global: Entry Points for Research*, ed. Hilary E. Kahn (Bloomington and Indianapolis: Indiana University Press, 2014).

40. Samuel Weber, *Theatricality as Medium* (New York: Fordham University Press, 2004), 29. Richard Schechner, *Between Theater and Anthropology* (Philadelphia: University of Pennsylvania Press, 1985).

41. Weber, *Theatricality*, 342.

42. Michael Fried, *Art and Objecthood: Essays and Reviews* (Chicago: University of Chicago Press, 1998), 163.

43. Fried, *Art*, 48.

44. Fried, *Art*, 153.

45. Michael Fried, *Absorption and Theatricality: Painting and Beholder in the Age of Diderot* (Chicago: The University of Chicago Press, 1980), 154.

46. Fried has continued his inquiry into picture and beholder in relation to photography. See his *Why Photography Matters as Art as Never Before* (New Haven: Yale University Press, 2008). That text addresses questions of surface and meaning making in ways that are, as might be expected, often divergent from my own thoughts on these issues.

47. Bruce Cumings, "Rimspeak: Or the Discourse of the 'Pacific Rim,'" in *What Is in a Rim? Critical Perspectives on the Pacific Region Idea*, Arif Dirlik (Lanham, MD: Rowman & Littlefield, 1998), 54.

48. Cumings, "Rimspeak," 68.

49. Arif Dirlik, "Introduction: Pacific Contradictions," in *What Is in a Rim? Critical Perspectives on the Pacific Region Idea* (Lanham, MD: Rowman & Littlefield, 1998), 10.

50. Epeli Hau'ofa, "Our Sea of Islands," in *Global/Local: Cultural Production and the Transnational Imaginary*, eds. Rob Wilson and Wimal Dissanayake (Durham: Duke University Press, 1996), 4.

51. See Katerina Martina Teiwa, "Frames: Reframing Oceania. Lessons from Pacific Studies," in *Framing the Global: Entry Points for Research*, ed. Hilary E. Kahn (Bloomington and Indianapolis: Indiana University Press, 2014).

52. Stuart Alexander Rockefeller, "Flow," *Current Anthropology* 52, no. 4 (2011): 557–578.

53. Elizabeth M. DeLoughrey, *Routes and Roots: Navigating Caribbean and Pacific Island Literatures* (Honolulu: University of Hawaii Press, 2010).

54. See Jameson, "Notes," 1998.

55. Arjun Appadurai, *Modernity at Large: Cultural Dimensions of Globalization.* (Minneapolis: University of Minnesota Press, 1996), 182.

56. Williams articulates his position in his chapter "Structures of Feeling" in *Marxism and Literature* (Oxford: Oxford University Press, 1977).

57. Appadurai, 192.

58. See Williams, *Marxism*, 131–132.

59. Shu-mei Shih, *Visuality and Identity: Sinophone Articulations Across the Pacific.* (Berkeley and Los Angeles: University of California Press, 2007), 189–190.

60. Arif Dirlik, "The Asia-Pacific Idea: Reality and Representation in the Invention of a Regional Structure," in *What Is in a Rim? Critical Perspectives on the Pacific Region Idea* (Lanham, MD: Rowman & Littlefield, 1998).

61. Manuela Ciotti, "Forms: Art Institutions as Global Forms in India and Beyond: Cultural Production, Temporality, and Place," in *Framing the Global: Entry Points for Research*, ed. Hilary E. Kahn (Bloomington and Indianapolis: Indiana University Press, 2014), 57.

1 ~ REELING

THE CHINESE ATLANTIC IS A CONCEPTUAL INTERVENTION TO think differently about the geographic rubrics that have organized ideas about oceanic spaces and capitalism, specifically in relation to cultural and social reproduction. This assertion implies the existence of empirical connections between China and Atlantic spaces, but here, the Chinese Atlantic functions principally to complicate or deconstruct other paradigms of Atlantic discourse, such as the green Atlantic, the red Atlantic and, most prominently, the black Atlantic.[1] This chapter engages in this task by looking at artistic productions that ostensibly discuss actual circulations of Chinese migrants in the Atlantic and, more specifically, the Caribbean world. Narratives invested in the quest for evidence across media platforms, the documentary films discussed in the following pages promise to bring previously submerged stories concerning Chinese people and things to the surface.

CHINESE CARIBBEAN DOCUMENTARY AS A MODE OF CHINESE ATLANTIC VISUALITY

Each of my examples identifies and visualizes Chinese subjects, so this chapter discusses the strategies of primarily cinematic representation (although later chapters will complicate the equation of visuality and human subjects). I analyze various kinds of testimony and visual verification organized to establish such a Chinese presence. I also ask, what sorts of narratives emerge in relation to material documentation, and what do such constructions tell us about globalization today?

In addition to narrative and visual evidence connecting purportedly real depictions or testimonies of Chinese experiences in the Caribbean with discourses of globalization, the chapter builds an archive of distinct cinematic seascapes. These seascapes frequently assist the viewer in locating the geographic coordinates that contextualize the narratives, but each film constructs and uses seascapes somewhat differently. A focus on seascapes provides a means to frame understanding of the films, and each cinematic work also shifts slightly how the seascape might be understood, particularly as it frames the "reality" into which the documentary purportedly provides insight. Insofar as each film unsettles truth claims in reference to actual people and places, the documentaries construct realisms in manners that can productively be read as theatrical. Films that exhibit facts and talking-head interviews as access to a relatively unmediated past, I term *Chinese Caribbean domestic ethnography*. Those instances where the films highlight and question perspectives narrating the past, turning also to visceral sensations produced through film, I call *Chinese Caribbean synaesthetic documentaries*. Subdividing the already niche genre of Chinese Caribbean documentary illustrates how the use of the seascape varies when deployed in contexts that offer contrasting perspectives on processes of documenting or representing the real.

Documentary film and on-location shooting have long promised an archive of visual knowledge that reflects the particularities of any given place. The camera differs from the painted seascape in its frequently presumed ability to index (in a semiotic sense) an empirical reality, notwithstanding the interventions and subjective desires of the director and crew. The index—in this case, the photographic trace of what existed in front of the camera—is, for my purposes, distinct from the painterly seascapist's impression and depiction of reality, which became highly conventional from the Dutch Golden Age forward. As Roger B. Stein wrote in *Seascape and the American Imagination*, a seascape is "as much a record of our thoughts and feelings about that outer fluid space and our attempts to map it and to impose upon it a conceptual grid as it is a documentary record of that space itself."[2] Put otherwise, seascapes depict unknown spaces as much as known ones. In this regard, the seascape in documentary might destabilize as much as establish the sense of place constructed through the film.

In relation to the tropical Atlantic, such visualizations have frequently highlighted exotic spectacles: beaches, palm trees, smiling islanders engaged in premodern practices. Such codification emerged forcefully as the Caribbean in particular shifted from an economy based on primitive accumulation (colonies providing raw materials through the plantation system to European metropoles) to one of tourism. This touristic gaze coincided with efforts to clean up beaches, build hotels, and render local cultures digestible; it has been cogently critiqued in the works of Atlantic and Caribbean studies scholars such as Francisco-J. Hernández Adrián, Patricia Mohammed, Leah Rosenberg, Mimi Sheller, and Krista Thompson. As a way of seeing, tourist imagery generates complex contradictions within and responses to such patterned processes of picturing and in attempts to mitigate or counter them. The clichés of the tropics, rendered through cinematic and literary seascapes, also occasionally animate discourses of diasporic nostalgia, where they may ground familial narratives or serve as devices to recontextualize the lived experiences of subjects inhabiting the region. Within such frameworks, I consider several documentaries that not only feature but also construct Chinese populations and notions of Chineseness in the Caribbean.

The selected films, therefore, constitute an archive documenting but also iterating and even inventing ostensibly Chinese cultural formations as they circulate through the Caribbean. Practical as well as conceptual concerns guide inclusion in this archive. In terms of the former issue, I have gathered films concerning this topic for several years and have talked to many of the artists about their work. My efforts in this regard provide a body of work to view or teach. Approximately a dozen examples of Chinese Caribbean documentaries exist; however, production of such work has boomed over approximately the last decade, so this number will likely increase. Such proliferation overlaps with several factors, including a decrease in the cost of film technologies and the ascendance of networks of Chinese capital that might help to fund such projects. In this chapter, I include discussion of those documentary films that have distribution channels that the interested English-speaking viewer can access.

In building this archive, I have also moved across geographical, linguistic, and ethnic/racial boundaries, because such destabilization occurs in the films themselves when considered as a group. Although Caribbean studies frequently organizes knowledge production in relation to language, imperial histories, or transitions within the region as a whole, the documentaries focusing on Chinese diasporic people deconstruct some of the assumptions frequently embedded in Caribbean and Atlantic discourses. The films highlight often occluded narratives in the dominant (and certainly productive) focus on a black Atlantic by demonstrating some of the ways in which such a formation is entangled with specific Asiatic racial formations and larger currents of cultural exchange. These cinematic productions shift focus from commonly evoked nodal points in triangular structures that reveal transnational links, usually among Africa, the Americas, and Europe.

The films thus implicitly propose new geometries that speak to Chinese Caribbean migrations as a subset of Chinese Atlantic seascapes. In so doing, the documentaries underscore the partiality of a black Atlantic vision or paradigm. My focus on several documentaries brings into view some surprising similarities among various locations, in addition to glaring differences among them. Chinese migrations have long occurred in the isles of interest to me. Nevertheless, in and of themselves, most of these islands tend not to register as particularly meaningful in popular discourses of globalization, given their small sizes and degrees of influence in the world, even though the Caribbean region as a whole is frequently described as the cradle of global capitalism because of the transnational slave trade and plantation system. However, when taken together, these selected sites suggest how contemporary Chinese investments of capital might reframe historical commercial and cultural circulations. Overall, this chapter reveals the ways in which Chinese Caribbean documentary archives seascapes that telescope between past and present, most often by drawing out narratives of generational migration. As perhaps the cultural medium of globalization par excellence (Hollywood imports, after all, eclipse nearly all national film production in countries outside the United States), film offers a set of visual technologies and conventions for (ostensibly) apprehending Chinese Caribbean populations reconfigured by domestic scenes to address, identify, and shape a specific locality.

REELING

I focus on the genre of documentary film because it traffics in and depends for its definition on signs of the real and the authentic. Rather than an ontological consideration of who or what is actually Chinese, the various works provoke consideration of how one comes to understand this label and what investments render this term meaningful in relation to the people and locations that the documentaries illuminate. Because film functions primarily through the use of optical and acoustic signs that generate epiphenomena, including affective and haptic sensations that form through surface encounters with projection screens, these works also point us to aesthetics that matter. In other words, they direct attention to the ways in which certain kinds of artistic devices reveal and produce material effects that facilitate spectators' cognizance of the Chinese Atlantic as both fantasy and, to a degree, materiality.

Reeling is the term I use to describe many of the characteristics of the films as a group. This word recalls the action of deep-sea fishing, which involves extensive amounts of line to catch anything beneath the surface. As a conceptual metaphor, I use it to suggest a search for apparent truth, because documentaries hinge on this sort of investigation of the real and suggest an in-depth engagement with their respective subjects. Reeling evokes a process, and even if the literal procedure of bringing in a fish from the sea depends on certain facts (speed of the boat, strength of the line, power of the fish), it also depends a bit on hope and educated guesswork. Although I elaborate these qualities in the pages that follow, I want to mark from the outset the resonance of this concept with the medium of film itself, in spite of the fact that celluloid has yielded to the digital. The film reel suggests a piece of a larger story or of a historical narrative. Although that technology became standardized in the industry, the possibility for changes in order, for reels to go missing, for incineration, and so on suggest how narratives about the past might be easily altered. In part, then, I turn to reeling to gesture toward the desires implicated in the documentary form: a pursuit of some sign of the real that is always a contingent and unfinished exercise.

The attention to signs moves alongside Anne-Marie Lee-Loy's study of the enunciation of Chinese Caribbean texts through Gilles Deleuze and Félix Guattari's work on minor literature. For Deleuze and Guattari, the deterritorialization of language, political contextualization, and collective value set conditions for literary expression by minorities working within the shadow of a tradition of "great literature" (their example is Franz Kafka, a Jewish, Czech-born writer who published in German).[3] Lee-Loy has herself written a survey of depictions of Chinese characters in Anglophone Caribbean literature. Pace these writers, I move through but also below and beyond nationalisms to articulate how Chineseness emerges through a particular set of films that suggests how Chineseness is constructed and might matter across antipodal, archipelagic, and insular imaginaries. The sensorial dimensions at work in this constellation guide viewers to ruminate on certain claims about ostensible empirical realities such as Chinese families (a subject common to many of the films, given the chain migrations that often fuel diasporic communities).

My inquiry through but also outside the frame of the national recognizes several factors that affect the ways in which people imagine Chineseness. China's soft power is being experienced across the globe, but, given the relative size and wealth of many countries in the Atlantic, a new sense of Chineseness is being felt acutely. As one example, China's Han Ban (also known as the Office of Chinese Language Council International) has rapidly set up Confucius Institutes in Cuba (2009), Jamaica (2010), the Bahamas (2012), Trinidad and Tobago (2013), Barbados (2015), Grenada (2015), Antigua and Barbuda (2018), and the Dominican Republic (2018). Although charged with language training, most of these institutions also offer cultural classes and programs. This kind of educational diplomacy pairs with financial circulations of Chinese capital, particularly on certain Caribbean islands, where such investment has been occurring on an unprecedented scale. Of course, here onlookers must note that the amounts invested, when viewed from individual islands, may seem vast, but in relation to China's overall international investment portfolio, only a small sum has been moved into a particular geographic area.[4] Nevertheless, China has invested billions of dollars in major infrastructural projects and loans to insular sites. One of the largest of these, for the moment, is the "Beijing Highway" that cuts across northern and southern Jamaica. Other ventures include new stadiums and performing arts complexes in various island locations. These massive undertakings indicate rapid physical transformations throughout archipelagos, transformations that owe much to China's current position in the global economy.

Another reason to think through imaginings of China and Chineseness across sites is connected to streams of historical migration. Significant numbers of Chinese migrants have lived in the Atlantic spaces under consideration since the nineteenth century, and their continued presence has generated a substantial amount of artistic production about and by Chinese subjects. This aesthetic history is, like all histories in the Atlantic, manifold, since the material conditions wrought through European and later American empires have played a significant role in how the term *Chinese* has come to matter in any particular place. To speak of, for example, the Chinese Caribbean or a Chinese Canadian can simplify what are complex negotiations of identification and political/economic power that occur at various scales, from the individual person to an insular community to the national to the regional to even larger transnational frameworks that link Asia to the Americas and beyond. The current social production of Chineseness depends in part on what sorts of historical contexts inform an understanding of *Chinese* in a given context.

My admittedly unusual assemblage of Chinese Caribbean documentaries—including material shot in Havana, Kingston, New York, Port of Spain, Toronto, and elsewhere—does not neatly correspond to area or ethnic studies rubrics, save for the fact that they all involve some element of realism in representing Chinese migrants. The gambit of amassing an argument in this manner is to think through but also to extend existing paradigms of knowledge, including the seascapes that I offer in this book. The nearly dozen works I examine in this chapter demonstrate how a focus on seascapes might be productive and, to a lesser degree, what my framework might miss. The films could be usefully regrouped into other analytic frames, and I do not mean to negate the value of such potential projects.

As one example, even a lens of national cinema that might include Jamaica and its diaspora (which provides a rich emergent body of film production) becomes clouded given that the crews and subjects might identify as much as American or Canadian as Jamaican. Certainly, the advantage of the national is that it focuses attention, in this case on the many screen productions touching on the topic of the Chinese Jamaican that have been produced in the last few years. Moreover, the 160th anniversary of Chinese arrival in Jamaica (2014) and the recent success of other cultural producers, from Tessanne Chin's victory on season 5 of NBC's *The Voice* (2013) to literary figures such as Easton Lee, Patricia Powell, and Kerry Young, might reinforce such a rubric. Nevertheless, I contend that ongoing documentary production—such as that of Jeanette Kong (including the shorts *The Chiney Shop* [2011] and *Half: The Story of a Chinese-Jamaican Son* [2013], and her feature in collaboration with Paula Williams Madison called *Finding Samuel Lowe: From Harlem to China* [2015]), Peter Chin and Jeremy Mimnagh's

Jamaican (2016), and Generoso Fierro's *Always Together: Chinese Jamaicans in Reggae* (in production)—resists such a framing even as it might conjure it. Rather than existing geopolitical labels, aesthetic terms like *realism* might better describe what links these films. In this case, realism is the dominant mode across these representations. Like all of the artistic works I discuss in this chapter, this set of cultural materials suggests a documentary impulse, here invested to various degrees in ostensibly empirical information concerning Jamaicans of Chinese descent. Reeling as an analytical term captures this quest for and effort to display "real" evidence.

REALISM AND THEATRICALITY

Scholar Janelle Reinelt's thoughts on documentary theater prove useful in unpacking this impulse. She has written that documentaries—whether "film, memoirs, photographs, internet sites, archives" or other forms—"can all be made to perform."[5] To avoid the potential entanglement with agency and intentionality, I would state this assertion otherwise: Documentary, perhaps contrary to normative assessments, is an inherently theatrical genre. As a mode of narrative creation through which one reels evidence together, it assembles signs usually in pursuit of some putative truth, evaluated in particularly affective terms. That kind of construction we could easily correlate, for example, with claims about Stanislavski-derived acting training. The investment in producing reality has been elaborated by Reinelt:

1) The value of the document is predicated on a realist epistemology, but the experience of documentary is dependent on a phenomenological engagement.

2) The documentary is not in the object but in the relationship between [the] object, its mediators (artists, historians, authors), and its audiences.

3) The experience of documentary is connected to reality but is not transparent, and is in fact constitutive of the reality it seeks.[6]

I use the term *Chinese Caribbean documentary* in part to foreground the theatricality of these works. In this vein, the "phenomenological engagement" Reinelt mentions might indicate "not only how we experience the world, but also what of it we experience"; theatricality emphasizes this idea of limited and situated experience that documentary filmmakers and viewers might nevertheless see as reality.[7] Moreover, the films I investigate stage, in different manners and to different degrees, terms of identification such as Canadian, Chinese, Jamaican, and Trinidadian. Such an assertion works against the idea that documentary functions as a straightforward recording of the real. Instead, the films stage reality, occasionally quite explicitly through reenactments. However, more often, the films juxtapose on-location shooting (a frequent strategy in documentary to show what happened in a specific location) with testaments by subjects who inhabit or have inhabited a place. Historical documents and photographs appear as verification of what happened, often as if those materials provided transparent windows into the past.

To mark documentary realism as theatrical is, therefore, to cast suspicion on these devices and to mark the ways in which filmmakers have constructed truth for the viewers. Documentary films, then, rather than simply attesting to the facts of Chinese presence in and migration through the Caribbean, assemble and create such knowledge. As a mode of Chinese Atlantic visuality, the Chinese Caribbean documentary reminds us of the tensions among events that have occurred, empirical observation, and the narration and visualization of those things.

CHINESE CARIBBEAN DOMESTIC ETHNOGRAPHIES

The strategies of staging ostensibly factual relations vary across the many films. The first group I investigate tends to function primarily as what Michael Renov, in his book *The Subject of Documentary*, has called "domestic ethnography."[8] Like Renov's examples, the set of films I discuss posits "a reciprocity between subject and object, a play of mutual determination, a condition of cosubstantiality. The desire (figurable as dread or longing) of the domestic ethnographer is for the Other self."[9] The documentaries I place in this subcategory seek to excavate and highlight narratives featuring Chinese ethnic, racial, and/or national identifications; indeed, the filmmakers often share similar ethnic backgrounds with the subjects they investigate. Their works exhibit an expository, if not always chronological, mode of presentation. They tend, or at least try, to work within a tradition of documentary "invested in rhetorical and stylistic conventions that minimize awkwardness" in the sense of not calling attention to the construction of the film or such things as the position of the camera (which, of course, shapes the extradiegetic viewer's perspective).[10] Moreover, these films exhibit positivism by insisting that we can recover the past directly, without much mediation. Ancestral connections frequently play a central role in this process. Despite these tendencies, the films do not necessarily expose some naïve faith in the seamless recounting of Chinese people's narratives or in the assertion that documentation produces transparent truth. Perhaps the most provocative moments in these films occur when the contradictions of competing histories come to the fore. Because individual films reveal specific complications in the search for signs and stories of Chinese affiliation, I unpack the narrative and formal features of each film to illustrate commonalities and differences that might push toward the Chinese Atlantic as an analytic.

Natalie Wei's *Chinee Girl* (2011) explicitly demonstrates how local contexts produce certain kinds of subjects. Largely reliant on a series of talking-head interviews, the film begins with a shot of the street sign for Trinidad's Charlotte Street, the location of Port of Spain's Chinatown, which grounds the narratives in a specific place.[11] The film immediately cuts from the sign to a handheld shot of the crowded thoroughfare, complete with vendors and passersby. Such visualization sets certain expectations: for example, that subjects will manifest the particularities of urban Trinidadian life. Given the title sequence in which Chinese characters—*zhongguo nuhai*—and then the English translation appear over a yellow background with computer-generated blossoming branches, the spectator might further anticipate an elaboration of gender and its intersection with Chineseness.

"Chinee girl," the viewer quickly learns, is a kind of hailing. The film describes several reactions to that specific address. Most of the women interviewed describe hearing "Hey, Chinee girl!" while walking on the street. "Hey, Chinee girl!" functions in the vein of Frantz Fanon's "Look! A Negro!" or Louis Althusser's "Hey you!" An ideological address to an individual identifies a subject and/or object within a given power structure. Some of the women acknowledge a split, familiar to readers of Fanon, as their subjectivities are reduced to singular elements of identity. Others find affirmation in this hailing. The explicit recognition of an individual's Chineseness seems to validate the ethos of Trinidad's imagined community in the sense of confirming the desirability of multiculturalism within the nation-state. Charlotte Street would seem to name a locus of this incorporation into the national body.

Wei's film ultimately confirms the women she interviews throughout Trinidad as subjects whose relation to Chineseness partially crafts each woman's sense of self. Although the documentary may not in itself provide a particularly novel perspective on issues of racialization or cultural amalgamation, it does emphasize the importance of the domestic as mediating individuals' identifications. Almost all the women appear in interior spaces; family photographs punctuate their respective stories. The director even downplays Anya Ayoung-Chee's public career as a beauty queen and reality television star, and the film instead offers an intimate reflection of interiority.[12] If, as I argue in the introduction, seascapes often demand that the scholar pay attention to the geopolitical, this film generally eschews such images and processes of imaging. On the one hand, *Chinee Girl* reminds viewers that geopolitical narratives are often quite gendered in the sense of not paying attention to the particularities of women's experiences. In this regard, the film refuses to let women's roles and their anecdotes recede into the background. On the other hand, identification or disidentification with the term *Chinee girl* occurs as part of an everyday practice within Trinidad, but neither the interviewees nor the director articulates these acts in relation to broader historical or economic dynamics (except for the stories of individual family migration). For my purposes, Wei's film nevertheless prompts a question about how quotidian anecdotes might suggest global phenomena.

Such an emphasis on the everyday reveals how the seascape sometimes occludes as much as it reveals. In Wei's film, the sea as such does not appear in any significant manner (glimpses appear as part of the background of the cityscape or in a photograph of someone on the beach). Instead, *Chinee Girl* frames women speaking interspersed with shots of the island—its parks, palm trees, and urban landscape—and some graphics relaying historical facts of Chinese migration. One sequence illustrating migration shows geographical outlines of China (with its current boundaries) and Trinidad, along with arrows that indicate passage from the former to the latter; it provokes thinking about how to represent such travel, since sea voyages did not necessarily follow a linear route across the Pacific (especially since the Panama Canal did not come into use until 1914). The geometry of migration thus remains out of view. This point contrasts with much of the rest of the film, which works as a kind of travelogue; *Chinee Girl* engages many of the visual tropes of the tropics. Perhaps this emphasis occurs because Wei is a Canadian-born filmmaker of Chinese and Trinidadian descent (all the women shown also identify themselves in terms of ethnic lineage early in the documentary) who has returned to one node in her genealogy. This celebrating of roots may have helped solicit financial support for the production from the University of the West Indies and the Trinidad and Tobago Film Company. In any case, *Chinee Girl* reveals a gendered space, one where Chineseness registers in discussion of chopsticks and food, language, physiological characteristics, and ancestral memories of the past. In reeling all of these details together, *Chinee Girl* borrows from extant imagery (family albums as well as tropes from other kinds of visual production) to construct a new but always partial and contradictory (as testified to by the women themselves) portrait of these women who claim belonging to this island.

Jeanette Kong's films constituting her self-proclaimed exploration of "documenting the historical past of the Chinese-Jamaican diaspora" complicate the perspectives in *Chinee Girl* and function to demonstrate more explicitly why seascapes might matter.[13] *The Chiney Shop* investigates a kind of institution in Jamaica, one well known across the Caribbean and elsewhere.[14] In the short documentary, community leaders, politicians, and artists all testify to the impact of shopkeepers on the island, particularly in the more remote areas where entrepreneurial individuals have provided different forms of service, from providing a lighted building where locals might congregate to offering cinematic entertainment to driving individuals in need to the hospital, which might be miles away. Largely a conventional expository narrative composed of talking-head interviews, archival stills, and voiceover, *The Chiney Shop* works largely to applaud Chinese labor that has contributed to island life.

Yet the film begins and ends with something of a tropical fantasy. In the title sequence, the camera tilts down to a cartoonish seascape of clouds, coconut palms, sailboats, and a map of Jamaica. The touristic image provides a reference point, one that owes much to various alignments of colonial and neocolonial power that create the image of Jamaica as a traveler's paradise. The film's opening shot captures this trope of the exotic.

In contrast, former politician Alvin Curling (a Canadian of Afro Jamaican descent) concludes the film with a somewhat different fantasy articulated in his assessment of Chinese-descended people in that location: "They are Jamaicans. And they are black, and we are Chinese." This statement coincides with Jamaica's national motto, "Out of many, one people." Curling's words

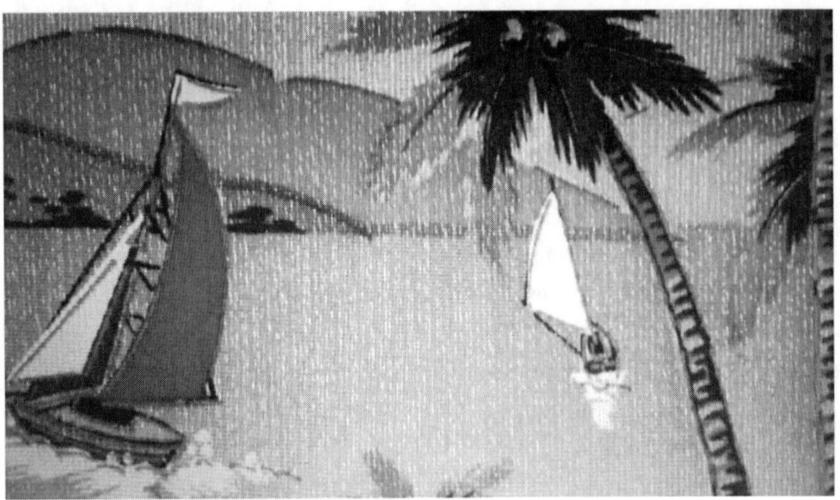

Fig. 1.1. The opening shot of *The Chiney Shop* suggests a touristic view.
Still from *The Chiney Shop*, 2011. © Ms. Chin Productions.

offer a succinct or curt (depending on one's perspective) assessment of the
islanders that the film would seem to track. Curling's punctuation to the narrative suggests that the Chiney shop demonstrates something about national
integration. Two very different imaginings thus bookend the documentary;
from this perspective, *The Chiney Shop* points to processes of world-making
(in this case, tourism and nation-building) that do less to stabilize reality
or claims of historical truth than to point to the processes that invent them.
Kong's declared documentation of "the historical past" pivots on theatrical
presentation (Jamaica presented as one imagines it to be) as much as on
material evidence.

Neither a paradigm of tourism nor one of national belonging fully encapsu-
lates what the film shows us. Instead, "Chiney shop" names a set of dynamic
relationships among people, money, goods, and services that shape particular localities. Posited as a space of Chinese social (re)production, commercial consumption, cultural exchange, and interpersonal/intergenerational
negotiation throughout the film, the stores evoked through the title exceed
definition as static sites where such developments occur. Rather, such processes generate the Chiney shop as an outcome in particular locations. The
postcard-like seascape and Curling's laconic account therefore suggest

imaginative inventions (with potential material effects) that denote not so much a process of documenting the real as a process of reeling.

Reeling means winding material together but can also indicate disorientation. Kong's film assembles different stories, various aural elements, and images into a cinematic narrative. But the real framed through Kong's own discourse proves elusive, and even the interviewees fish for some apt description of all that a Chinese Jamaican grocery might signify. Reflecting on her perspective as a child, Jamaican author Olive Senior (who left the island in 1989 and currently resides in Toronto) reminisces that the interiors full of "barrels of salted fish" and jars of "sweeties" impressed her as "part of a magical world." Curling himself recounts a kind of joke that he and his friends used to tell—"We think the Chinese didn't have any feet"—because they always saw the Chinese retailers behind the counter. Such enchanting narratives reveal how much subjective memory shapes experience. When Carol Wong, labeled in the film as a "community leader," remembers a "certain affection and fondness" that grew over the years between her family and their neighbors in Jamaica, her tone also indicates a nostalgia for the society that raised her, an affective casting into her story that frames the past in terms of the present investments of the documentary. This use of temporality—thinking through fragments of what has been to project what might be—is, of course, what reeling does. In pursuit of something in the future (arranging something for later use or angling in order to catch a fish), reeling looks back in hopes of obtaining a richer future.

Half, the familial story of Vincent Lee, connects South Dakota (the site of his current residence) to Jamaica to China (where he spent a large portion of his childhood). As a formal construction, Kong's documentary again consists almost entirely of still photographs from the past and talking-head interviews. Snapshots occupy most of the backgrounds; Vincent usually appears speaking in front of a collage of family photos, some of which come into focus as a detail or an entire frame in the course of the documentary. In other sequences, the story told closely correlates with the image. When the film explains that it takes forty-five days to reach Hong Kong, it shows us three sepia-colored stills beginning with a ship in what the sequence suggests is Hong Kong Harbor.

This seascape is the only time that we see the ocean for the approximately twenty-five-minute duration of the screening. Although frequent stories

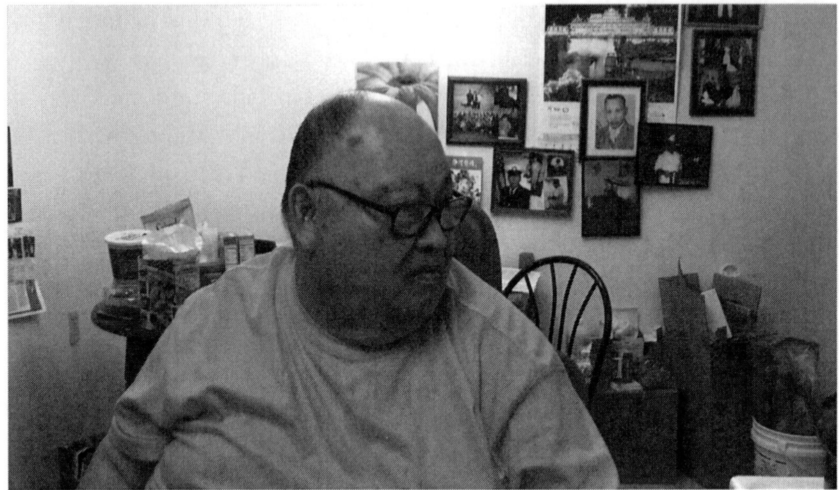

Fig. 1.2. In *Half,* Vincent frequently occupies the foreground of a domestic mise-en-scène containing family photos. Still from *Half,* 2013. © Ms. Chin Productions.

about China and Jamaica occur, the film tends to use portraits or landscapes to establish place. When Vincent tells his interlocutor that his grandmother intervened to prevent his beating and potential death, the image of an elderly Asian lady appears; most of the background is the gray sky, so identifying a location anywhere other than generically "outside" is difficult. Earlier in this particular sequence, he discusses the rice field (cue still of rice field). The spectator must take on faith that narrative and image coincide. Whereas the previously discussed documentary uses graphics of the sea to destabilize correlations between truth and memory, here the emphasis falls much more on creating a linear narrative for the central subject, despite the fact that the interviews, particularly with the women in the family, emphasize trauma and the fracturing of the household unit.

This attention to domestic ties permeates the film's interview subjects as they search for connection to one another. For his part, Vincent states that he did not initially remember his mother and sisters in Jamaica (cue image of black woman in a white dress against the grass). In the interview with Chow Me Lee, Vincent's daughter born in China, she describes her paternal grandmother as a "foreign woman" who eventually called for her son's return to Jamaica. Chow Me Lee describes a dramatic elision in her father's story: his abandonment of his wife and child for twenty years. Vincent later describes his black Jamaican girlfriend, with whom he had three other children. Shots of the father and his three sons, now grown, suggest contentment, and Chow Me Lee later tells her interlocutor that she welcomes all her brothers when they come to visit, an interesting note when earlier in the interview she described her mother crying for years because she had not received letters from her husband. The film insists that family, in some form or another, stays connected—the tears of Chow Me Lee's mother notwithstanding.

The film turns to foodways to affirm cultural and familial affiliations, to establish a locality in which Chinese and Jamaican might exist in some harmony.[15] For example, when the professor and author Anne-Marie Lee-Loy says in her interview that her "uncle seemed Chinese," her words become a voiceover that occurs while Vincent cooks black mushrooms. Indeed, the film's many scenes of meal preparation and consumption—dumplings made and eaten, green beans washed and then sizzling in a skillet—reinforce Vincent's claim that food sparked his memory when he returned to Jamaica from China. Cinematic visions often pair the phenomenon of Chinese cooking, frequently in the home, with people assumed to have some organic link with these practices. Such ostensible Chinese connections follow logically from the etymological associations of the term *diaspora* itself. Denoting the scattering of seeds, diaspora literally conjures the roots that produce foodstuff. This sort of rooting has long spread through the routing facilitated by transnational commerce. This historical traffic, fusing diverse cultural traditions at different sites, in turn speaks to the kind of rhizomatic linkages of which Deleuze and Guattari speak.

The logic of reeling provokes thinking about the rhizome. In the films I have discussed, the quest for true stories of migration produces a number of berthing points, none of which guarantee access to anything but expressions of memory that have been reassembled like so much flotsam to create something like a structure of, in these cases, familial belonging. A multiplicity of ostensible authorities anchors these historical narratives of lineage, from individual testimony to old photographs, each given relative weight by the filmmakers and their interviewees. As an ensemble, these sources generate affect, but their solicitation of emotive response has less to do with specific claims (as might be the case, for example, in relation to documentaries on the Holocaust) than a more amorphous charge: a kind of disorientation in the wake of an assortment of various possible kinds of evidence.

The dynamism of rhizomatic thinking opposes a singular agency potentially suggested in spooling something together. But I want to suggest that such agency is often illusory. Anything wound together might easily become entangled. Moreover, if one thinks of reeling in an object at sea, it becomes quite easy to imagine how one collects unanticipated things, how the object ostensibly being harvested might itself disappear or pull the line in its own direction. The films I have discussed also operate through a logic of reeling in the sense of continually constructing or reconstructing an ostensible empirical reality. Following this logic, the Chinese Atlantic is, therefore, never fixed but rather a shifting representation that elicits feelings through certain foods or sensations of loss generated by boats, photos, and stories floating across the sea.

That sense of incompleteness can also produce physical manifestations. Jeanette Kong's feature-length collaboration with Paula Williams Madison entitled *Finding Samuel Lowe: From Harlem to China* (hereafter *Samuel Lowe* to distinguish the film from the memoir of nearly the same title) demonstrates this phenomenon. Unlike Kong's other two films, the film's temporality reaches backward quite far into the past for very explicit reasons. The documentary opens with Paula Williams Madison's address in 2012 to the Congressional Black Caucus. Arguing that people need to know from whence they come, she declares emphatically, "We have to stop defining ourselves around slavery. . . . It was a moment in time" in a long history of "Africanness." This sentiment recurs in the book entitled *Finding Samuel Lowe: China, Jamaica, Harlem* and leads her to emphasize the familial fragmentation produced by the slave trade, specifically to move outside of that framework to understand her subjectivity. Ultimately, Williams Madison will update the genealogy (*jiapu*) of her ancestral village to include the Afro diasporic lines of the family; she exchanges a history of enforced labor for one of entrepreneurial savvy, shifting a potential story of enslavement to freedom and to one that spotlights the contradictions of neoliberalism.

From its outset, the documentary film explicitly marks linkages among the African slave trade and the Chinese coolie trade. A cinematic seascape composed of titles superimposed on shots of waves informs the viewer to expect "one family's story," one whose migration patterns have led to a family of mixed race descendants, including Williams Madison.[16] She seeks information about her Chinese Jamaican grandfather, Samuel Lowe, a former

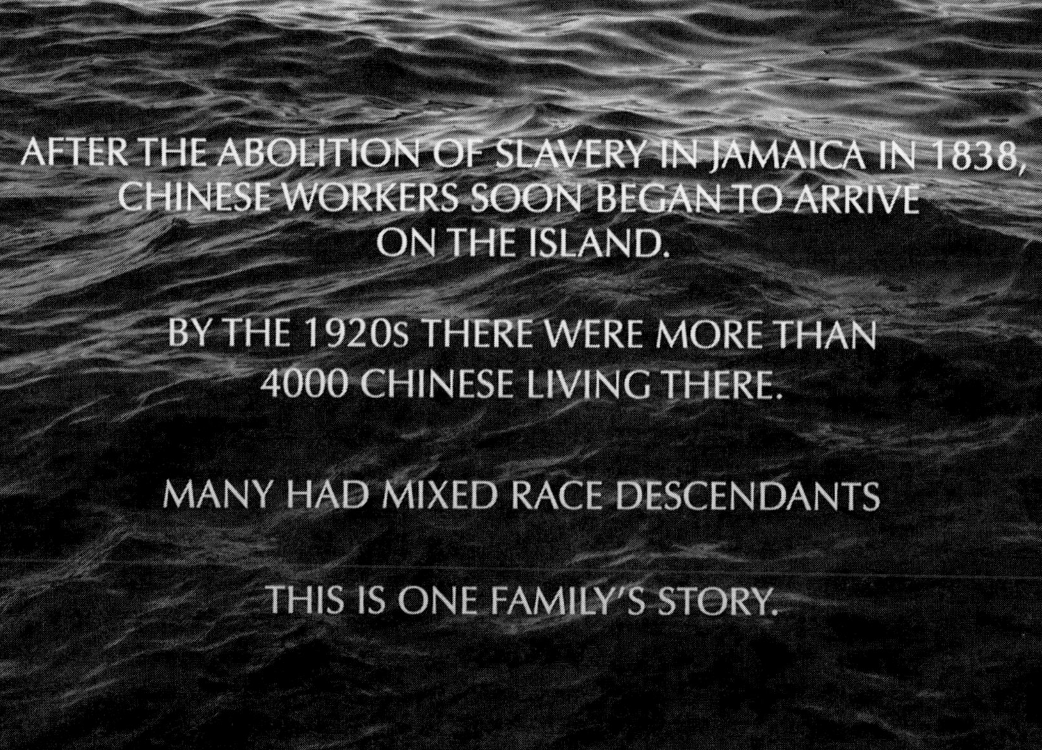

Fig. 1.3. *Finding Samuel Lowe* contextualizes familial history with intertitles superimposed on a seascape. Still from *Finding Samuel Lowe: From Harlem to China* (2015). © Paula Williams Madison.

shop owner on the island who returned to China in 1934. Ultimately, the film pivots around the quest to find the extended family of this Chinese business-man, whose Hakka roots would seem to provide the trinity around which the granddaughter he never met has organized her life: "Family. Prosperity. Education."

Shots of the water and stills of ships and their passengers anchor a particu-lar migration story that the principal subject of the documentary (Williams Madison) states might universally resonate with "children of immigrants." In this vein, the film establishes a relatively conventional narrative of immi-grant success, but the details of this tale provide insights into some of the economic and human flows that shape the Chinese Caribbean and the larger frame of the Chinese Atlantic. Williams Madison and her brothers recount, in the first few minutes, their impressions of their grandfather based on their recollected conversations with their mother, Nell Vera Lowe. Photographic seascapes punctuate mentions of Samuel Lowe's departure from Jamaica in this introductory section. As Williams Madison explains, "Sometimes when you pick up and go somewhere else, you leave a part of yourself. Even if you're going to a new place, you're leaving a part of yourself in the old place." The film illustrates this idea with footage of individuals disembarking at a port superimposed on a shot of moving waves. The movement in the background and foreground suggests the continuing evolution of sites of departure and arrival. Williams Madison sets as her task the linking of these shifting locations.

Ultimately, both the literary and cinematic versions of *Finding Samuel Lowe* validate a particular narrative structure—one that Asian American literary scholar Erin Khuê Ninh has more generally described as the "debt-bound daughter"—in which filial expectations produce a model minority.[17] From various shots of China and Jamaica, the film cuts to a satellite view of Manhattan and then to black-and-white found footage featuring the streets of Harlem. The film visually links what would otherwise appear as unrelated places. The Harlem sequence further conveys a neoliberal ethos in its insistence that the individual should overcome poverty and that familial wealth indicates happiness and success. Of course, this drive for accumulation occurs in the wake of immigrant precarity. As performance scholar Lara Nielsen has observed, "neoliberal disciplinings reconfigure the laboring subject in a way that requires attention to a subtle if seismic shift in the operations of late capitalism."[18] The articulated drives for financial gain respond to the family's previous monetary struggles; according to Williams Madison, she and her eldest brother had "always strategized about building wealth." At the same time, the siblings insist that capital accumulation does not determine worth; instead, the film attributes value to forms of familial desire: for siblings to look after one another and for parents, although separated, to take custody of their kids. Harlem serves as the locus of these early bonds. As one of the brothers notes in regards to his siblings, "It's about us three first." *Samuel Lowe* thus insistently centers kinship.

This family-centered approach proves more complex than it might seem. What begins as a story of struggle for opportunity morphs into a case study in technological, financial, and, finally, cultural globalization. Williams Madison achieved success in New York television before moving to an executive position dealing with diversity at NBC Universal. She tells her interlocutor that her eldest brother, Elrick, launched an "algorithmic trading company," which led to the amassing of an "unbelievable amount of money" and facilitated the birth of the Williams Group Holdings LLC. She describes this enterprise as a "family investment company" whose portfolio includes the Los Angeles Sparks WNBA basketball team and The Africa Channel. From this discussion, the film cuts to yet another set of seascapes, the first of which is a shoreline with titles identifying it as Martha's Vineyard, Massachusetts, where Williams Madison apparently vacations. Eventually, the film shows a shot of family members aboard *Miss Nell, Harlem, New York*. The vessel that bears both the matriarch's family and her name (if not her body) to ports of leisure counters the relative lack of mobility that Nell Vera Lowe experienced for most of her life. The sequence ends in the Williams family compound. The shots of seascapes in the film help to establish a triumphant celebration of rags to riches that reinscribes neoliberal discourse.

Notwithstanding this potential critique, the film shows us specific contradictions of late capitalism. Paula Williams Madison and her brothers successfully guide this mode of production with filial rhetoric and actions. Although they narrate their bourgeois present as a direct response to earlier experiences of racialized disenfranchisement, Williams Madison also links her business acumen to an essentialist Chinese (specifically Hakka) entrepreneurial spirit. Indeed, much of the film emphasizes the filial connections that seem to supersede divisions of language, nationality, and upbringing. Witness the shot of Williams Madison hand in hand with one of her Chinese elders at a banquet that brings dozens of extended family members together in China, including twenty-two she herself flew there from the United States.[19] Such events would seem to have sown the seeds for an even larger network of family capitalism extending across continents. This is one example of what anthropologists Aihwa Ong and Stephen Collier might call a "global assemblage," in this case a structure of dispersed familial relations resulting from particular flows of labor mediated by shifting governance structures in Jamaica, the United States, and China and eventually reconfigured as a corporate entity with the power to write new cultural norms through various media platforms including television (The Africa Channel), literature (her memoir), and live performance events (the WNBA).[20]

Within the film, the politics of such transformation of local family to corporation (for it is her financial resources that enable Williams Madison to connect her extended relatives, as she herself notes) to extended transnational family remain rather obscure; however, these kinds of assertions become more nuanced in her published memoir. Establishing the late 1960s as the context for her coming of age, she explains her attachment to the Black Power Movement, facilitated through both the Students Afro-American Society and the support of her mother, who identified as "'colored,' then 'Negro,' then 'Black'" despite her physiognomy.[21] Such contextual notes situate, however problematically, financial success as linked to particular US politics of race. The family-cum-corporation in turn has responded to such a state of affairs in part by creating businesses that facilitate (although not exclusively) class advancement for black subjects.

In other respects, the book overlaps with but also departs from many Asian American family memoirs and Caribbean autobiographies, genres that offer some useful comparisons to Williams Madison's writing.[22] Within the latter, as literary scholar Sandra Paquet has argued, women frequently assume the role of a kind of primordial mother (she speaks here of men's narrative specifically, from fictional accounts like Sycorax through the marginalization in a text such as C. L. R. James' *Beyond a Boundary*).[23] Certainly, maternal figures loom large in Williams Madison's text. Within Asian American autobiography, Williams Madison offers a new transnational approach—not exactly comparative, as scholar King-Kok Cheung has recently advocated, but one attentive to women as actors whose agency takes on different meanings in light of different cultural contexts (for example, the Asian American woman actively creates familial memory in ways that challenge patriarchal accounts).[24] In terms of structure, Williams Madison's text begins in the author's contemporary moment, shifts back to the story of her mother, then moves forward to Williams Madison's own childhood, then to her efforts to reconstruct her grandfather's life and find her maternal relatives. This multigenerational story coincides in form with many other tales of Asian immigrant success.

However, Williams Madison also complicates this genre of life writing through the details of her trajectory. In this vein, the scope of the published autobiography offers much more than the film in terms of describing political and social dynamics, specifically by highlighting 1960s Harlem as well as offering a comparatively greater emphasis on the meeting of her parents in Jamaica and the societal norms that affected their relationship. These elaborations account for the slight shift from the film's subtitle, *From Harlem to China*, to that of the memoir, *China, Jamaica, Harlem*. Nevertheless, the written text also begins with a question that centers both epistemological and ontological concerns, although the book offers this inquiry as part of an intimate setting as opposed to the very public scene of the congressional address shown in the film. Roosevelt, Williams Madison's husband, asks, "Baby . . . do you know you're Black?"[25] The question recurs roughly halfway through the memoir. The text elaborates such ontological claims; in this case, kinship verifies them. As Williams Madison explains in celebratory fashion, "eventually we will mourn our elders whom we have been blessed to know and love."[26] The Asian American memoir here is recast as an intersectional narrative that finally reconciles the generational gaps common to that literary genre and that also destabilizes what *Asian American* might mean. The author reveals how terms like *black* and *Chinese* vary in connotation across various locations and times. She also suggests the inextricability of these descriptors when thinking about Chinese migration to Jamaica in particular and the Caribbean in general.

An illustration of these dynamics occurs in a section called "Where Love Begins"; this segment describes a Jamaica striated by social divisions that nevertheless facilitated the pairing of "outside children" (those born out of wedlock). This section also includes some of the few departures from the otherwise intense investment in conventional autobiography that emphasizes temporal progression and relations of cause and effect in order to naturalize the unfolding historical narrative. The departures here include recounting of a "fabulist tale" and undocumented migrants mistaken for duppies, or spirits.[27] However, such inclusions also reinforce the ethnographic tone of the text (a standard feature of Asian American autobiography and one long burdened with debates about real and fake cultural articulations), since the other sections of the author's family quest deal principally with various empirical forms of evidence. For example, mention of "a lovely pen-and-ink drawing" indicates the author's mother's attachment to "China, which she never saw but to which she felt connected."[28]

The author renders these professedly organic bonds to China in literal terms throughout the book. According to Williams Madison, rediscovered relations transformed her "from a tourist to a local" when she visited China.[29] Elsewhere, she wonders if something in her "DNA . . . facilitates making money," an entrepreneurial predisposition that she retrospectively locates in her Hakka lineage.[30] These claims essentialize Chineseness in a problematic manner, yet the narrative as a whole contextualizes these contentions in relation to her upbringing as a youth from a relatively poor single-parent home in Harlem. This household structure thus informs her later articulated desires for a larger, prosperous family unit. Indeed, Williams Madison's narrative fulfills the wishes of her mother, a person who, in the most striking scene of claiming biological linkages, pulls out a box of her children's umbilical cords, which would ostensibly validate their parentage.[31]

This investment in the identification of genealogy propels the memoir, and it contextualizes the book's one use of the word *reeling* as an emotional jolt that erodes distinctions of private and public. Williams Madison wonders specifically whether her mother was reeling from the news that her husband (from whom she had separated but not divorced) had a child out of wedlock.[32] The concern over outside children earlier in the story recurs with an affective charge. The documentary turns on issues of familial discovery and the transmission of intimate knowledge to the world at large. Although all of the documentaries I have analyzed thus far investigate varying feelings of disorientation in the wake of personal disclosures, the two versions of *Samuel Lowe* foreground the solicitation of affect in the most pronounced manner. Whether the outrage that Williams Madison's prose recounts when she relates the scene of her father with his new wife or the film's visual close-ups of Williams Madison as she begins to cry, the search for Samuel Lowe produces emotional engagement as verification of the impact of actual events on life stories.

My point in offering this fragmentary analysis is not to offer a close reading that privileges the formal dimensions of either the film or the autobiography; instead, I offer four conclusions. First, the film uses a number of shots that tie Chinese immigration to literal and conceptual seascapes (which constitutes the link to this book). Such scenes demonstrate the fluctuations of identification in relation to different contexts and the knowledge assumed to correlate with them. Second, these seascapes pull together several forms of evidence in solicitation of an affective response from the viewer. Third, the autobiography and film suggest a particular version of family capitalism, one structured by a first imagined and then materialized filial kinship structure from the perspective of Paula Williams Madison. This sort of reconnection emerges through a particular transnational nexus, one that imagines Confucianism as allegiance and obligation across the spaces of Jamaica, the United States, and China. This formulation displaces a narrative that might otherwise be conceived through an American model of neoliberalism. Here, that economic structure is iterated in a complex fashion that both avows and disavows the asymmetries of power, including factors like racialization and national politics. To some degree, Williams Madison suggests that the entire edifice of global capitalism resting on Atlantic slave and later (ostensible) contract labor is an inadequate model. The shift in paradigms of understanding brings me to my fourth conclusion: Williams Madison's conceptual move away from slavery roils several Atlantic currents.

This last point requires significant elaboration. Sociologist Michaeline Crichlow and her frequent collaborator, economist Patricia Northover, likewise suggest that lived experiences of creolization, what they understand as "selective creation and cultural struggle" following the Haitian anthropologist Michel-Rolph Trouillot, move outside of American iterations of blackness determined by the plantation system writ large.[33] Crichlow and Northover offer an alternative and quite expansive model of creolization that has a worldwide reach: "When empirically examining the interdependent and dynamic relationships implicated in *creolization*'s politics of place, one is forced to move beyond the confines of the Caribbean nation-states, if only (as a start) for the simple reason that reticulated Creole identities are produced and refurbished in and beyond Caribbean spaces."[34] Crichlow and Northover offer a means to consider how Williams Madison's search for relatives reveals and produces entangled notions of home and homing.[35] Her search recalibrates her grandfather's networks in China and Jamaica to become a new site of social reproduction, now moving through and beyond China, Jamaica, and North America.

In other respects, however, Crichlow and Northover's work would complicate Williams Madison's expressed desire to disarticulate blackness from the slave trade. They work in a similar current as the Martinican intellectual Édouard Glissant, who wrote extensively on creolization as an open-ended process, one that involves what he called *Antillanité* (frequently translated as "Caribbeanness") and *mondialité* ("worldliness") as methods that bring people into relation with others. Glissant's lifelong explorations of these issues open certain possibilities for thinking about creolization, some of which Crichlow and Northover extend. Crichlow, Northover, and Glissant differ significantly from the narrative provided in either version of *Finding Samuel Lowe* because the scholars see the Atlantic as what Glissant calls the womb and the abyss. That is, the ships that crisscrossed the Atlantic and the ocean itself, which so often were the site of literal death, also created new forms of relation. Williams Madison clearly distances herself from such ideas. What is the effect of that positioning?

Like the other documentaries I have analyzed, *Samuel Lowe* pivots on affective responses to home. The directors have usually staged these affective moments as intimate encounters in interviews. However, the interpersonal dynamics link to larger displacements, notwithstanding the desires of, for example, Williams Madison to imagine otherwise. Individual chronicles of often quite mundane activities point to the complexities of globalization routed through if not rooted in the Atlantic world. The human subjects who participate in or are left reeling in the wake of such processes reveal not the negation of histories of slavery but the ways in which streams of people and goods intersect precisely because of their legacy.

CHINESE CARIBBEAN SYNAESTHETIC DOCUMENTARIES

The category of what film scholar Bill Nichols calls "performative documentary" expresses a different relationship to empirical evidence than the Chinese Atlantic domestic ethnographies; according to Nichols, the former rubric "addresses the fundamental question of social subjectivity, of those linkages between self and other that are affective as fully as they are conceptual."[36] He argues that this mode shifts from "the referential as the dominant feature."[37] Thus, in the performative documentary, the object of analysis may not always be clear. In using a mix of "expressive, poetic, and rhetorical" elements to create an experience rather than a linear narrative that supports claims with evidence, the performative documentary shifts attention from the world captured and referenced in the frame to the spectator and the possibilities of transforming the viewer through aesthetic engagement. Implicitly following linguist J. L. Austin and philosopher Judith Butler, Nichols suggests that the performative does something as opposed to simply describing it. Yet Austin writes that the performative is a category of speech acts; Butler writes more broadly of the "reiterative power of discourse to produce the phenomena that it regulates and constrains."[38] These definitions do not necessarily coincide with Nichols's elaboration, which seeks to develop an existing taxonomy that includes expository, observational, interactive, and reflexive documentaries.

Nevertheless, the articulation of the performative against the ethnographic in Nichols facilitates my own formulation of a subcategory of Chinese Caribbean documentaries that offer significant departures from the domestic ethnographies I discuss in the first half of the chapter. The documentaries I discuss hereafter perhaps overlap with what Nichols would term performative, but I emphasize synaesthetic qualities: that is, the ways in which these films use visual stimuli to elicit kinaesthesia, proprioception, and thermoception in the spectator. In other words, these documentaries offer a particularly theatrical experience understood as engaging sensory perception in ways that frequently interrupt narrative progression and destabilize avowals of accuracy. Selected films of Peter Chin and Jeremy Mimnagh, Richard Fung, and Rigoberto López best illustrate this classification of Chinese Caribbean synaesthetic documentary, which provides different framings of genealogy, migration, and empirical evidence than the Chinese Caribbean domestic ethnographies.

All of these filmmakers have benefited from government support for their work. Rigoberto López obtained backing from the Instituto Cubano de Arte e Industria Cinematográfica. Chin and Fung reside in eastern Canada, and the projects included have been funded at least in part by provincial and national funds. Such financial investment recognizes in part Canadian multiculturalism (visible minorities), and the projects to differing degrees fulfill expectations set within that rubric. The videos enable spectators to learn about otherness or to affirm a particular cultural articulation. Fung is something of a pioneer in this regard, but he was soon joined by others who addressed this topic, sometimes more obliquely.

In terms of individual examples, I begin and end this section with Fung because he has directed the most work pertaining to Chinese communities in the Atlantic region; his work combines original narrative and visuals with found footage (from 8mm home movies to educational documentaries to clips from Hollywood). Fung's films on familial relations—*The Way to My Father's Village* (1988), *My Mother's Place* (1990), *Sea in the Blood* (2000), *Islands* (2002), and *Nang by Nang* (2018)—provide a poignant commentary on his familial experience while elaborating the form of Chinese Caribbean synaesthetic documentary. I focus here on the films as a quintet about kinship, notwithstanding the fact that Fung filmed them over thirty years and produced a number of other videos during this time.[39] This project follows Fung's lead insofar as he has written an essay that discusses the first three of the five.[40] Insofar as the quintet coheres, it integrates Richard's voiceover commentary with a variety of other speakers. The narratives frequently offer conflicting oral reminiscences that facilitate the viewer's questioning of what one sees on screen. Water figures prominently as an image, often suggesting the ways in which culture continually drifts and transforms.

The Way to My Father's Village opens with a suggested seascape: sounds of breaking waves and images of a stone pathway. This trail cuts to a typewriter, where Fung's unseen father, Eugene Fung (1909–1986), registers his information with the state bureaucracy. Such a beginning suggests that the video will direct the spectator to some concrete location where the patriarch of the Fung family will emerge from history through some expository reconstruction of his life. However, the journey indicated by the title is much more complicated. Peter X. Feng, in an essay appropriately titled "Getting Lost on *The Way to My Father's Village*," has written in detail about how the film departs from conventions of exposition common in the documentary genre; it highlights gaps in the visual field, disruptions in linear narrative, and breaks between the story Fung ostensibly wishes to tell and the materials (people and documents) he marshals for that purpose.[41] In the film, the father's story moves rapidly from Canton to Hong Kong to Vancouver to Montreal to Halifax and, finally, to Trinidad before returning to Canada (Toronto) and China. From the Pacific through the Atlantic into the Caribbean, the itinerary becomes visible through partial images of the mechanisms of travel: passports, trains, boats, and planes. The film resists the long establishing shots that might assist the spectator in feeling located, and this visual assemblage seems to reflect the perspective of Richard Fung himself as he narrates the many impasses encountered in trying to reimagine his

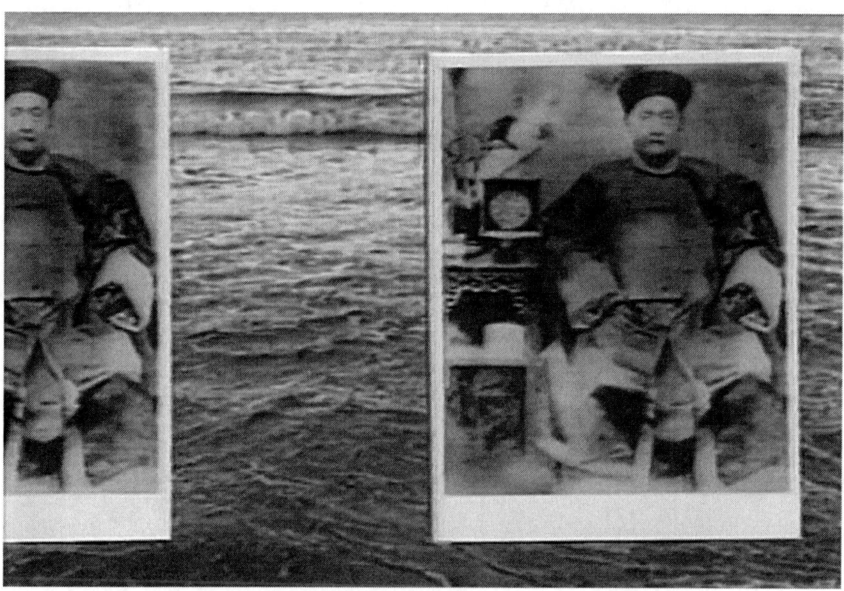

Fig. 1.4. *My Mother's Place* includes photographic images of Fung's ancestors moving across a shoreline, emphasizing the seascape as the background for familial history. Still from *My Mother's Place* courtesy of Vtape. © Richard Fung.

father's life. Although most of the film depicts scenes that have little to do with seascapes and the physical sensations that such images might engender, I have called attention to certain sequences to establish a reference to the sea, which becomes increasingly more pronounced in this body of Fung's work.

Indeed, *My Mother's Place* repeatedly shows us a seascape that interrogates ancestral lineages. During the third episode (entitled "mother"), several portraits of Asian men pass across the screen, superimposed over an image of the shoreline. This device recurs three times during the course of the documentary's forty-nine minutes. Portraits on the sea suggest not so much cultural drift (since the streaming across the screen occurs at an even pace) but rather a more purposeful process of image making. Here, the sea becomes the ground against which a line of cultural or blood relations takes shape. Fung insistently reminds viewers that Chinese people have inhabited and continue to inhabit the shores of Trinidad; they constitute what José Muñoz, one of the most astute commentators on Fung's work, called a contact zone, following Mary-Louise Pratt. For Muñoz, Fung's contact zones are liminal locations of hybridity that "allow for new social formations."[42] The social formation Muñoz seems to have in mind is a space of conjunction in which Fung's various positionalities as a Torontonian, gay male, English-speaking, Chinese Trinidadian artist might assemble in sometimes unexpected ways to reveal the fissures among Trinidadian communities and the sorts of political possibilities of both identification and disidentification with that rubric.

The formal construction of the film, as Julianne Pidduck has observed, also marks Fung's own presence both inside and outside the frame.[43] Pidduck links this inside/outside framing to Fung's queer aesthetic practice. She follows Diana Fuss in suggesting that Fung's formal composition of inside/out "functions as the very figure for signification and the mechanisms of meaning production. It has everything to do with the structures of alienation, splitting, and identification which together produce a self and an other."[44] The beach is one space of encounter, where cultures meet but where the materiality of borders also takes shape. The scenes of portraits superimposed on the surf suggest the human movements across oceans that set the conditions of possibility for Fung's life even as they imply the ways in which connections might drift apart.

My Mother's Place situates the Fung lineage in Trinidad and Canada at the same time that it gestures toward the more explicitly queer register of some of his other work.[45] The filmmaker states, in the voiceover accompanying the opening shots, his desire to use snow falling outside a suburban house to create a mood for the inquiry into the tropics that the film projects. The chilly exterior creates a contrast to the interior scenes. "That old Patois song" Richard's mother Rita used to sing and that constitutes part of the soundtrack not only in the opening of the film but as a kind of recurring refrain throughout it reinforces the play, or perhaps dialectic, of divergent tones. In the beginning, the music links a home in the snowfall, family pictures arranged on a mantel, and a shot of the open water. The progression transitions from black and white to color once the camera depicts the sea. This effect reverses the conventions of representing the past. The stills that follow show various moments of Rita's interview in both black and white and color. Fung's narration explains the tactics of interviewer and interviewee in this domestic conversation between mother and son: "We eliminate details to protect the guilty." Whereas the spectator might expect to gain intimate knowledge of the film's third-generation Chinese Trinidadian subject, the narration prepares viewers from the outset to retain a level of suspicion about what *My Mother's Place* depicts. When, for example, the film shows a young Richard as "an ordinary boy doing ordinary boys things," the spectator can almost see the wink behind the camera. The footage shows a frolicking boy, and eventually a title about Richard being caught by his mother in one of her dresses. As promised from the outset, the speakers in the video do not talk candidly about such things.

Offsetting the limits of familial disclosure, other women either appear or otherwise receive recognition in the film. For example, four talking head interviews—with sociologists Himani Bannerji and Dorothy Smith, poet Ramabai Espinet, and producer Glace Lawrence—offer feminist perspectives on why stories matter and what the political stakes of a production like *My Mother's Place* might be in different contexts from Canada to the Caribbean. Rita mentions various Trinidadian folktales, such as the story of the *soucouyant*, a kind of eastern Caribbean vampiric witch, and the Warahun traders.[46] These various narratives, both implicit and explicit, tie the imagination of Chineseness to several frames of analysis, from more academic discussions of race, representation, and empire (including the later Commonwealth as well as the American occupation during the 1940s) to the empirical knowledge gained from living in Trinidad and taking part in its many embodied traditions.

Among these frames that shape the family, the most interesting figures occupy the margins. Aside from himself as a youthful sexual subject, Fung calls attention to a scene with Violet, the Afro Chinese caretaker who lived with and worked for the Fungs. This brief story raises more questions than answers. A descendant of a former slave, Violet, according to the narrator, gossips with Rita in French patois. However, her precise affective and material relationship to the Fung clan remains unclear; Rita does not discuss her. Moreover, the transition from this brief segment to the two following—one concerning the Catholic Church and its particular instantiation in Trinidad and the other about the visits of the royals as well as several renowned figures in international politics—reframe the particular relations of Violet within the family to larger geopolitical affairs. How are issues of faith, intimacy, and race perceived and managed at different scales of social organization?

Such queries linger at the end of the film, and they partially open a larger conversation about why this story about one Chinese Trinidadian mother, who subsequently migrated to Canada, might matter.

Sea in the Blood interweaves two principal storylines: that of Richard's sister Nan, who died of thalassemia, and Richard's long-term partner Tim, who lives with HIV. The film opens with shots of a waterline; two figures come into view, swimming through one another's legs. A jocund encounter, this scene transitions to slides held in front of the camera as Richard's voiceover introduces his younger self and Tim, depicted on them. Shots of handwritten prose contribute to a series of superimpositions fading in and out that describe the men's relationship; a red subtitle reads, "We met at a gay Marxist study group." These introductory moments provide, in formal terms, a structure of memory, alternating images of a mixed-race couple that relies both on subjective accounting and mnemonic materials from photographs to documents. The voiceover becomes a travelogue informing the viewer of mundane aspects of travel, including correspondence, through which Richard learns of Nan's relapse. The film cuts to footage from an educational interlude on thalassemia.

This next section underscores how race takes on material meanings linked to a seascape. Initially understood as a Mediterranean disease, thalassemia did not register as a potential blood disorder that might afflict Asian or Asian diasporic people. Here, proximity to an oceanic world shapes the understanding of human biology and etiology. Doctors in Trinidad would not have expected to find thalassemia in the Fung children, and therefore, they did not immediately diagnose the symptoms that presented in Nan. As Priscilla Wald has demonstrated, medical conditions—their identification and treatment—depend on narrative and social construction.[47] Richard's first travels outside of the Caribbean coincide with the family's efforts to obtain the proper medical care for his sister; footage from these journeys appears on screen. In this manner, this film, which might seem to have the least to do with Chineseness of those under discussion, continually demonstrates why the meanings associated with Chinese matter. The correlation of racial characteristics in medical discourse (often as if this were not itself a construction but merely a presentation of facts) and illness points to the value that identificatory language might have, for better and for worse. The social position of this family engaged in entrepreneurship to access a transnational health system indicates how a term like *Chinese* might figure in class relations. In this case, many of the costs for the procedures appear to have been waived because doctors wished to study an ethnically Chinese patient with thalassemia.

Tim becomes a kind of medium that enables Richard to inquire about Nan's death. This sort of posthumous reconciliation occurs in the film's depictions of the water: Richard and Nan as children playing on the beach take a different form through Richard and Tim's swimming together. The images contrast the information provided at different times, either in voiceover or typed across the screen, that Richard and Tim missed the last months of Nan's life because of their travels and that Nan had always wanted to meet Tim but passed the morning before Richard returned to Trinidad. The visual parallels in the film establish, if not a meeting, then some meaning in the sense that a life now expired enables the narrator to act and empathize differently in the present. In the final sequence, Tim and Richard surface from the water, concluding a breathtaking eulogy and also a celebration of those who continue to live.

Islands is the shortest piece in the quintet, running less that nine minutes, but it serves as an appropriate coda for the works that precede it. It begins with the Caribbean picturesque. A soundtrack containing splashing waves, calling birds, and chirping crickets accompanies a traveling shot of Trinidad's coastline. The film splices scenes from the Hollywood feature *Heaven Knows, Mr. Allison* (John Huston, 1957), starring Robert Mitchum and Deborah Kerr, with a little bit of original footage. The plot ostensibly unfolds on a Japanese-controlled island in the Pacific, but the actual shooting took place in Trinidad and Tobago. The Hollywood sequences have been recontextualized with text on the screen describing the production process, including Fung's uncle Clive's move to Tobago to play a Japanese soldier in the film. This textual supplement describes the mundane reality of Clive's life—"ordinarily he slices meat in his brother-in-law's shop"—and contrasts it with what should be an extraordinary experience of playing a role in a Hollywood feature. Instead, the film depicts anonymous, ostensibly Japanese soldiers running about the seashore. The film ends with the note that "he strains to see himself." The extraordinary event of the film reproduces the very ordinary invisibility wrought through the dominant neoimperial gaze of Hollywood, in which all Asians look alike and one tropical backdrop substitutes for any other. The commentary of visuality and performance here reverses the intentional reconstruction of the seascape in Fung's earlier documentary *In My Mother's Place*.

The titles on screen offer some historical context and record the perceptions of local audiences on the film's release. Fung's work investigates how media industries shape dominant perceptions and the fungibility of Hollywood Orientalism: a Trinidadian Chinese man assumes a Japanese role, and one tropical isle serves as the equivalent of another. The film also picks up on the ongoing material relationship of Trinidad and Tobago with the United States, particularly after the United States established military bases there and, more implicitly, in relation to the calypso craze that swept the United States (which will be noted by anyone unfortunate enough to remember Mitchum's calypso recordings).[48] How does culture circulate, and what do such cultural flows produce? Fung's oeuvre offers complicated responses to such inquiries; they track the distance between Rita's affecting performance of an old patois song and Mitchum's oddly affected vocalizations in his calypso phase.

Fung's four films that I have discussed deconstruct the insular world of the Chinese Trinidadian family and its quotidian experiences. Memory screens out as much as it captures. The spectator sees moving images, but the films emphasize the difficulty of contextualization, of producing coherent meaning. Instead, each work seems to hinge on an affective relationship to the visual: a longing for connection that the pictures promise to wind together. The films further elicit physical sensations from the spectator in the forms of kinesthesia (for example, the perception of the regular flow of an ocean current) to thermoception (the ambiance of a warm living room juxtaposed against flurries of snow). Through visual and aural stimuli, the films enjoin viewers to feel something. But Fung's work does not prompt such bodily experiences in a manner that clearly correlates each film with a desired corporeal response (as do body genres like horror or pornography). Instead, these physical sensations work on a more impressionistic level. Again, reeling produces a kind of disorientation, an affective charge that the spectator processes over time in the wake of movements of people across the globe.

These concerns recur in a different manner with Fung's most recent work on extended kin, titled *Nang by Nang*. That film offers something of a commentary on the Chinese Caribbean documentary as a whole, so I defer my elaboration of its work until the end of the chapter. Genetic links, however, also inspire other Chinese Caribbean synaesthetic links, and I turn next to an example that overlaps with and also departs from Fung's engaging practice of filmmaking.

Certainly, fragmentation of familial bonds into amorphous expressions of affect informs López's *The Longest Journey*. López explores relationships among China, Cuba, and Havana's *barrio chino*. The film shows López's contemporary moment and alludes to, although it does not completely bring into focus, the *trata amarilla* ("yellow trade"), or traffic in Chinese coolie labor in the nineteenth century.[49] The narrative assembles fragments that inform the director's own background and uses a mélange of historical reenactments, interviews, and other devices to inquire into how Chineseness might have shaped and continues to circulate within Cuba.

The Longest Journey opens with the clash of a gong on the soundtrack and an intertitle on screen: "The longest journey begins with the first step. Chinese proverb" ("*El viaje mas largo se iricia con el primer paso. Proverbio Chino*"). The camera tilts down from darkness to the corner of a brightly decorated table on which sits a dark ovoid object. A hand reaches into the frame and picks up the object, which turns out to be a pair of stones for casting lots. A high-angle shot reveals an altar at which a male figure picks up joss sticks and reads a pamphlet, but the writing is not discernible. Cuts juxtapose this take with a man seated half in darkness, a set of candles, and a fu dog in black stone with a candle behind it; smoke rises from below the statuette. The bang of a gong punctuates each cut until a Cantonese monologue occurs on the soundtrack. The film cuts from the black stone figurine to a rear view of the man at the table, which, from this angle, now appears as part of a larger altar. No translation of the Cantonese appears in the subtitles.

In the opening shots, the viewer witnesses a ritual space, exoticized with incense smoke and shadowy figures. The tone of this sequence is both somber and mysterious. The lack of subtitles, once the soundtrack includes spoken language, marks through absence Chinese as untranslatable. This theme persists to varying degrees through the remainder of the film. But the Orientalist mise-en-scène and soundtrack do not code as feminine, as is typical of classic Hollywood cinema. The perspective is masculine, from the voiceover to the bodies that inhabit the frame; men occupy the world projected through the camera. As the opening credits begin to appear, this world of men comes into view in increasingly fetishistic fashion.

The film cuts from the image of the singular figure at the altar and his apparently read monologue to a series of stills of various men. The mood shifts thanks to a lively piano with orchestral accompaniment on the soundtrack. The camera focuses on each person individually, revealing the images in pieces through tilts, zooms, and pans. Superimposed on the stills are the opening credits. This series of stills—black-and-white photographs of mostly elderly chaps—features people racially marked as Asian. These images become part of a ritual invocation; they provide a potential context for the actions starting the narrative.

If ritual is a performance of conventional elements designed to suture a subject into a larger historical frame, then this film would seem to announce itself as a performative mediation of individual and community from the outset. However, the goal of the ritualistic behavior remains unclear, as does its import; in this case, then, the ritual would seem to be a theatrical staging of Chineseness (that is, the ritual substitutes for a more expository explanation of what might constitute Chinese in Cuba). The central question to which the title gestures also raises spatial demarcations as central to what might otherwise be more of a temporal investigation. What are the nodal points of the journey? In what might be an answer to this provocation, the film next cuts to a seascape of a large sailing vessel cresting the waves. Various shots of the boat are sutured together with the following masculine voiceover: "This story began in the twelfth moon of the forty-seventh year of Emperor Tocon's reign: on January 2, 1847, when more than three hundred poor laborers embarked on the frigate *Oquendi* at the port of Amon, in Canton."[50] The voiceover informs the viewer that these men were sojourners with eight-year contracts to work in Cuba, and that one hundred and forty-two days after their departure, two hundred and six survivors entered the port of Havana. In elaborating its opening ritual through this specific story, the film becomes a technology that not only describes historical events, but also tries to construct an experience for the viewer to connect to the past.

The next sequence displays a torch moving through a catacomb-like space. The flame recalls the visuals of the many candles in the opening. The formal element here suggests that the ritual has transported the viewer elsewhere. This space, however, is never exactly defined. The voiceover describes it as a *barracon* (which the subtitles translate a bit euphemistically as "temporary living quarters"). The film stages these particular transitional spaces through dramatic reconstructions. The camera wanders through a space filled with rats and soiled limbs (particularly feet) and faces. In this explicit re-vision of the material conditions of Chinese laborers who journeyed to Cuba, the film relies on gaps in the visual field—in this case, bodies viewed always partially, in medium and close-up shots—to supplement a fragmented narrative.

Indeed, much of the film offers footage without much context. The images include several men who stand outside and bow, a graveyard, an interview in Spanish with one Kwan Kimfu, and several shots of religious iconography. These last images occur in tandem with a voiceover explanation of the syncretic religious traditions apparently practiced by the Chinese Cuban population. However, the voiceover seems to connect all of these diverse elements through a sense of nostalgia, although that nostalgia takes different forms throughout the piece. For example, Kwan Kimfu opines, "All Chinese are homesick." Certainly, the verbal recounting of various Chinese myths in the narrative would further suggest that the mourned object is China.

However, later images of busy streets are juxtaposed against the comparative emptiness of Havana's Chinatown. Several interviews and a shot of a monument to Chinese revolutionaries repeatedly express the Cuban nationalism of the interview subjects and return to an immigrant assimilation paradigm in which the film documents Chinese contributions to Cuban life. At one point, the voiceover intones, "Middle-class Chinese from California arrived in Havana and opened up small businesses"; this segment features both stills and the director's own footage of men involved in quotidian activities—eating food, getting haircuts, shopping for and selling goods. As the opening of this documentary short might portend, the film is finally quite ambivalent about how it constructs Chinese Cuban as a category. The filmmaker's explanation of his relationship to his father doubles this cultural ambivalence; he states succinctly in the context of his discussing the wooing of his mulatto mother that "my father, Lan Yan, was a great mystery to me." The final voiceover states, "They are a part of us, yet their essence remains a mystery hidden behind a tenuous but impassable barrier of sandalwood smoke and Chinese reserve protecting their identity." A Chinese motif on the soundtrack concludes this reverie, which yields to Jose Urfe's musical theme that began the film. The final image of the film is a pair of masculine legs accompanied by a cane walking away from the camera. The image of calves and thighs offers a final fetishistic view of travel. This emphasis on peripatetic travel depends nonetheless on the sea as its condition of possibility, given the film's own allusion to the *Oquendi*.

Peter Chin, who immigrated to Toronto from Jamaica in 1966, also seems interested in processes of theatrical ritual that connect individuals to larger histories. Initially trained as a classical musician, Chin studied fine arts at York University, where he began to create intermedial pieces. In Chin's case, that term would come to refer not only to influences from the Western avant-garde—including modern dance, fluxus, and performance art—but also to the intercultural investigations that his creative work engages—that is, the collaborative processes of creation that reveal connections linking and gaps separating societies and their aesthetic practices. Chin's touchstones in this endeavor include a number of Asian performance traditions, including those of Indonesia and, later, Cambodia. To facilitate such work, Chin in 1999 founded the company Tribal Crackling Wind, through which he produces what he has called an Asian model of total theater, integrating dance, music, and other forms of performance. For example, his piece *Woven* (2015) draws on craft histories and techniques from several regions of the world, suggesting the persistence of a category of folk traditions across the globe.

Outside of a concert dance or larger performance setting, bodily movement is characteristic of migration and, as *Woven* illustrates, also indigenous cultural production connected to particular places. Given such contexts, the fact that Chin's codirected film *Jamaican* features dance prominently elicits little surprise. Indeed, the collage-like assemblage of elements, including Chin's choreography, the soundtrack by Gordon Neil Allen, the diegetic drumming of Kevan Douglas, and interviews of a dozen individuals (including scholars and artists), enables viewers to understand the prismatic quality of the film's title. At once embodied in and subject to the productive ecologies that give the term meaning, *Jamaican* is, as the first interviewee, Veerle Poupeye, the former executive director of the National Gallery of Jamaica, states, "a complicated set of cultural dynamics," both an open-ended concept and a continually morphing lived experience. In this film, Chineseness inflects the meanings of *Jamaican*.

The film begins with Chin's voiceover, which declares, "I am a kind of Jamaican that might not be familiar." From the start, this project announces itself as insular in the sense of being about Chin's own experience of what he terms "Jamaican-ness" and eccentric (as in, having an axis off-center) in that it seeks to understand how this term means in different locales to various people. The city of Kingston provides the initial location for the shoot, and its institutions obviously play a role in the perpetuation of certain definitions of Jamaican. For that reason, perhaps, the film opens in St. Peter and Paul Preparatory School. The voiceover continues noting that the national motto of Jamaica, "Out of many, one people," incorporates the diversity embodied not only by Chin but by what he calls the Jamaica matrix: "Chinese, Black, and White." In this way, Chin's own background serves as a hermeneutic for the national project itself, especially since Chin sees the coincidence of his own birth and that of Jamaican independence in 1962 as significant.

However, Chin also notes, in these opening moments of the film, exclusions that contradict the national slogan; the Coat of Arms displays Taino people, often believed to be absent in the nation-state. The voiceover ponders this assertion, wondering how certain traditions and the people who practiced them might remain in the island space. In contrast to these verbal musings, children play in front of the camera and frequently directly address it. The tension between the past, evoked through a national image of an indigenous group, and the future, suggested through the children, raises questions about how Jamaican-ness might be shifting even as the filmmaker constructs and records a certain version of it. Such plays between visions of what might have been and what might be recur in the film and reproduce, again, what I have described as a logic of reeling. For example, a machete-swinging man in a medium shot might seem to index a continuing history of manual agricultural labor on the island until the camera cuts to a long shot showing a backhoe mechanically excavating the same plot of land.

As the film challenges stable timelines from, for example, tradition to industrial modernity, it also works to undo a binary of emplacement and displacement; this is, again, the eccentric perspective that Chin's film offers. His interview with Poupeye implies that Jamaican-ness is not reducible to some essential core; in her words, Jamaica is "a country that has produced a large number of migrants who have spread all over the world," with products such as music that circulate globally. These streams of Jamaican-ness produce a situation in which any definition of Jamaican depends on what happens within but also outside the nation-state. Chin analogizes this complexity in the form of the interview, which begins seated in a parlor and abruptly shifts to the interviewer and his subject seated in the middle of a parking lot before showing them again in the interior room.

Space functions not just as a theme in the film but as part of the overall hermeneutics of Jamaican-ness. This embodied, physical investigation in specific ecologies—city streets, shipping ports, highland outlooks, aboraceous glens—provides certain conditions of possibility for moving the body. The film emphasizes this aspect of Jamaican-ness through the many dance and drumming sequences that punctuate the film. Many of these involve Chin's peripatetic performance that moves through municipal or countryside landscapes. Both diegetic and extradiegetic spectators see Chin's often lyrical movements, which tend to register within the film as out of place in the contexts of pedestrian comings and goings. This interruptive spatial practice frequently facilitates a denaturalizing of the background on screen. The extradiegetic spectator becomes conscious, for example, of the disjuncture between a voiceover interview on the singularity of Jamaica as Chin dances in front of a Digicel outlet and National Commercial Bank, corporations that imply the homogenizing pressures of global communication and financial networks.

The film's shift from Jamaica to Panama underscores the ways in which various political and cultural spaces inflect Jamaican-ness, further emphasizing its eccentric articulation. In her reflection on how "the Jamaicans live," Anna Graciela Rose Mature states baldly, "Everybody's one.... God made us all, and we're one set of people.... I's white and you's black, and I's Chinese, and you's Indian and we, we didn't have that here." Like most of the interviews throughout the piece, this speaker offers a complicated rumination, one to which the viewer has only partial access. For example, Mature discusses faith without much elaboration. However, during the segment, Chin dances in the Cementerio Chino. The setting of his performance challenges Mature's claims. To what extent does Christianity inform her understanding of Jamaica? What exactly is the relation of the Chinese colony to the construction of a Panamanian Jamaican? What kinds of embodied practices link faith and national or ethnic belonging? Panama's relationship to Chineseness is especially multifaceted, because it remains one of more than a score of countries that officially recognize Taiwan.[51] The concrete manifestations of a very specific diasporic community as materialized in the graveyard's headstones unsettle the feeling of unity expressed by Mature. Or they may suggest incongruities between the past and the present.

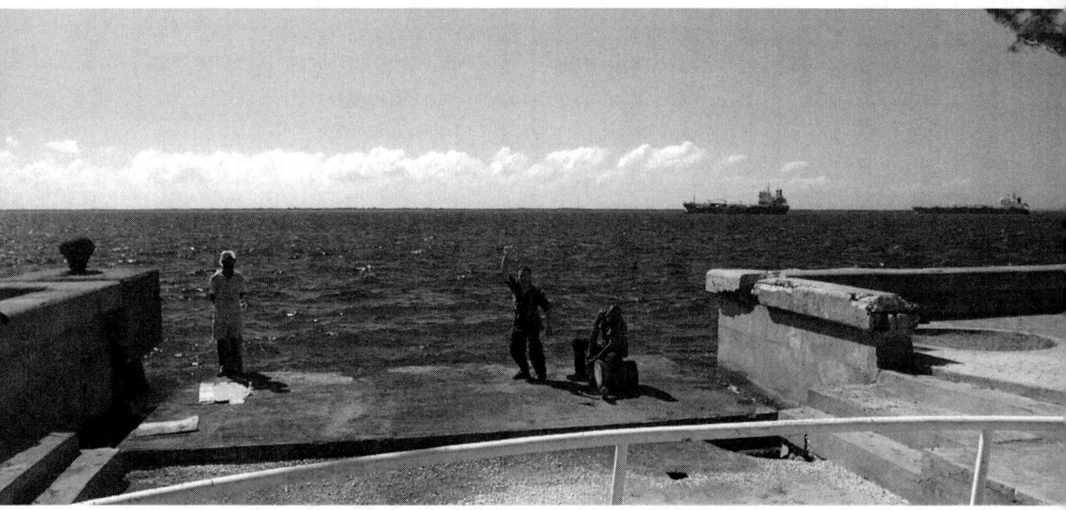

Fig. 1.5. Peter Chin dances with the sea at his back. Still from *Jamaican*.
© Peter Chin and Jeremy Mimnagh.

Certainly, some of the other interviews in Panama—including those with Braudia Corina Dixon Warren de Conquet, Kevin Antonio Fortuné, and Sheriff Eunice—indicate how one might "feel Jamaican." Each interviewee provides at least one example, albeit many overlap: most mention familial ties, but individuals respectively discuss skin color, speech patterns, and Bob Marley. These indicators link the affective dimensions of Jamaican-ness to bodily surfaces, linguistic features, and transnationally circulating commodities. Collectively, they suggest the slipperiness of the term *Jamaican*, its contingency on everything from local to global referents. The alterations in meaning coincide in the film with shifts in physical location. Moving across Panama from Bocas del Toro (including Isla Bastimentos) to Panama City (including the canal), the continually changing images on screen resist attempts to fix Jamaican-ness to one site. The seascapes that form the background of many of the shots indicate transnational linkages that seep past national boundaries.

As a contrast to this watery vision, the Panama sequence suddenly cuts to a scene in artist Margaret Chen's studio and then to a bamboo forest. Chen identifies herself as a Chinese Jamaican Canadian at the same time that she contests the utility of such labels, because they "try to capture something that's uncatchable." Her sculptural work, which appears on screen only as part of the background, would, on closer inspection, materialize some of her more philosophical commentary on processes of identification. She contends that "things seep through" from the past into the present in ways that one can only apprehend through retrospection. This belief structures her most exhibited works: her Steppe series of nearly a score of wood-based mixed media panels, or reliefs. Her family's furniture enterprise inspired these often large-scale works that involve layering various materials, carvings, and images over one another. The sedimentation calls attention to what Chen has called "subterranean" in the sense of drawing on unconscious Asian influences (thus the title's allusion to the Eurasian Steppe).[52] Like Peter Chin, Margaret Chen does not focus on incorporating specifically Chinese aesthetic traditions in her work, yet they both emphasize Chinese circulation (either through the allusion to the steppe or through physical bodies).

Nonetheless, Chin perhaps finds a better bedfellow in Richard Chen See, with whom he has an interview that largely addresses concert dance. Chen See has a history with Alvin Ailey American Dance Theater, among other companies, especially Paul Taylor Dance Company. This segment explicitly discusses the value of nonverbal communication and also the kind of access that a Caribbean person of Chinese descent might have to certain African traditions in comparison to an African American. Chen See has a high level of formal training in dance and actively sought to shape the international dance world. His expressed interest in the institutional politics of the dance world do not seem as operative in Peter Chin's practice, whose work is a bit more self-motivated (sometimes more self-reflexive) and less committed to concert dance as such. A commitment to an exploration of corporeal movement and how bodies embody cultural difference and connection links the two men's practice.

Chin intercuts his interview with Chen See with Chin's solo in what appears to be the kitchen of a commercial bakery. Close-ups of flour and sugar measurement, and of dough produced via assembly line mechanization, suggest physical labor in the service of capitalism. The images of bags of Jamaican cane sugar might remind viewers of a historical context, as the drudgery on sugar plantations marked a transition in the Caribbean and shaped it into a cradle of globalization. In this case, women compose the bulk of the workforce in the factory. Chin's performance to Douglas's drumming breaks up the space, interrupting the work stream, and it also calls attention to the gendered dynamics of the floor, albeit without elaborating them. Meanwhile, the soundtrack transmits not only the beat of the drums but also Chen See's thoughts on being called a "Chiney boy" and his own movement vocabulary, beginning with a sense of community derived from his island roots. This scene, then, offers a different way to think about bodies and communities coming together through food and/or dance. Habits of the body bring what might be otherwise disparate social groups into some sort of relation, at least for a while.

The final interview, with Erica Neeganawedgin, returns the spectator to a discussion of the Taino people and the ways in which she ties identity to "rootedness in the land." Although not a particularly long sequence, it forms a kind of bookend with the mention of the Taino at the beginning of the film. The dialogue yields to shots of Jamaican mountains under time-lapse photography. Again, the film would seem to ask how Jamaica and ideas about what *Jamaican* might mean have changed and will continue to change. The precise relationship of indigeneity to Chineseness remains unexplored here. The film's explorations of Taino cultural legacies nevertheless remain to question how Chineseness might matter and in what ways Chinese people and finances might occlude or otherwise complexify native connections to the island and the larger region.

The last section of Chin's film, which takes place in the mezzanine space opposite a proscenium stage, reinforces the sense of theatricality of the film. This final sequence casts what has come before as a culmination of different local performances that also enact connections among the terms *Chinese*, *Jamaican*, and *global*. From this perspective, globalization is theatrical insofar as it is a set of enacted practices that demonstrate the way in which Chineseness might structure and be informed by other terms: *Canadian*, *Jamaican*, and *American*. Chin's film culminates his exploration of these conjunctions not through exposition but through dance. Significantly, his moving response does not occur on the stage but in the space for the audience. The film implies not that we witness globalization inflected by Chinese circulation but that we experience it on a visceral level. Like the other films I have examined, *Jamaican* enables spectators to see but also perhaps to feel the vicissitudes of Chineseness, drawing attention to different assemblages of Chineseness across an antipodal imaginary.

DOCUMENTARY, THEATRICALITY, AND THE SEASCAPE

All of the works examined in this chapter evoke complementary and also competing sensations of Chinese-inflected globalization through discursive as well as (if to differing degrees) affective and phenomenological engagement. The kinds of movements they show us—migration, foodways, dance—highlight different but interrelated aspects of Chineseness and how that term accrues meaning as it circulates in, through, and outside the Caribbean. The evidence the films assemble in this regard may work through some expository framing, but they also provide different ways of apprehending the global, questioning the epistemologies of rational deduction that would give that term meaning. Whereas the domestic ethnographies tend to invest heavily in linear narratives and expository framing, those I have called synaesthetic documentaries elicit impressions of feeling Chinese, often without attempting to encapsulate such sensations in a fully coherent manner.

Theorists of the Caribbean, such as Glissant, Crichlow, and Northover, animate my own thinking on theatricality, Chineseness, and the region's relation to the world. That said, my perspective on these issues begins with a critique of Glissant. His occasional writing about Chinese things is, like some moments in the documentaries I have discussed, not coherent and can be exasperating. When discussing the country or its people, Glissant tends to offer inanities in what is otherwise an amazingly insightful and productive body of writing. For example, in the *Poetics of Relation* (first published in French in 1990), he speculated on what he understood as the endogenous quality of Chinese language, although he avowed a lack of knowledge in this area.[53] I have shown in the introduction how terms like *typhoon* came into Western language, and, in my previous book, I have discussed the import of words like "brainwashing" (*xinao*) and *qipao*, or *cheongsam*. Chinese has, of course, long borrowed from other lexicons everyday vocabulary words, from those pertaining to religion, like *amen* ("amen") and *anjier* ("angel"), to cultural practices, like *baleiwu* ("ballet") and *yujia* ("yoga"), to commercial and social formations, like *bazha* ("bazaar") and *kuer* ("queer"). On the basis of language alone, China exhibits historical and ongoing connections to many parts of the globe.

Although the role of China in Glissant's thought deserves its own study, I would note simply that, even twenty years after the publication of *Poetics of*

Relation, Glissant continued to speak of China with something of an unapologetic, sometimes Orientalist flair. In an interview with Malian cultural theorist Manthia Diawara, he explained his thoughts on the potential of Chinese *mestizaje*: "Historically China has not exploded onto the world. . . . There have always been Chinese in the world, but that's been an individual phenomenon. They've been merchants and traders; in every country of the Antilles, there is a Chinese shopkeeper. . . . But there hasn't been a fundamental Chinese diaspora."[54]

Perhaps my disagreement with Glissant here concerns semantics and what constitutes "fundamental." However, later in the interview, he elaborated in a discussion on borders his sense that the Chinese "have rarely been invasive."[55] From the perspective of Tibetans and Uyghurs, that statement would seem quite ignorant. In any case, Glissant linked these thoughts to his general understanding of China's migration policies; he succinctly stated, "I believe that the Great Wall was built to prevent the Chinese from leaving China."[56] Such rhetorical positioning ultimately means that he did not substantively address China and the circulations of Chinese goods and people in his archipelagic thought, despite the fact that they have helped to transform even his home isle of Martinique (see chapter 3 of this book).

The Chinese Atlantic is partially a response to Glissant, whose work would be enriched by thinking about China as fundamental to his respective oeuvre. Nevertheless, as I have already suggested in my discussion of *Samuel Lowe*, Glissant offers a dynamic notion of relation that I see in productive relationship with Crichlow and Northover's take on creolization. Moreover, and notwithstanding my criticisms of Glissant on the import of China and Chineseness, his work intersects Crichlow and Northover's in asserting that theatricality matters in perceiving and establishing the Caribbean's relationships to the world. Glissant, of course, would eventually divide worldliness (*mondialité*) from globalization (*mondialisation*), which he sees as homogenizing.[57] In his earlier work, one finds an emergent sense of the complicated role that theatricality can play within this frame. In *Caribbean Discourse* (originally published in French in 1981), he wrote several pages on what I would term the theatricality of the everyday (*dans la rue*, the street scene) and stage performance (*théâtre*), neither of which is a diversion (*détour*, a key concept for Glissant in terms of Caribbean cultural production and one he especially associated with Creole language) that facilitates awareness (*prise de conscience*).[58] Yet collective theatricalization can be one of the first drivers of resistance (the French reads, "*Mais le délire individuel et la théâtralisation collective, en tant que forces de résistance, sont les premiers 'conducteurs' de cette conscience*").[59] Collective theatrical acts would embody and generate politics that might move against the passive enjoyment of representations in which the formerly colonized are, for example, relegated to folkloric traditions. Glissant pointed toward South America as an illustration of the variety of necessary theatrical production that needs to happen in Martinique.

Crichlow also implicitly refers to theatricality in her case studies. She discusses the Rastafarian King Arthur in Jamaica and the Lucians in her native St. Lucia. The former figure's mode of self-presentation involves a Toyota emblazoned with his name and stuffed with a desultory array of things including photographs, dolls, and flags. The latter group staged political satire. These case studies argue that the presentational venues of car and stage create intimate interactions through which signs and processes of globalization might be witnessed. Both Crichlow and Glissant explore the paradoxes of globalization through various embodiments of theatricality. This point winds me back to the Chinese Atlantic documentary.

Given that each film offers a slightly different investigative project, I have tried to analyze each on its own terms; nevertheless, all of the documentaries use and frequently stage seascapes. Sometimes such visualization works to establish a sense of place by revealing a specific shoreline or port. In other instances, the seascapes call attention to migratory travel and to the sensation of being adrift yet connected to others. Here, I am reminded of the last sequence of Richard Fung's *Nang by Nang* (much of which takes place in New Mexico, far from Trinidad and outside of any aquatic frame). The last two minutes of the film reveal Richard and Nang walking on the beach. A pair of fishermen appear in a long shot, their lines cast into the water. Nang, a former dancer with Geoffrey and Boscoe Holder, dances in the beach grass (a plant that has its own history of migration, given its historical distribution to control sand dune erosion). A final image of the surf appears. The view of the coast here inspires a search for sustenance and a creative improvisation. Fung reels these different images and ways of looking at the ocean together, asking what new forms of relation might emerge through the tides and the transit they facilitate. Rather than an empirical given, the seascape sequence constellates various forms of visual evidence, asking what new forms of being assemble in their wake. In so doing, Fung reveals the efficacy of Chinese Caribbean documentary and the analytic of reeling. Like the other films I have analyzed, Fung's *Nang by Nang* recasts the relations among people and places by denaturalizing images and the transparent histories and current social realities they might seem to depict. Sensorial engagement, this time created through the kinesthetic aspects of a dancing body captured as a moving image, destabilizes how Chinese circulations might mean in and through the Caribbean.

NOTES

1. Paul Gilroy has provided a strong lead in conceptualizing the Atlantic, even if he did not initiate it. A general overview of critical currents is provided in Jack P. Greene and Philip D. Morgan, *Atlantic History: A Critical Appraisal* (Oxford: Oxford University Press, 2009), and, of course, the journal *Atlantic Studies,* launched in 2004. On the green (Irish) Atlantic, see Peter D. O'Beill and David Lloyd, *The Black and Green Atlantic: Cross-Currents of the African and Irish Diasporas* (New York: Palgrave Macmillan, 2009). The editors are interested not only in the antagonisms but also the solidarities among these groups. For a specific performance lens, see Kathleen Gough, *Haptic Allegories: Kinship and Performance in the Black and Green Atlantic* (Routledge: New York, 2013). The attempts to push the conversation beyond discussions of black and white are fewer; a summary of indigenous peoples' roles in shaping the Atlantic can be found in the introduction of Jace Weaver's *The Red Atlantic: American Indigenes and the Making of the Modern World, 1000–1927* (Chapel Hill: University of North Carolina Press, 2014).

2. Roger B. Stein, *Seascapes and the American Imagination* (New York: Whitney Museum of Art, 1975), 1.

3. Anne-Marie Lee-Loy, "Identifying a Chinese Caribbean Literature: Pitfalls and Possibilities," *sx salon* 15 (February 2014), accessed March 24, 2014, http://smallaxe.net/wordpress3/discussions/2014/02/28/identifying-a-chinese-caribbean-literature/. Gilles Deleuze and Félix Guattari, "What Is a Minor Literature?" *Mississippi Review* 11, no. 3 (Winter/Spring 1983): 13–33.

4. See Richard J. Bernal, *Dragon in the Caribbean: China's Global Re-Dimensioning Challenges and Opportunities for the Caribbean* (Kingston and Miami: Ian Randle, 2014). See also Ronald C. Archibold, "China Buys Inroads in the Caribbean, Catching US Notice," *The New York Times,* April 7, 2012.

5. Janelle Reinelt, "The Promise of Documentary," in *Get Real: Documentary Theatre Past and Present,* eds. Alison Forsyth and Chris Megson (New York: Palgrave Macmillan, 2009), 6.

6. Reinelt, "The Promise of Documentary," 7.

7. Maaike Bleeker, Jon Foley Sherman, and Eirini Nedelkopoulou, eds., *Performance and Phenomenology: Traditions and Transformations* (New York: Routledge, 2015), 1.

8. Michael Renov, *The Subject of Documentary* (Minneapolis: University of Minnesota Press, 2004).

9. Renov, *Documentary*, 219.

10. Jason Middleton, *Documentary's Awkward Turn* (New York: Routledge), 7.

11. Although the designation of Charlotte Street as Chinatown has been an informal one, Port of Spain's mayor stated in 2018 that he intended to mark the street with two monuments. See Julien Neaves, "'Chinatown' for Charlotte Street, PoS Mayor Says," August 4, 2018, *Trinidad and Tobago Newsday*, https://newsday.co.tt/2018/08/04/chinatown-for-charlotte-street/.

12. Chee was a Miss Universe contestant and the winner on the reality fashion show *Project Runway* in 2011.

13. See her website, "Ms. Chin Productions," accessed June 29, 2016, http://www.mschinproductions.com/#home.

14. The Chinese shop in Jamaica has been particularly well narrated in both academic and creative prose. See Easton Lee, *From Behind the Counter: Poems from a Rural Jamaican Experience* (Kingston: Ian Randle, 1998) and *Encounters: Voices and Echoes: Poems from Chinese-Jamaican Experience* (Kingston: Ian Randle, 2003); critical analysis of his work can be found in Anne-Marie Lee-Loy, *Searching for Mr. Chin: Constructions of Nation and the Chinese in West Indian Literature* (Philadelphia: Temple University Press, 2010), and Tzarina T. Prater, "Labrish and Mooncakes: The Meeting of Vernaculars in the Work of Easton Lee," *Small Axe* 43 (March 2014): 149–160. Aside from literature and its study, see Winston Hayden Chang Jr., *The Legacy of the Hakka Shopkeepers of the West Indies* (Scarborough: Wanata, 2004). Jeanette Kong has written that she specifically works in the tradition of Lee Tom Yin, Patrick and Loraine Lee, and Ray Chen. See Sean Metzger, "Roundtable: Imaging and Imagining the Chinese Caribbean: Jeanette Kong, Maria Lau, and Laura Fong Prosper," *Asian Diasporic Visual Cultures and the Americas* 5 (2019): 183–193.

15. The attention to foodways overlaps with other documentaries of this type. I have discussed elsewhere Cheuk Kwan's multiepisode work, *Chinese Restaurants*, particularly the fifth vignette, which concerns one of Trinidad's major cities, San Fernando, and one of its hallmarks, Soong's Great Wall Restaurant. See my "Chineseness in Caribbean Cinema," *sx salon* 17 (October 2014) http://smallaxe.net/wordpress3/discussions/2014/10/22/chineseness-in-caribbean-cinema/.

16. Unless otherwise noted, quotations are taken from the film.

17. Erin Khuê Ninh, *Ingratitude: The Debt-Bound Daughter in Asian American Literature* (New York: New York University Press, 2011).

18. Lara D. Nielsen, "Introduction Heterotopic Transformations, the (Il)Liberal Neoliberal," in *Neoliberalism and Global Theatres: Performance Permutations*, eds. Lara D. Nielsen and Patricia Ybarra (New York: Palgrave Macmillan, 2012), 2.

19. A similar image appears in the published book as part of the insert of photographs.

20. Aihwa Ong and Stephen Collier, *Global Assemblages: Technology, Politics, and Ethics as Anthropological Problems* (Hoboken: Wiley-Blackwell, 2004).

21. Paula Williams Madison, *Finding Samuel Lowe: China, Jamaica, Harlem* (New York: Amistad, 2015), 109 and 110.

22. Rocio Davis, *Relative Histories: Mediating History in Asian American Family Memoirs* (Honolulu: University of Hawaii Press, 2011).

23. Sandra Pouchet Paquet, *Caribbean Autobiography: Cultural Identity and Self-Representation* (Madison: The University of Wisconsin Press, 2002).

24. King-Kok Cheung, "Chinese and Chinese American Life-Writing," *Cambridge Journal of China Studies* 10, no. 2 (2015): 1–20.

25. Williams Madison, *Lowe*, 3.

26. Williams Madison, *Lowe*, 268.

27. See Williams Madison, *Lowe*, 41 and 55 respectively.

28. Williams Madison, *Lowe*, 74.

29. Williams Madison, *Lowe*, 146.

30. Williams Madison, *Lowe*, 202 and 221.

31. Williams Madison, *Lowe*, 84.

32. Williams Madison, *Lowe*, 100.

33. Michaeline A. Crichlow, *Globalization and the Post-Creole Imagination: Notes on Fleeing the Plantation* (Durham: Duke University Press, 2009), 21.

34. Crichlow, *Globalization and the Post-Creole Imagination*, 70.

35. Their article "Homing Modern Freedoms: Creolization and the Politics of Making Place," *Cultural Dynamics* 21, no. 3 (2009): 283–216, elaborates this suggestion from *Globalization and the Post-Creole Imagination*.

36. Bill Nichols, *Blurred Boundaries: Questions of Meaning in Contemporary Culture* (Indianapolis: Indiana University Press, 1994), 104.

37. Nichols, *Boundaries*, 94.

38. Judith Butler, *Bodies That Matter: On the Discursive Limits of Sex* (New York: Routledge, 1993), xii.

39. As a sidebar, these works are all single-channel videos, although I use "film" to describe them.

40. Richard Fung, "Remaking Home Movies," in *Mining the Home Movie: Excavations in Histories and Memories*, eds. Karen L. Ishizuka and Patricia Zimmermann (Berkeley and Los Angeles: University of California Press, 2008).

41. Peter X. Feng, "Getting Lost on *The Way to My Father's Village*," in *Like Mangoes in July: The Work of Richard Fung*, eds. Helen Lee and Kerri Sakamoto (Toronto: Insomniac, 2002), 30–39.

42. José Esteban Muñoz, "Revisiting the Autoethnographic Performance: Richard Fung's Theory/Praxis as Queer Performativity," in *Like Mangoes in July: The Work of Richard Fung*, eds. Helen Lee and Kerri Sakamoto (Toronto: Insomniac, 2002), 55.

43. Julianne Pidduck, "Queer Kinship and Ambivalence: Video Ethnographies by Jean Carlomusto and Richard Fung," *GLQ* 15, no. 3 (2009): 445.

44. Diana Fuss, "Inside/Out" *Inside/Out: Lesbian Theories, Gay Theories*, ed. Diana Fuss (New York: Routledge, 1991), 1.

45. For different queer readings of *My Mother's Place*, see Muñoz, "Revisiting the Autoethnographic Performance," and Thomas Waugh, *The Romance of Transgression in Canada: Queering Sexualities, Nations, Cinemas* (Montreal: McGill-Queen's University Press, 2006).

46. I use Fung's own spelling here from his article "Remaking Home Movies"; I believe the legend is connected to the Warao people.

47. Priscilla Wald, *Contagious: Cultures, Carriers, and the Outbreak Narrative* (Durham: Duke University Press, 2008).

48. For an illuminating analysis of the American obsession with calypso, see Shane Vogel, *Stolen Time: Black Fad Performance and the Calypso Craze* (Chicago: The University of Chicago Press, 2018).

49. Kathleen López, *Chinese Cubans: A Transnational History* (Chapel Hill: University of North Carolina Press, 2013), does a remarkable job of tracing the movement from indenture to wage laborer in Cuba. The period of coolie traffic has been extensively discussed in the scholarship of Denise Helly, Evelyn Hu-Dehart, Moon-Ho Jung, Rebecca Scott, Lisa Yun, and myself, among others.

50. I am not sure what this name references. The seventh emperor of the Qing Dynasty, the daoguang emperor, ruled from 1820–1850. Perhaps Tocon is a transliteration.

51. On the ways in which Taiwan complicates belonging to ethnic, national, and other communities, see Lok C.D. Siu, *Memories of a Future Home: Diasporic Citizenship of Chinese in Panama* (Palo Alto: Stanford University Press, 2005).

52. See Veerle Poupeye, *Caribbean Art* (London: Thames and Hudson, 2012), 176–178.

53. Édouard Glissant, *Poetics of Relation*, trans. Betsy Wing (Ann Arbor: The University of Michigan Press, 1997), 23.

54. Manthia Diawara, "One World in Relation: Édouard Glissant in Conversation with Manthia Diawara," *Nka Journal of Contemporary African Art* 28 (Spring 2011): 8. The word *mestizaje* appears on page seven and elicits Glissant's elaboration.

55. Diawara, "World," 15.

56. Diawara, "World," 15.

57. See *La Cohée du Lamentin/ Poétique V* (Paris: Gallimard, 2005).

58. Édouard Glissant, *Le Discours Antillais* (Paris: Gallimard, 1997), 683.

59. Glissant, *Discours*, 684.

2~INCORPORATING

From September 2017 through February 2018, the artist Nicole Awai (b. 1966), who originally hails from Trinidad and Tobago, exhibited *PS: Simultaneity* (2017), a rectangular 50″ × 159″ collage mounted on the wall of the gallery space in Los Angeles's California African American Museum as part of the exhibition *Circles and Circuits: Chinese Caribbean Art*. An observer might best describe Awai's contribution to the show as a sculptural mural that incorporates a collage of various materials, including acrylic, foam, graphite, paint, paper, and polish. Composed of four square panels arranged on a horizontal axis, the materials protrude, sometimes quite dramatically, from the base as if oozing out of the sections. In actuality, the artwork has incorporated these materials to provide the impression of a kind of dynamic seepage and accumulation.

The work brings together recurring elements from the artist's corpus. As Awai has explained to me, *PS: Simultaneity* reflects back "on the last decade of the visual investigation in my work as a whole." She adds that it "resonates with the particularity and presence of Caribbean space . . . the work is also about the history and malleability of the Caribbean (including issues of displacement and replacement) space/landscape as a site of discovery, creation, and always, a perpetual material, economic, and cultural resource for the world."[1] Awai has frequently rendered such concerns in her corpus through sedimentation and imbrication providing a layering of material that

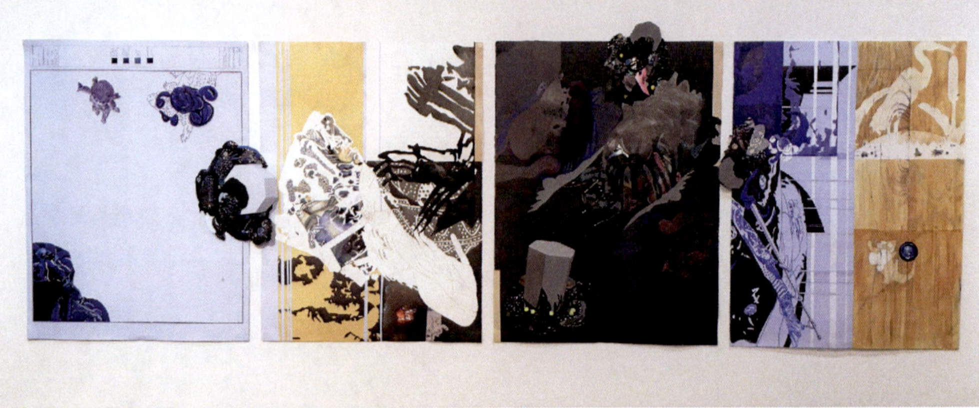

Fig. 2.1. Nicole Awai, *P.S. Simultaneity*, 2017. Graphite, acrylic paint, nail polish, resin, construction foam, flocking, reflective paper, collaged prints, mirrored glass, plastic and glass beads, synthetic paper on/in paper. 158 × 50 in. Four-panel painting installation with relief elements created for *Circles and Circuits I: History and Art of the Chinese Caribbean Diaspora* at the California African American Museum as part of the recent PST LA/LA Getty Initiative.

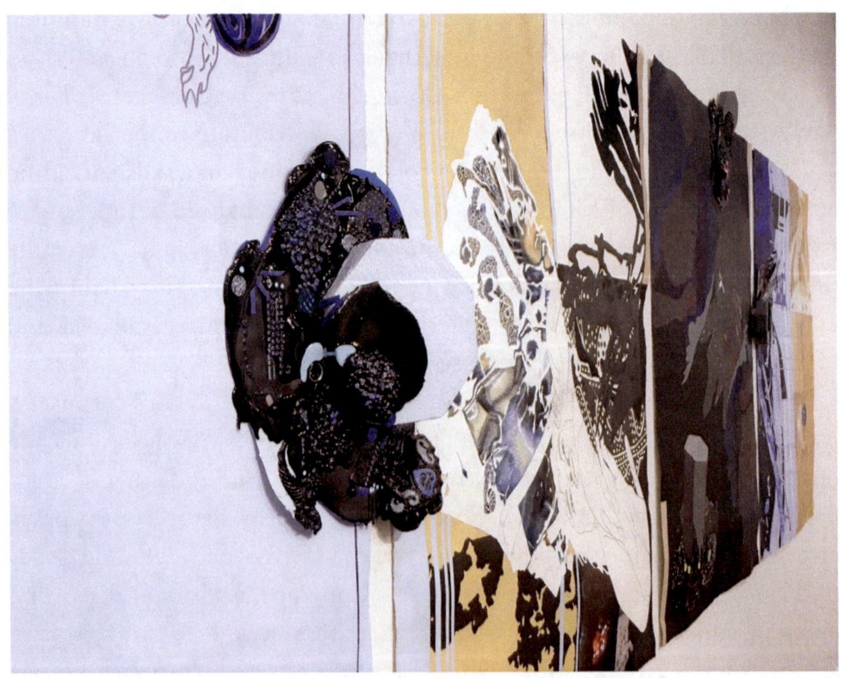

Fig. 2.2. Nicole Awai, *P.S. Simultaneity*, detail, left side with relief elements.

her art seems to secrete. Scholar Michelle Stephens has written a compelling analysis of Awai's earlier work describing how "Awai's ooze marks a quality, an action, a motion, that is, the permeability of the boundary between two-dimensional, surface stereotypes and three-dimensional, material objects... between what we (think we) see and the inapprehensible world of the real that we can never quite capture straight on in our vision."[2] One of Awai's installations in this regard, *Asphaltum Glance* (2013), used bituminous paint to provide texture and an olfactory component. She created that piece after a funded research trip to Trinidad's Pitch Lake.

PS: Simultaneity also draws inspiration from Pitch Lake, the largest natural deposit of asphalt in the world. Located on the southern portion of the island, the lake covers some one hundred acres and has an estimated depth of two hundred and fifty feet. Naturally occurring pitch, bitumen, or asphalt (I use those terms interchangeably) is a solid or semisolid form of petroleum. From the mid-nineteenth century through the 1990s, petroleum and related prod-ucts became a major part of Trinidad and Tobago's economy (indeed, by per capita GDP, Trinidad and Tobago is the wealthiest country in the western hemisphere after the United States and Canada). Although the country has shifted to natural gas to some degree, oil in its various forms continues to register as the major source of revenue in the national imaginary. To look at a map of the now-expanded energy industry is to see Trinidad as simply a central node in a series of underwater drilling and ocean bed exploration projects that fuels the nation-state's economy. As Awai's work helps to clar-ify, these economic investments also help to drive the cultural sector. This phenomenon results in part from the appropriation of, as the most visible example, oil barrels for steelpans (music and carnival—both of which have relied on steel bands   have largely characterized Trinidadian expressive cultural forms). Awai has herself used a more abstract approach, integrating what looks like bitumen into her sculptural creation.

I begin with Nicole Awai's *PS: Simultaneity* because it encourages a con-ceptual linking of Trinidadian art with the industrial seascape that such art frequently references. As an artist of Chinese descent, Awai might still rep-resent certain genealogies that inform the personal stories of the larger Chi-nese Caribbean and Chinese Atlantic that I discussed in chapter 1. However, *PS: Simultaneity* also fits within a series of specifically Trinidadian artworks that deemphasize autobiographical and familial stories like the ones that anchored the seascapes I examined in relation to documentary film. Awai uses a more abstract form that nonetheless engages seascapes. In this chapter, I trace a number of such abstracted representations, including Awai's work and those by three other important Trinidadian artists (two of whom happen to be of Chinese descent). The movement of the chapter decouples the circulation of Chineseness from familial bonds and associates it more with processes of commodification and exchange.

In spite of such delinking, Awai's own ethnic background might still evoke a loose connection between Chineseness and Pitch Lake's oil reserves that constitute her subject; in this manner, she turns up the history of Chinese labor, albeit in an oblique manner. Here, I do not mean to equate artistic invention with the human toil involved in resource extraction but merely point to the general figuration of Chinese bodies and how they render visible certain dynamics of capital circulation. In other words, Awai's artwork evokes a longer history in relation to Pitch Lake, specifically that of the coolie. The coolie in the Caribbean brings into focus certain seascapes featuring cargos of people from Asia. In this framework, Awai's *PS: Simultaneity* constitutes part of a genealogy of visual art that figures Chineseness through nonhuman representational forms in relation to both local and transnational referents.

This genealogy includes Carlisle Chang (1921–2001), who was instrumental in visualizing the national project of Trinidad and Tobago; Willi Chen (b. 1934), who is arguably the best-known living artist of Chinese descent in the country; and Christopher Cozier (b. 1959), perhaps Trinidad's most internationally renowned artist today. Although curators frequently place the three men's artworks in national or regional (Caribbean) frameworks, I here expand that interpretive structure to think about the ways in which Trinidad, and even more specifically, Chinese figures in Trinidad, reflect and might shape contemporary discourses of globalization.[3] In order to further this perspective, I first historicize the coolie as a figuration of capital (following the productive work of several scholars but also tracing the figure back to Karl Marx's own writings). I center on the coolie's relevance to a discussion of primitive accumulation, since Marx writes of the coolie in that context and because Trinidad's place in the world owes much to its efforts in resource extraction and the circulation of the subsequent products as commodities. I elaborate these discourses as what I call crude accumulation to gesture to the localized connotations that render the figure of the coolie meaningful in Trinidad specifically. The next section further refines the *contemporary* meanings of Chineseness on the island. Turning to discourses about Chinese visiting workers as well as Chinese Trinidadians in newspapers and in a brief example from Willi Chen's fiction, I investigate how writings by and about Chinese-descended people found certain claims in relation to seascapes. Finally, I turn to the artworks themselves and the ways the various examples facilitate a logic of incorporating that offers a useful lens for thinking about how seascapes by Chen, Chang, and Cozier bring Chinese-inflected globalization into focus and how they might align with the sorts of concerns that Awai's work suggests.

I recognize that incorporating might seem like a departure from the watery discourse that suffuses the chapters in this book. However, I insist that incorporating evokes aqueous discourse. Cecilia Chen explains that "As a responsive and promiscuous solvent, water is rarely pure and is always picking up, carrying along, dropping off, and bonding with other elements."[4] The Deepwater Horizon oil spill in the Gulf of Mexico in 2010 illustrates how the ocean incorporates even toxic materials; sea life and the seabed itself were not only covered in but also absorbed particles of oil and the dispersants used in the clean-up effort. These substances continue to be found in sediment samples and throughout the marine ecosystem. Such ongoing alteration of an ecology can be productively extended as a metaphor to think through how Chineseness has altered and continues to alter the imaginary of Trinidad and Tobago and the country's relationship to a larger global context. Again, Trinidad's economic vitality has owed and continues to owe much to oil and petroleum products, but two of the dominant forms of expressive culture associated with the isle—carnival and pan—also owe a debt to this industry. In focusing on a logic of incorporating, I turn to the streams that propel such cultural forms as suggested in one genealogy of visual art.

UNDERCURRENTS: THE COOLIE WITHIN CAPITALISM

The history of the Chinese coolie links the specificity of Trinidad's representations of Chineseness to larger cultural currents. The coolie foregrounds some of the complex forces shaping Trinidad even as that figure expresses more generally the contradictions of transnational capitalism. Literary scholar Lisa Lowe provides a lead. As the first New World site to experiment with the importation of Chinese labor in anticipation of gradual manumission and the demise of formal transatlantic bondage during the nineteenth century, Trinidad served as an experiment for the British Empire "to adapt and improvise combinations of colonial slavery *with* new forms of migrant labor, monopoly *with* laissez-faire, and an older-style colonial territorial rule *with* new forms of security and governed mobility."[5] Lowe has further written of the ways in which the coolie (in her study, a discursive figure specifically produced in archived "colonial and parliamentary papers") came to signify an "alleged transition from slavery to freedom," or what she more broadly conceives as the contradictions of liberalism.[6] Following Moon Ho-Jung's work (and in implicit conversation with Lisa Yun's), the coolie here emerges as the sign and embodiment of a particular transition in racialized labor, a move that expanded the cultural currents and imagination of the Atlantic world to include bodies from China (and then India).[7] The rhetorical power and persistence of the coolie may raise an eyebrow given that, as historian Walton Look Lai has observed, the arrival of Chinese in the Caribbean might be seen "as a continuation, on a more massive scale, of something that had been taking place on the fringes of hemispheric colonial life since the late sixteenth century."[8] Rather than emphasize scale in terms of the numbers of Chinese migrants arriving, I stress the qualitative shift in seeking in such a labor pool a resolution (or at least a stopgap) to a problem attendant to transnational capitalism: what Marx called "the so-called primitive accumulation."[9]

For Marx, primitive accumulation, which he associates with the colonial system writ large, draws on the power of the state; it precedes but also overlaps with the expansion of capitalism as a mode of production. The state and its relationship to overseas trade through mercantilism had long been in transition by the dawn of the nineteenth century; thus, companies that once operated on the behalf of a given European monarchy assumed more and more autonomy in their operations, including their capacity to garner greater profits by engaging in actions that increasingly resembled and overlapped with those of sovereign powers. I return to this point shortly, but I emphasize here that the new commercial and political alignments set the conditions of possibility for the emergence of the coolie.

Lowe elaborates the figure of the Chinese coolie (within and beyond the Trinidadian imaginary) through a reading of C. L. R. James's *Beyond a Boundary,* a text central to the island's literary tradition and intellectual history. This work combines memoir, social critique, and a commentary on the game of cricket. According to James, the Chinese migrant set up shop on the island and slowly assumed a role in the community by becoming the benefactor of a local team. Lowe's gloss of James's recollection of Chinese men in Trinidad stages the paradoxes associated with the coolie: a figure brought to the New World to sustain the plantation economy fueling the acceleration of capitalism on an increasingly worldwide scale.

> The "Chinese" . . . may figure as part of an allegory for the way in which capitalist imperialism expands by means of colonial differences, not through rendering equivalent all labor, resources, and markets, but rather precisely through calculations that differentiate lands to appropriate and develop and those to ignore, which select certain populations for exploitation and civilization, and others for neglect or elimination. In this allegory, not only does the "Chinese" provide material support for a common project shared with the cricket players, but the figure performs James's recognition of provisional unity across difference, in his "vivid" recollection of the "Chinese."[10]

The category of the coolie serves as a linchpin sustaining the exploitation of laborers (even if it nominally marks the transition from a slave- to a wage-based economy) but nevertheless also indicates potentiality, creating new relations that might contest the erosion of more collective affiliations.

I use the term "stages" quite self-consciously, for James insists that cricket be viewed as a specific form of art. He emphatically writes, "Cricket is first and foremost a dramatic spectacle. It belongs with the theatre, ballet, opera, and the dance."[11] In other words, the "Chinese" person matters in James (extending Lowe's reading of *Beyond a Boundary*) because he assumes a role in a public, *theatrical* spectacle. James develops the implications of this assertion. For him, a "major consideration in all dramatic spectacles is the relationship between event (or, if you prefer, contingency) and design."[12] The Chinese man's import depends on particular actions in a given time and the structure in which such actions take place. James's Chinese example reveals how individuals negotiate capitalist circulations that are informed by but also shape localities.

The Trinidadian Chinese coolie focalized anxieties about labor in very different ways than was the case, for example, in the United States. Eric Hayot has written that the perceived problem in the late nineteenth-century United States was that Chinese migrant "labor produced a growth inimical to the health of the country as a whole, largely because it rerouted the flow of capital around the European worker."[13] Hayot continues, arguing that the uncanny endurance of the Chinese worker hyperbolically described by the American Federation of Labor around the turn of the twentieth century reinforced desires for and structures of racialized exclusion (various laws severely restricted immigration from 1882–1943). Trinidad and the British Empire more broadly took another position on Chinese migration.[14] Nevertheless, in both the case of the United States and Trinidad, the Chinese coolie figured transitions between paid and slave labor even as the American discourse, to a much greater degree, overlaid attendant distinctions of human and inhuman. The different spaces to which this figure helps to give form also construct the image of the coolie in markedly different ways. The most notable distinction is, of course, the fact that in the British context, coolie labor referred as much if not more to labor sourced from India than from China.

These elaborations of the coolie intersect Karl Marx's references to the Opium Wars (1839–1842 and 1856–1860) and the increasing amount of labor transported overseas in part VIII, "The So-Called Primitive Accumulation," of *Capital, Volume I.* For example, both C. L. R. James and Karl Marx posit the rise of the coolie coeval with a theatrical worldview enabled by colonial circuits of cultural encounter. According to Marx:

> The discovery of gold and silver in America, the extirpation, enslavement, and entombment in mines of the aboriginal population, the beginning of the conquest and looting of the East Indies, the turning of Africa into a warren for the commercial hunting of black-skins, signalised the rosy dawn of the era of capitalist production. These idyllic proceedings are the chief momenta of primitive accumulation. On their heels treads the commercial war of the European nations, with the globe for a theatre. It begins with the revolt of the Netherlands from Spain, assumes giant dimensions in England's anti-jacobin war, and is still going on in the opium wars against China, etc.[15]

The preceding text uses "with the globe for a theatre" as a translation for *mit dem Erdrund als Schauplatz.*[16] This phrase has been translated by Fredric Jameson as "with the globe as its battlefield," but *schauplatz* can also mean play area or theater.[17] I call attention to the German to note the possibilities for signaling a kind of theatrum mundi in Marx's own configuration of nineteenth-century world events that lead to relations of production organizing increasingly interconnected societies.

In light of this notion, I extend Jameson's comments on Marx's "so-called primitive accumulation." Jameson compellingly demonstrates how this portion of *Capital, Volume I* addresses problems of "historiography . . . periodization and historical causality" (for Marx attempts to answer the question of what precedes capitalist production).[18] Marx's response moves through the English countryside (the expropriation of land for use as sheep pastures to supply the emergent textile market, for example) to overseas trade, exemplified in part by the "English East India Company," which had gained, in his view, "the exclusive monopoly of the tea-trade, as well as the Chinese trade in general, and of the transport of goods to and from Europe."[19] Put otherwise, Marx's origin story of capitalism shifts from a grounded understanding of the dynamic processes that shape a particular territory to one that drifts toward maritime trade and the structures that facilitate these exchanges (such as banks). These transformations steer us toward the financial wars waged by European powers in this new theater of oceanic activity.

One privileged figure staging this economic nexus—implicitly in the work of Marx and somewhat more explicitly in that of James—is the coolie. For my purposes, these otherwise very different discourses suggest the ways in which the coolie signifies commercial traffic among Asia and the overseas networks established by colonial powers. The seascape provides a means to see such phenomena and the historical legacies of the transportation of Chinese labor from one place to another, in this case, from Asia to the Caribbean. The submerged details of these cultural and economic flows haunt later cultural production in Trinidad.[20]

CRUDE ACCUMULATION

The figure of the Chinese coolie morphs in Trinidad from the nineteenth century to the present in very specific ways because of the unique material conditions that give rise to capitalist production there. The completion of indenture contracts in Trinidad without the continual contract deferrals experienced in, for example, Cuba meant that workers could move from the plantation system into other livelihoods. During the mid-nineteenth century in Pitch Lake, commercial oil drilling began in fits and starts (so Trinidad possibly became the earliest site for this kind of commercial venture in the world). However, by the early twentieth century, oil companies boomed on the island, leading to the development of infrastructure to support these economic ventures.[21] These transformations also facilitated radical shifts in class mobility; the story of John Lee Lum (1842–1921) is one such story.[22] Lee Lum left China in 1870 in pursuit of California gold. From there, he migrated to Trinidad in order to open a grocery, which he eventually expanded into a chain. Such growth eventually resulted in his establishment of plantation estates as well as speculative investments in, notably, oil. Literal accumulation of crude may have only shifted the fortunes of a few individuals, but I use the term "crude accumulation" here to name shifts from coolie to capitalist enabled through resource exploitation as well as other forms of opportunistic speculation. I also elaborate this notion of crude accumulation to account first for the ways in which oil shaped and continues to shape a national image of Trinidad as a seascape and second to think through the ways in which China relates to Trinidad today.

The early entrepreneurial endeavors on the island led to very specific developments. Lee Lum's grandson, James, explained in an interview, "The partnership worked out in such a way that Rust [a business partner] was to go and do most of the fieldwork because his background gave him more of that capability, and my grandfather did virtually all the early financing. And that was the involvement that gave, I would say, potential for the oil industry to grow."[23] That particular industry inadvertently fueled an emerging class consciousness through events like the watershed 1937 strike.[24] Even within the British Empire writ large, this foundation proved pivotal. Winston Churchill's decision to fuel the Royal Navy with oil as opposed to coal led to Trinidad becoming, for a time, the largest oil producer within the empire. Moreover, such industrial expansion helps to explain events like the American occupation of Trinidad from approximately 1941–1947. Historian Harvey R. Neptune has analyzed the lingering effects of maintaining military bases in the Caribbean colony, including nationalist debates that centered on the American production of a stage revue, *Land of the Calypso* (1944).[25] This production followed shortly on the heels of other performance events that staged Trinidad's place in an evolving realignment of global power, including the return of local-born dancer Si-lan Chen.[26] As I have repeatedly argued, Trinidad's cultural exports also owe much to the oil industry, since recycled oil drums became the base for steelpans beginning in the 1940s. These sorts of artistic projects expressed some of the thorny political issues in Trinidad's colonial entanglements and became flashpoints for decolonial thinking.

However, the legacy of the US occupation has the most significance in my study because it transformed the literal seascapes surrounding the island. To replenish depleted reserves, Trinidad shifted from land to marine drilling beginning in 1954 with the development of the Soldado Field off the coast. Such industrial moves have resulted in the continual presence of oil rigs and tankers in the waters surrounding Trinidad (if not Tobago, which has maintained several ecological preserves). These offshore explorations continue today, as evidenced by the 2015 energy map of Trinidad and Tobago that I referenced at the beginning of this chapter.[27] Michaeline Crichlow, Francisco-J. Hernández-Adrián, and I have argued that "fantasy, politics, and economics work to produce islands" as *particularly* meaningful.[28] Indeed, the energy map of Trinidad and Tobago, with its carefully demarcated zones of corporate and national offshore claims, provides a different view of sovereignty that a terrestrial orientation simply does not enable one to see. Seascapes are, therefore, crucial to understanding the relations of nation-states, corporations, and governmentality in insular spaces complexly connected through waterways.

Crude accumulation also speaks to China's relationships to Trinidad and Tobago today. China has invested a significant amount in Trinidad and Tobago, creating new business opportunities in oil and natural gas as well as putting forward a deluge of other proposals. Such business negotiations involve high stakes; in 2014, one bid from Trinidad and Tobago attempted to attract investment from China for solar energy valued at nearly 7 percent of Trinidad and Tobago's overall GDP.[29] China's requirements in its energy sector thus help to drive financial markets both within the nation-state and the region (Trinidad is a banking hub of the Caribbean). The international exchanges between the nation-states of China and Trinidad and Tobago have produced new flows of goods and people; this circulation of products and laborers redefines how people understand Chineseness and the characteristics that Trinidadians associate with Chinese things.

THE DEPTHS OF CHINESENESS

Trinidad holds further interest for a study of globalization and the Chinese Atlantic. In March 2010, Trinidad launched *Chinese Weekly,* a Chinese-language newspaper subsequently recast in a bilingual format during July of the same year. Editor-in-chief Johnny Chow expressed hope that the journal would strengthen the ties between the Chinese and the local community to "help both individuals to understand each other's culture a bit more."[30] This rhetoric positions the Chinese in an awkward relationship to the articulation of the local, given that a Chinese minority has long existed in Trinidad, occasionally occupying a central place in the construction of a national imaginary (as when the artist Carlisle Chang designed Trinidad and Tobago's coat of arms and collaborated on the nation's flag, adopted in 1962 with independence). However, the meanings attached to "Chineseness" within the country have recently shifted as both capital investment and migrant labor from China have begun to appear in substantial numbers. The former phenomenon is exemplified in the energy deals I have already mentioned as well as large-scale construction projects such as the National Academy for the Performing Arts (NAPA) North (Port of Spain) and South (San Fernando), which owe their development to loans from China.[31] These massive complexes have changed the cityscapes; in Port of Spain, the buildings dominate much of the surrounding architecture; the half-dome roofs recall sails, much like the structures of the Sydney Opera House. The landscape of this port city has thus become more like a seascape, but one built through Chinese financing.

Public discussions around the projects funded and often built with the labor of Chinese guest workers have occurred in news reports and blogs describing tensions among locals and migrant Chinese contract employees as well as around more general conditions for these hired hands.[32] The Urban Development Corporation of Trinidad and Tobago Limited (UDeCoTT) revealed little to the media about the contractual stipulations of overseas Chinese workers, but a cover story in *Newsday* indicated that at least five hundred such laborers lived in the country in 2007.[33] While this number may seem minuscule, only approximately 1 percent of the country's total population of nearly one and a half million identifies as Chinese, so the proportion of Chinese people in Trinidad actually increases with the influx of a foreign-born workforce. The development of resources such as *Chinese Weekly* undoubtedly serves not only Trinidadians of Chinese descent and the fluctuating population of overseas workers, but also revises perceptions of Chineseness as they alter with these demographic shifts.

Chineseness can be viewed productively through a logic of incorporating. Although the emergence of *Chinese Weekly* registers a contemporary moment in which the flows of Chinese capital and people challenge and, perhaps, alter the national imaginary, Chinese cultural iterations have long shaped the "local," particularly in Trinidad. Marking Chineseness on the island foregrounds notions of belonging and its apparent opposites, alienation and insecurity, as they manifest in a site of the oldest experiments with Chinese contract labor in the New World and where racial rhetoric has long centered questions of intermingling and integration.[34] Incorporating serves to name particular iterations of national inclusion. It also indexes Chinese financial circulations that far exceed the national frame as Chinese funds flow through and well past the borders of Trinidad and Tobago. These currents become visible through various seascapes, particularly but not exclusively those in the medium of visual art. Indeed, as Derek Walcott has observed of himself and his fellow residents, "We knew the names of Trinidadian painters . . . before the writers emerged."[35] One such artist is Willi Chen. I contextualize my analysis with some of his literary production and in the wider context of intellectuals and writers who consider the importance and impact of Asian flows through the nation-state.

WILLI CHEN AND THE CHINESE TRINIDADIAN

Probably the best-known writer of Chinese descent in the Anglophone Caribbean, Chen has enjoyed a protean career. Formerly a baker and an oilman, he continues to run a printing shop.[36] As an artist, he works as a painter, sculptor, set designer, and playwright. He has also authored several collections of short stories. The various occupations in which he has engaged over the last six decades of his life imply the wide range of professional positions that the Chinese in Trinidad and Tobago have occupied from the islands' independence forward. Chen avowedly draws on these experiences to mold artistic representations that insistently incorporate Chineseness within his artistically rendered nation.

However, rather than being representative in some mimetic fashion of some generalized "Chinese Trinidadian" experience, Chen's work demonstrates how such a term might signify in the first place. I eventually turn to Chen's sculpture *Solar Marinorama* because marinorama is a seascape by definition, so this work brings into focus the concerns of this book with discourses of nationalism, economics, and Chineseness. However, given the lack of context provided through its exhibition, I offer in this section a larger historical frame—one provided in part by Chen himself—that assists in elucidating Chen's sculpted seascape.

Insofar as I invoke history, I understand it as a form of narrative that structures the past, but I wish to interrupt the particular construction that would lodge Chinese Trinidadian as an element in a developing yet uncritical nationalism: a story that generally begins with a seascape manifested through the docking of the *Fortitude* in 1806. While I understand that all nationalisms partake of the imagined, to summon Benedict Anderson's phrase, the varieties of Chinese Trinidadian historical works that have appeared in the last thirty years often participate in recovery efforts that produce hagiographic accounts.[37] As a counter to this ecstatic mode of biographical exegesis, I deploy fiction as one contextual element of my analysis precisely because it foregrounds the act of narration as such; visual art further demands scrutiny and invites projection. Both forms, therefore, conjure alternative imaginaries that confound an easy claiming of a nationalist paradigm. Thus I gesture toward an iteration of what Michaeline Crichlow has called the "post-creole imagination."[38]

The post-creole imagination names "selective creation and cultural struggle" both through and beyond the frames that have generally contained it: beyond linguistic usage, beyond reference to the Caribbean, and even beyond plantation economies writ large. This intervention does not entail disregarding the Caribbean as such. Instead, Crichlow proposes to locate "the Caribbean's experiences as an entangled site and a portal."[39] Etymologically, these words remind us of the ships that have heretofore anchored much discourse in Caribbean and Atlantic studies. To *entangle* is thought to have originated as a term to describe getting one's oars trapped in the weeds (*OED*). But entanglement is also historically related to land ownership, and often describes, even still, illicit sexual liaisons. Such meanings, of course, have often served to register the complexities of cultural collisions and the dynamic processes of creolization over time. *Portal* might also conjure the image of a ship: the *port hole* that might allow clandestine access or escape. Even in its more proper etymological association with gates, portal connotes a barring (that is, restricted access) at the same time it more frequently signifies an entryway: a passage to somewhere, be that through the ostensibly global technology of the internet or through the ostensibly national technology of the state (e.g., doors that enable passage through customs from one country into another). The portal, then, is linked to citizenship both in the sense of a regulatory matrix of rights and responsibilities and as a morphing system of informal actions cum attributes that constantly challenge and sometimes shift that formal structure. Chen's fiction illustrates a post-creole narrative.

Indeed, the surfacing of Chineseness in the Caribbean in general conjures a post-creole imagination. This period saw the decline of the Chinese empire and, with its fall, the scattering of its one-time subjects as overseas entrepreneurs and (more commonly) as a cheap workforce for hire. In the wake of the so-called Opium Wars, the British Empire occupied an especially privileged position in relation to the Middle Kingdom, enabling the former to set terms of exchange with the latter, not only in terms of goods but also overseas workers. To facilitate the growth and internal regulation of such migrant networks, associations often based on region of emigration and/or familial affiliation formed in the new areas of both temporary and more permanent settlement. In the case of Trinidad, such connections fostered the development of predominately Hakka (*Kejia*) enclaves. These migrants differed in background from the waves of migrant labor currently landing on Trinidad's shores, and it is these older travelers that Willi Chen's work usually invokes as part of Trinidad's racial mélange.

Chen's art invites dialogues not only with other Chinese artists who have preceded him on the island but also with other notable figures, such as V. S. Naipaul. Indeed, Chen's writing usually depicts the ethnic majorities of Afro and Indo Trinidadians, with Chineseness figuring as part of the background in the complicated Trinidadian racial nexus. This representational strategy in his writing often partakes of a certain realist aesthetic that might initially seem to reproduce Chen's real-life social position as a Hakka entrepreneur. But the quotidian role of Chinese people in Trinidadian life surfaces infrequently within Chen's large oeuvre. Indeed, Chen's visual art tends toward the abstract, and his writings, particularly in his first two collections, usually figure Chineseness only through the businessmen who inform the settings of his stories. When Chineseness explicitly emerges, it usually serves as evidence of a national formation based on the continual integration of difference into its structure.

As I have suggested, critics have noted that Willi Chen's short stories tend to consign Chinese characters to minor roles; they tend to appear, when they appear at all, as the bar owner, the middleman, the local entrepreneur.[40] Thinking of other ethnicized writers from the island, like V. S. Naipaul, we might remember that Kamau Brathwaite celebrated in his 1963 essay "Roots" Naipaul's emphasis on character and its introduction of the East Indian into the realm of literature: "Before Mr. Biswas the West Indian East Indian was without form, features or voice."[41] Chen is positioned very differently than Naipaul in terms of how the author's life is perceived to correspond to the fiction. Nevertheless, Chen's collection, *Crossbones and Other Stories* (2009), participates more than any of his previous creative writing in a sort of sinography (an explicit writing of Chineseness), in which "China" as a construction redefines "crucial problems of contemporary thought: problems of translation, of subaltern subjectivity, of the universal human."[42] The collection includes three stories that prominently feature Chinese characters, but the first is most relevant to Chen's understanding of the contours of historical Chinese migration and the use of a seascape to frame such concerns.

The collection opens with "First Arrival," a story fewer than four pages in length. The Chinese protagonist Zukong arrives at Cocorite on the northwestern part of Trinidad, having swum ashore after jumping overboard. The plot is straightforward: He arrives, sees a pair of people, offers gifts to both, and disappears with them, holding the young woman's hand. The first sentence emphasizes displacement: "He came at twilight as if from no-where, as seagulls winged across a warm red sky."[43] Avian flight in this instance reinforces the idea of Zukong being out of place. Literary scholar Shin Yamamoto has noted the prevalence of birds in Chen's prose more generally, and he suggests that they establish a bird's-eye view of Trinidad's social dynamics; while I might question the objectivity that Yamamoto reads in such images, certainly the birds predict both themes of visualization and movement tied to a sentiment of freedom that pervades this story and much of the collection as a whole.[44] Moreover, the birds here reiterate the literary seascape that suggests a particular way of seeing, one that conjures visions of oceanic travel. In this case, the titular protagonist has narrowly escaped a "secret voyage of death" by braving the tides in near darkness.[45] The impending doom in this phrase conjures the title of the book and its relation to the inaugural story. The term "crossbones" alerts the reader to the plunder and clandestine trade in which the renowned, if often hyperbolized, pirates of the Caribbean engaged. As a memento mori figure, the image of crossbones not only evokes mortality, but also a scattering of bodies (since the bones here are separated from the skull, with which they are usually associated). Zukong has plunged into the ocean as a means of avoiding his fate at the hands of seaborne human traffickers. The tale alludes to the histories of illicit and forced migration of Chinese coolie laborers to the Americas that document the actions of imperial agents, who measured people as units of profit. Zukong's (net) worth depends on market value and its assessment of the relative price of labor from particular cultural backgrounds. Zukong continues this chain of associations, describing his transport ship through metonymy: *Fortitude, Wanata, Lady Flora Hastings*. The reference to these boats that brought to Trinidad shipments of coolies places him in the context of the contract laborers mentioned earlier in this chapter as much as his explicit narrative about recruiting agents and broken promises.

Sandwiched between the story's opening and conclusion, Chen repeats historical details that he never quite brings into focus and that he rather abruptly drops. Zukong's onboard experience records the plight of Chinese laborers generally and testifies to those now forgotten in the hearsay that the omniscient tale provides; Zukong "heard of a ship that never arrived at Brazil. He heard, too, the Panama Canal was a destination of certain death."[46] From the perspective of Zukong, these rumors of missing Chinese bodies across the Americas validate and extend his experience of losing two companions in the "swirling current of a rising tide."[47] The drowned men form a chain in a repetition of disappearing units, lives that register only in tales of cargos lost, or in larger reports of the contract labor system's injustices. What is surprising, then, is that this tale also ends with an image of disappearance occasioned by the shifting sea: "dried, wind-shifted leaves covered their tracks, and in the bay the swelling tide rose to blot out footprints on the sand."[48] Zukong also disappears as a corporeal body, his fate left unknown to the reader.

This logic, continually at play in Chen's corpus, incorporates the figure of Chineseness into the racial calculus of Trinidad and Tobago. This absorption involves more than integration of a minority subject into a political structure. In Chen's oeuvre, Chineseness figures most frequently as the embodied movement of capital. As I have argued elsewhere, Chen repeatedly depicts institutions of and people involved in or as exchange.[49] Therefore, incorporating suggests the consolidation of an ever-evolving financial body as much as a political one. In Chen's Trinidad, the circulation and imagination of Chineseness as embodiments of finance connects the Pacific and the Atlantic. Thus, while Trinidad witnessed an early failure of Asian migrant labor in the Americas in the inability of the *Fortitude*'s cargo to function as a viable plantation workforce, the island has nevertheless provided a frame to imagine how Chinese bodies assist in shaping a project of national formation through the repeated equivalence of Chinese people and capital investment. Such continued financial currents, flooding from China to the Caribbean, as well as to Africa and elsewhere, evince a realignment of global power in which China comes to stand on par with or even displaces the United States as today's economic superpower. The stakes of Chen's artistic production lie not only in a description of Chinese contributions to a relatively small nation-state, but in the barometric reading of the streams of Chinese capital, now nearly ubiquitous in the world.

Incorporating forges one part of a larger intellectual mapping that attempts to track Chineseness in relation to Atlantic spaces; a logic of incorporating facilitates thinking through the circulations of Chineseness because such flows now (and historically) constitute forms of transnational capitalism and globalization that challenge the easy equation of that term with Americanization. Indeed, the referents for entrepreneurial savvy and economic infrastructure on Chen's imaginatively constructed island are often the Chinese small business owners and rarely the American corporate conglomerate. Figuring financial structures in this manner suggests forms of incorporating that open up artistic, economic, and political domains often held apart.

In its subjective reimaginings of a Trinidadian nationalism, and the ways in which Chineseness in and through Trinidad assists in thinking about issues of globalization and migration, the notion of incorporating informs and complicates the seascape. I have argued in chapter 1 that nautical imaginaries and economies have shaped labor and the conditions of possibility for subject formation. Moving to a comparative Anglophone context in the Caribbean, Chen's work suggests a refinement of this organizational structure. The Trinidadian case hinges on two particularities: first, the fact that Chinese immigrants never amounted to more than one or two percent of the total population, and, second, the fact that they formed what Selwyn Ryan calls "one of the most upwardly mobile communities."[50] Ryan attributes this phenomenon at least partially to pigmentation and its relative value in the "old colonial order" shaped by Afro and Indo Trinidadian labor from 1797–1919. I do not propose to affirm or contest these propositions. Rather, their utility lies in helping to establish a dominant narrative of a Chinese Trinidadian population. Central to such a narration is the idea that value inheres in thinking of this group *as* a group, actual numbers and patterns of exogamy notwithstanding, *and* that a salient characteristic of the Chinese Trinidadian is a productive relation to capital. Trinidad's experiments with the organized shipment of potential Chinese fieldworkers, ostensibly as contract laborers whose productivity on the plantation was expected to be two and a half times that of a field slave, constitute the earliest mass movement of Chinese labor to the New World. This mythology of the industrious Chinese worker endured despite, for example, the failure of this historical project. These early connections of Chineseness to production resonate powerfully with Chen's Chinese Trinidadian descriptions across many of his short stories.[51]

Two public art pieces in Port of Spain illustrate this point and enable an elaboration of incorporating within the Trinidadian context. These public displays also reveal something about the ways in which private and public art markets are enmeshed on the island. I conclude the chapter with an investigation of Christopher Cozier's *Made in China* series and also his *Gas Men* installation. Unpacking the idea of incorporating through these aesthetic forms highlights the fantasies that might facilitate new considerations of the imbrication of space, politics, and economics.

TWO SEASCAPES

Port of Spain's central bank on the southern edge of Independence Square in the Eric Williams plaza has sponsored many of the visual artists on the island. Because of the lack of a developed art market in the relatively small nation-state, banks and hotels have served as primary supporters of individual artists. As a 2007 exhibition catalogue explains, "The Central Bank Art Collection is the largest art collection in this country with more than 150 pieces, of which seventy-five percent is in the form of paintings."[52] Much of that collection remains restricted from regular public viewing. However, one can see Chen's *Solar Marinorama* within the interior of the bank, hanging near the money museum; in the words of curator Geoffrey MacLean, the "mural is considered to be one of Trinidad and Tobago's most important

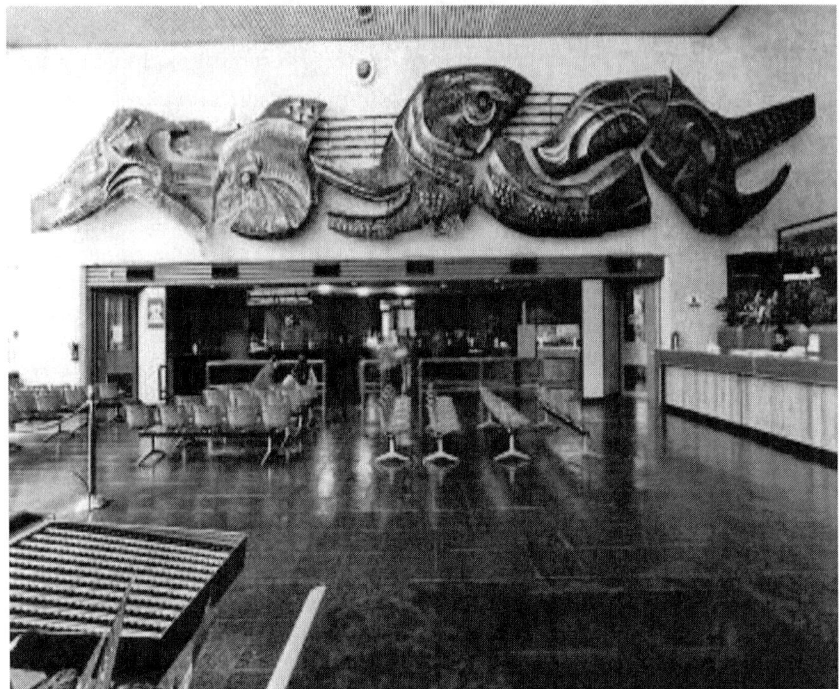

Fig. 2.3. Willi Chen, *Solar Marinorama*, 1988. Photo courtesy of Willi Chen.

artistic treasures from the twentieth century."[53] Glancing upward, one encounters Chen's imposing, 64′ × 14′ sculpture on the wall; its ongoing exhibition results from Chen's winning first prize in a 1988 art competition sponsored by the Central Bank (the selection also came with a substantial cash prize).

As one moves close to the sculpture, the material of composition becomes evident—steel, copper, and brass covered in enamel—as does the fact that this dragon (a term I use for reasons that will become apparent) actually appears to consist of nine individual pieces assembled to create a unified visual spectacle. The placement of the sculpture reminds the spectator of the flying fire-breathers hoarding treasure in the Western mythic tradition. The nine sections may also conjure a Chinese cosmology, as that number was often associated with both the Middle Kingdom's emperor and dragons. Such icons of prosperity would seem appropriate to the fortune of the national bank. But the invocations of Chineseness never quite come into full relief.

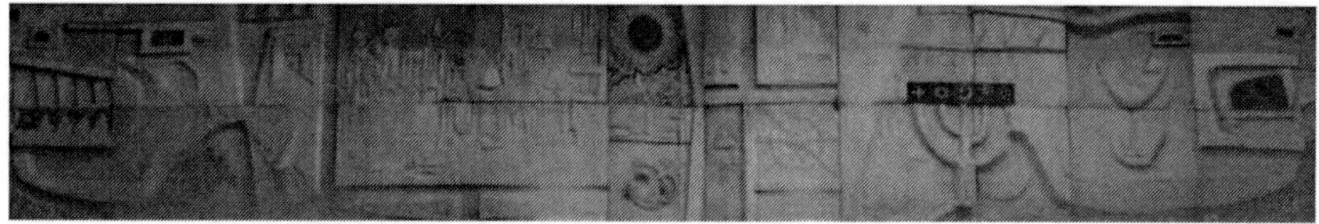

Fig. 2.4. Carlisle Chang, *Conquerabia*, 1964. From Kim Johnson, *Descendants of the Dragon* (Kingston and Miami: Ian Randle, 2006).

Nevertheless, the shapes abutting one another recall another façade in Port of Spain by artist Carlisle Chang.

In particular, Chang's 41′ × 7′ sand-cast mural *Conquerabia* (1964) depicts a different type of dragon, the body of which contains panels of images, including the city itself as well as various symbols such as a tree of freedom with icons of the five principal religions.[54]

As a composite of sand and stone, the sculptural form uses materials indigenous to Trinidad and Tobago.[55] The represented city consists of a fusion of architectural styles that infer a number of influences from around the world. The prominent displays of both Chang's and Chen's respective seascapes on or within institutions of governance and finance, indicative of independence and self-sufficiency, evoke a dialogue about Chinese Trinidadian contributions to the national project of Trinidad and Tobago.

This sort of conversation often includes mention of the visual artists Amy Leong Pang (1908–1989) and Sybil Atteck (1911–1975), and the formation of the Society of Trinidad Independents (active 1929–1938). Although the group disbanded, these women's efforts paved the way for the founding of The Trinidad Art Society (now the Art Society of Trinidad and Tobago) in 1943, which explicitly influenced figures like Chang and Chen, and more obliquely a later generation of artists that includes Cozier and Awai. Both born in Trinidad, Amy Leong Pang had studied in China, while Sybil Atteck had worked with the Ministry of Agriculture (which may explain her interest in flora and still life) after secondary school. Atteck later studied in the UK and the United States. Despite their influence on Trinidad's art scene, their contributions still remain in some obscurity, partially because their work never achieved a level of international success like that of their Caribbean contemporary Wifredo Lam (1902–1988). Notwithstanding this elision, more recent efforts have attempted to situate the artists as significant figures within national and regional genealogies.[56]

The emphasis on murals or mural-like work also intersects the Mexican mural movement from the 1920s through the 1940s in the address, specifically in Chang's case, to a newly constituted national political body.[57] Diego Rivera remains the most famous artist working in this vein. Mexican muralism was frequently masculinist and bound with a certain mission sometimes read as propagandistic and other times as empowering for the masses. Whether celebratory or condemnatory, such inscriptions assume the political teleology of national formation as the condition for intelligible subjects. How else might *Chinese Trinidadian* signify? What kind of work might such a term perform if the affirmation of the Trinidad and Tobago national project were not always mobilized as that which organizes and rationalizes it?

In a 1977 interview, Carlisle Chang stated that *Conquerabia* was "the most important structural mural" that he had done to that point.[58] The content of Chang's mural is sandwiched between a serpent's mouth on one end and a dragon's on the other. That anatomy may refer to the historical use of *dragon* to refer to large snakes, but it might also be read as a cultural collage of the Mayoid (that is, native) tradition, Chinese iconography, and other facets of the multicultural nation. The serpent's and dragon's mouths name a certain geography, each representing one of the straights that provide access into the Gulf of Paria and separate Trinidad from Venezuela (thus, the work is a seascape). *Conquerabia* also recalls the moniker of Port of Spain in days past. But the structure does not attempt to reclaim a linear history, despite the primary horizontal axis that seems to organize its constituent images. Instead, Chang's construction might be seen to evoke multiple and contradictory time frames—colonial, religious, geographic—that exist in simultaneity. The Trinidad on display lays bare the incongruent imaginaries that exist both inside and outside of a national framework. The juxtaposition of so many elements does not anchor a national narrative so much as it exposes the shifting grounds from which such a narrative might emerge. Chang's work functions as a tectonics of potential nation formation in which each of the square plates indicates not only fusion, but also fissure. While the mural holds different pieces together, they might literally fall apart. The artistic structure concretizes a national ideal insofar as such a notion depends on the coalescing of difference under the sign of Trinidad and Tobago, but it also gestures to a larger oceanic world.

Chen's work, also a rectangular structure in which gaping gullets appear prominent, serves as an artistic response to Chang's earlier creation. As early as 1961, Derek Walcott had compared Chen to Chang and other ethnically Chinese artists like Atteck and Patrick Chu Foon.[59] The title of Chen's sculpture, *Solar Marinorama*, likewise suggests a visualization of space. This emphasis on fire and water contrasts with the earthy *Conquerabia*. Although *Solar Marinorama*'s construction in the year of the dragon, according to the Chinese zodiac, may be serendipitous, this fact further links the piece to the efforts of a series of Chinese Trinidadian artists like Chang, whose particular oeuvre Chen acknowledges as a major influence. The shift from ground to sea, however, reorients the spectator. What can it mean to conjure a seascape that one must enter a bank to see (literally, as the bank itself does not allow photography for security reasons)? The exhibition area does not offer an ocean view, and the only suggestion of water, if any exists, is the reflection of the sculpture in and out of the slats of the ceiling.

Here, the two murals diverge, but they also provide an interesting counterpoint. Chang's town hall décor situated on the exterior addresses the passersby; its symbols juxtapose and fuse difference on a national emblem to comment on a national narrative, for a country that gained its independence only two years prior to the mural's construction. Its placement and the stories suggested through its representations would materialize a kind of Habermasian idealization in relation to a newly formed public sphere. This is a type of incorporation in which individual elements, including those that have sailed or otherwise drifted across the sea, might coalesce into the national body. By contrast, Chen's more abstract figuration appears inside a financial center, a place of a markedly other sort of incorporation, one where the individual may in fact have fewer rights than the incorporated entity and will almost undoubtedly possess less capital and influence. If, in the first instance, Chang depicts a certain rootedness to a particular place despite signs of marine voyages that extend beyond one location, a placeless circulation defines the second. Indeed, the many curved lines in Chen's sculpture convey the sense of interlocking currents. To see *Solar Marinorama* is to compel a confrontation with flow—of desire and capital. Constructed at a very different historical moment, the later piece marks an era when the sea is not the primary arbiter of exchange, and when the capacity to do business with the rest of the world potentially exists in any given room with access to electricity and a modem.

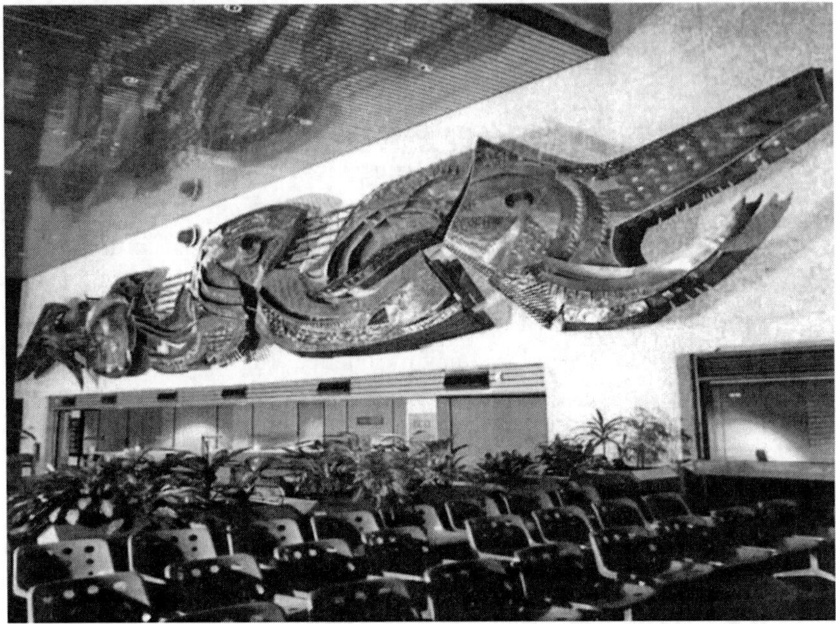

Fig. 2.5. Willi Chen, *Solar Marinorama*, 1988. From *The Art of the Central Bank of Trinidad and Tobago* (Port of Spain: Central Bank of Trinidad and Tobago, 2004).

This comparison should not suggest that the two murals embody an opposition. *Solar Marinorama* also connotes an amalgamation, for it evokes the completion of an elemental totality. Marinorama suggests water, while the composite materials suggest earth. The manipulation and grafting of the metals betray the blowtorch used in construction, and the sculpture's suspension above ground provides a sense of flight through the air. This combination would seem to function as a metaphor for the multiracial reality of Trinidad and Tobago's population. Carlisle Chang's *Conquerabia*, for its part, also depicts various forms of exchange, most noticeably the Iberian caravel that sailed into numerous harbors of the New World to extract riches for the crown. Both connotations of incorporating, then, figure to different degrees in *Conquerabia* and *Solar Marinorama*. This double resonance helps to define a logic of incorporating, which binds political subjects to institutions and histories of economic transaction. However, in the current historical moment, the idea of a fiscal entity also registers the archaic use of *incorporate* as "without body," or "incorporeal." A tension springs from the notion of a Chinese

Trinidadian subject within the nation, as well as a more abstracted form, a registering of the flows of capital that might structure life in some way but do not materialize in what we might expect: a citizen–subject with some sort of agency vis-à-vis the state. What I am suggesting is that Chinese Trinidadian is recast via *Solar Marinorama* not in some ethnic or racial calculus but as a symptom of a peculiar consolidation of capitalism that Chineseness comes to represent. Indeed, the spectator too may find herself reflected in the ceiling of the Central Bank, an unclear image that suggests not so much personhood as a sort of virtual life, but one that circulates through a sea of financial institutions of which the subject may even be unaware.

MADE IN CHINA

Christopher Cozier began the *Made in China* series in response to seeing a particular image on the docks: the increasing presence of Chinese guest workers as he drove his son to school. Shipping containers marked with Chinese characters and brand names frequently dotted the area surrounding the harbor and suggested to him contrasts between Trinidad–China trade relationships and the apparent working conditions of the migrant laborers. These observations encouraged Cozier to think through both contemporary and historical contacts between the two nation-states. In the postmillennial period, Cozier also witnessed Chinese workers on planes flying around the Caribbean and in certain parts of Africa; these chance encounters raised questions about labor relations and the circulation of Chinese goods and products.

Such global circulations materialized in a quite spectacular way in the construction of NAPA North in Port of Spain, which was ostensibly finished in 2010. Built for an estimated cost of $500 million by a Chinese-based construction firm, the building was shut down in 2015 because of structural flaws and safety concerns, including air quality.[60] For Cozier, the structure is also connected to impressions gathered with his son, Isaac, who dubbed it a "Decepticon" (after the toy company Hasbro and its Transformers series, in which evil machines masquerade as ordinary objects and vehicles). In this loose metaphorical description, NAPA is the result of a shady economic transaction disguised as a very striking but apparently very expensive and very unsound building. As an example of the concerns that motivated the creation of the *Made in China* series, this gigantic construction project conveys the scale of Chinese investment, the ubiquity of Chinese products and labor, the sometimes shoddy quality of Chinese goods, and the frequent mistrust of government-level Sino-Caribbean exchanges. As I have previously suggested, the performing arts complex also suggests a kind of futuristic seascape in which the cityscape of Port of Spain assumes new form. The location at the edge of Queen's Park Savannah, now a green space, evinces a history of other colonial ties. Once a site for the cultivation of sugar (a crop with deep ties to Chinese labor in the Caribbean), the edge of the park along Maraval Road also contains seven Victorian structures that remind the viewer of the British influence on the island. This area also contains the largest roundabout in the world, suggesting the development of urban infrastructure to which Chinese investment now contributes in an eye-catching manner, for better or for worse. NAPA's story provides one context for understanding Cozier's work.

For the first iteration of *Made in China*, Cozier used a found object, an ink stamp purchased at a mall in Port of Spain that printed the series title. The stamp produces an impression, one that is obviously reproducible. Indeed, as I suggest in the introduction to this book, Chineseness is often linked to anxiety because of China's capacity to build and destroy on a seemingly unprecedented scale. The stamp might appear at a far remove from the seascapes I have discussed in Chang and Chen's structural murals, but Cozier's work builds as a kind of assemblage. The larger formation constituted through his work continues the evocation of seascapes that we see in Chen in terms of moving toward a more abstracted vision of what that term might signify. But it also connects seascapes to other geographies. The ink stamp uses a rubber mold; Trinidad's historical development includes the seeding of rubber plantations, and that product links Trinidad to the forests of the Amazon, where such trees originated, but also to a booming colonial trade not only in South America but also in Asia.

Perhaps to suggest the mutability of both the object and the Chinese manufacturing it would seem to represent, the stamp has taken different forms. Engraved on a hollow wooden box, the phrase "Made in China" adorns a photo of the artist from the calf down wearing formal black slacks and shoes while standing on the box. When he won the Prince Claus Award (2013), visitors, including several members of the diplomatic corps and well-to-do arts patrons, were invited to stand on the Made in China box at the exhibition

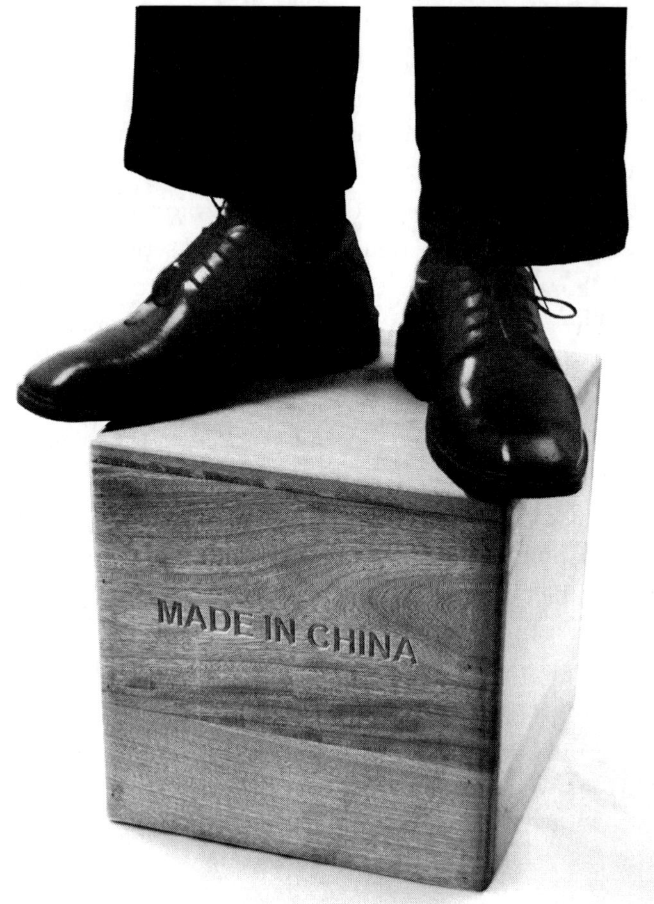

Fig. 2.6. The wooden box instantiation of Christopher Cozier's *Made in China* series expresses his concerns about Chinese-inflected processes of globalization. Photograph courtesy of Christopher Cozier.

venue, Alice Yard, in Trinidad and Tobago's capital. Cozier implicates himself, various governments, and his supporters as being made by China even as he would critique any such connections. The cube may connote a microversion of the shipping container and more literally recalls the soapbox, which was originally named as such to stand for various retail products that were transported to retail stores in wooden crates. The linguistic message in the photographs would seem to expand rather than restrict the rhetoric of the images that Cozier provides. Even the medium, the photograph, used to capture all of these images—of the stamp, the artist, and others on the box—suggests forms of technological reproduction that increase copies and, therefore, scale. China is everywhere, indeed. And the artist himself seems to be attached to Chinese networks.

Another iteration of *Made in China* is the *Now Showing* print, sometimes indicated simply by a date, *12.30*. Produced as a limited series of one hundred prints in collaboration with the Trinidad and Tobago Film Festival but also elaborated in several different paintings, this set of works displays certain visual elements that recur in Cozier's oeuvre arranged in new ways and through various media. These elements usually include an image of a loaf of bread on wheels, a tree in front of the forensic center, feet (sometimes bare, sometimes clad in shoes), the sketched busts of several film stars, an empty lot, the number *12.30*, a silhouette of a head on which rests a box with the words "Made in China" on which stands a pair of legs, and breezeblocks (usually called cinderblocks in North American English), either painted or cut out.

The trio of small heads (which are absent in the image included in this book but present in a print that I own) require scrutiny, as they are difficult to see; the faces represent film stars popular during the 1970s, including Amitabh Bachchan, Clint Eastwood, and Jimmy Wang Yu (Wang Zhengquan). Bachchan achieved breakout success with the 1973 film *Zanjeer*, in which he popularized the character type of the angry young man in Bollywood cinema. Long associated with spaghetti westerns and tough guy roles like Dirty Harry, Clint Eastwood rose to fame slightly earlier in the late 1960s and early 1970s. Wang earned his success through collaborations with the famed Shaw Brothers Studio in hits such as *One-Armed Swordsman* (1967), which promoted the *wuxia* genre. These actors all portray aggressively masculine types across a wide range of transnational film industries. The distribution networks of Bollywood and Hollywood as well as the influences of the Shaw empire across East and Southeast Asia and the Italian auteur Sergio Leone around the world suggest mediated intimacies that connect large sections of the globe through mediascapes. The circulation of these screen images not only helps shape local sites, but, insofar as Trinidad and Tobago's emergent film production draws on such referents, suggests how local productions might in turn affect the transnational dissemination of images. The spaghetti

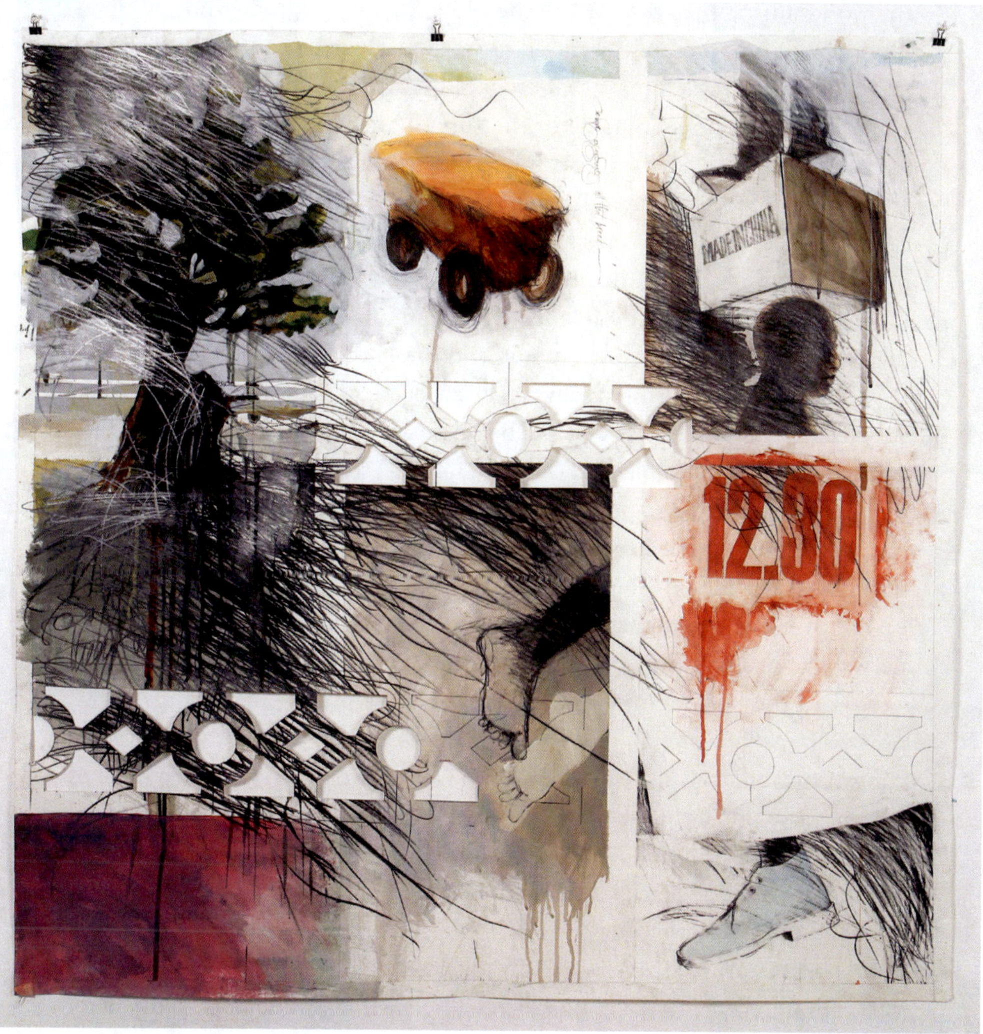

Fig. 2.7. Christopher Cozier, *Twelve Thirty 2*.

Western is, of course, a good example of this phenomenon from an earlier historical moment. As a film advertisement, then, the print works to condense global flows and personify them through the likenesses of screen persona.

The mediascape registers alongside a very local referent: a large tree that stands outside of the Forensic Center by Federation Park in Port of Spain. Per capita, Trinidad had one of the highest murder and kidnapping rates in the world during the early part of the new millennium. This criminal activity resulted in part from the island's locations close to South America and the dense mangrove forests that enable smugglers and other traffickers to store their loot largely outside of the surveillance of authorities. Drugs in particular seem to have led to a high level of violence, particularly among young men. People frequently gathered outside the forensic center to identify recently deceased loved ones. The tree, then, provides an organic counterpoint to the images manufactured by film industries around the world. To juxtapose icons of screen violence with a literal site of death and mourning brings into relation global media and the quotidian experience it often informs. In Cozier's print, of course, every element is part of an image. The very technology renders what could be very different experiences as relatively equivalent signs. The relay between fiction and reality forestalls a privileging of a kind of depth experience over a surface experience. Cozier himself has asked whether the level of mediation in which we live means that we are now living in a movie. The materialization of violence depends a great deal on the overseas traffic that uses Trinidad as nodal point in a transnational network of drug traffic.

Toward the bottom of *Now Showing*, a couple of bare feet appear juxtaposed against a foot clad in a blue Clarks shoe. Feet constitute part of the central vocabulary with which Cozier has been working over the course of several years, including their display in his *Tropical Nights* series. Here they convey a sense of dynamic motion. Again, Cozier offers a metacommentary on mediation. Clarks is a shoe company that extends back to England in 1825; on its website today, it continues to commemorate the successful nineteenth-century display of its products at the "Great Exhibition of the Works of Industry of All Nations."[61] The English lineage suggests colonialism but it also indexes the neocolonial relations that might instantiate economic dependencies for small island states. In this case, the Clarks shoes convey what we might call certain insular relations between England and its former colony.

The controversial Jamaican musician Vybz Kartel has a recurring lyric in a song called "Clarks": "Everybody haffi ask weh mi get mi clarkes"; the video shows enough footwear to satisfy even the most intense fetishist. Cozier has noted the artist as a reference point. The circulation of commodities suggested in this part of the image contrasts the unadorned feet next to it.

Moreover, the allusion to Vybz Kartel (currently releasing music from prison, after being convicted of murdering his associate in one of the longest trials in Jamaica's history) plays with ideas concerning freedom, violence, and neoliberalism that constellate in complex ways. Here one thinks of Cozier working in the company of artists like Jamaican-born Ebony Patterson, who has constructed a body of work on the motif of what might be called gangsta dandyism, but Cozier is a bit more subtle in his approach to this theme. Cozier's image conjures the messiness of its imbricated themes by having the various elements bleed into one another. The dark washes lend the work a foreboding atmosphere. And the macabre tree seems rooted to all of the other features.

Images of feet and trees also hark back to one of the earliest Chinese Caribbean artworks to achieve major recognition: Wifredo Lam's *La Jungla* (1943). Comparison to the earlier gouache on paper furthers the links between the seeming binary of cosmopolitanism and primitivism into which critics have placed many Caribbean artists. In both cases, the feet suggest various kinds of mobility, including forms of fugitivity that facilitated leaving the plantation as well as the circulation of artists across international borders. Like Lam's painting, Cozier's offers a commentary on the organic and the manufactured using local landscapes that are nevertheless connected to cultural streams and events far from the island that would seem to be the artwork's ostensible subject.

This point leads to the breezeblocks. This element also recurs in a series of independent works by Cozier. Concrete has a long history as an industry in Trinidad and Tobago, albeit one shorter than oil's, connected to the nation-state's infrastructural development and self-sufficiency. Cozier's breezeblocks might remind viewers of the island's distinctiveness in terms of development even as they more generally suggest the mediation of an encounter, a structure that facilitates certain forms of perception of and contact throughout and beyond the Caribbean. Given the tropical climate, breezeblocks frequently appear in architectural designs in this region. Cozier often includes the likeness of the breezeblock as a structural element of the print (that is, the image is cut into the paper itself). This change in the texture of the print means that one looks at but also through the image. In this manner, Cozier enjoins the viewer to ponder the background, to contemplate what is or is not visible. In building construction, the use of breezeblocks also helps to regulate temperature. Breezeblocks enable certain kinds of phenom-enological experiences, particularly thermoception. Our ability to sense heat or get the chills might result from not only external stimuli, but also internal processes. In this manner, the static print also provides a commentary on a quite theatrical experience, because elements like the tree in Cozier's work reference and potentially produce affect (remember, this is a site where families identify bodies of the deceased).

Made in China coalesces a vast array of elements that address the financ-escapes connecting Trinidad and China, and the series also contextualizes such exchange through Trinidad's appropriation of an array of transnational cultural flows. To be made in China, it would seem, is part and parcel of larger flows of goods and people throughout even a relatively small and seemingly bounded space like an individual isle in the Caribbean. Even specific events, such as murders that occur in or near Port of Spain, become part of a larger picture, the understanding of which depends on cultural circulations from different parts of the world. In Cozier's work, the local takes shape through the global and vice versa.

INCORPORATING, THEATRICALITY, AND VIEWING VISUAL ART

The art examined in this chapter references Chineseness in some manner and helps demonstrate Trinidad's connections to China through the extension and elaboration of large-scale movements of goods and people. These flows have characterized the island to lesser and greater degrees since the beginning of coolie importation in the nineteenth century through the current moment, when Trinidad's economic status increasingly depends on China. At the same time, the flows from China into Trinidad involve frequent and rapid accommodation that, for example, incorporate Chinese circulations of capital into infrastructural as well as aesthetic projects. The artworks enable spectators to envision and imagine a world inflected by these forces. Consistent with Samuel Weber's notion of theatricality (discussed in the introduction), Trinidad as expressed through the four artists in this chapter cannot be imagined outside of Chinese influence.

Each artist has focused on different aspects of such intersections, but they also overlap in their concerns. Although the prints function differently than the art by Awai, Chen, and Chang (which demand a certain degree of bodily movement in terms of viewing the work), Cozier's *Now Showing* overlaps with these other works in several ways. First, all of them suggest circulations of Chineseness without necessarily depicting any Chinese people. These circulations suggest economic flows and, as I have argued, incorporate Chinese bodies into other figures. Second, each piece uses elements ostensibly derived from but that also help to represent the locality of Trinidad. At the same time, each one suggests different ways in which transnational streams of finance and people linked to a seascape mold visions of the multicultural nation-state. Third, each static artistic creation nevertheless elicits from the viewer or otherwise references phenomenological experiences. In this sense, the works function as theatrical, whether that means standing on a wooden box, moving one's body to find an appropriate perspective, or peering through an artwork.

Immersing oneself within a perspective—that is, calling attention to the ways in which bodies orient themselves in relation to the artworks—recalls Michael Fried's ideas about absorption and theatricality. In his writing on minimalism, Fried cited the artist Robert Morris, who stated that "physical participation becomes necessary" for viewing works of a certain scale.[62] To varying degrees, in the cases of the artworks I have discussed by Awai, Chang, Chen, and Cozier, such assertions also hold true. One can survey, for example, Awai's *PS: Simultaneity* at a distance, but the textures and materials of the composition only become apparent as one studies the panels within reach of them. The placement of Chang's mural means that one must deal with not only its size but the conditions of light that frequently cast some of it in shadow. Again, the details of this piece require one to walk along its horizontal axis to view them. The imposing scale of Chen's *Solar Marinorama* also demands that one move back and forth to and from the wall to see the individual pieces that create the overall sculpture. Cozier's box asks the spectator–participant to engage with kinesthesia and proprioception as one mounts and balances on top of it. If Cozier's print works in a more expected manner to elicit an appreciation of spatial arrangement, color contrasts, media (pencil, paint, wash, etc.), and style (freehand, stencil, cutout) that might pertain to many artworks on paper, the literal holes of the represented breezeblocks draw the spectator's eye not only to the image but through it.

To look differently at an object further suggests the ways in which Awai, Chang, Chen, and Cozier mark Chinese cultural flows explicitly or implicitly, and they suggest the utility of theatricality in analyzing elements that have already been incorporated into an artwork. In this regard, Cozier's recent installation, *Gas Men*, or *Globe*, offers a coda for this chapter. A video shot on location on the banks of Lake Michigan, *Gas Men* does not lend itself to ready identification of that body of water (it is a much more generalized waterscape that lends itself to comparison with the other art of concern in this chapter). However, information about locale does contextualize the image, since a crude oil spill occurred at BP's Whiting refinery in northwest Indiana in 2014. Here, one sees the continuing relevance of discourses of crude accumulation. Staged as if in a Western shootout, a pair of suited men in silhouette point nozzles at each other. In another image, the duo spins gas pump hoses in the air as if about to lasso something. This citation of popular cinematic imagery replaces the iconic rugged individual of the Western genre with the corporate clone. Rather than the more specific backdrop of the Old West, the expanse of the horizon here suggests worldwide commercial intervention, specifically by those invested in the petroleum business. The relationship of the Trinidadian artist to this particular scene is complicated, since, as I have argued, the island's infrastructure depends to a large degree on the energy sector of the economy. Yet the silhouette, as I have argued elsewhere, is a form of becoming.[63] Although the immediate reference point in the installation might be the company formerly known as British Petroleum, the shadowy form has yet to come into focus. What the viewer can see is a kind of attachment of a person to mechanical device. The theatrical image of person with prop shows how humans can manipulate technology, and it also illustrates new organic-mechanical interfaces. The ecological costs of such relationships remain to be calculated in any specific place, but the images trigger questions about what shape the Chinese quest for resources around the globe might take.

The question that my analysis of these various artistic productions proposes is what happens when we articulate Chinese Trinidadian not as a rights-bearing subject, but as a figure of and for capitalism? Might such a figure help us to reimagine Chineseness in relation to structures of governance? How might we revise persistent tropes deployed in relation to Chineseness in the Atlantic, exemplified in, for example, Anne-Marie Lee-Loy's work, where she writes, "the question of belonging and nonbelonging in relation to Chinese West Indians is not, of course, abstract . . . belonging is

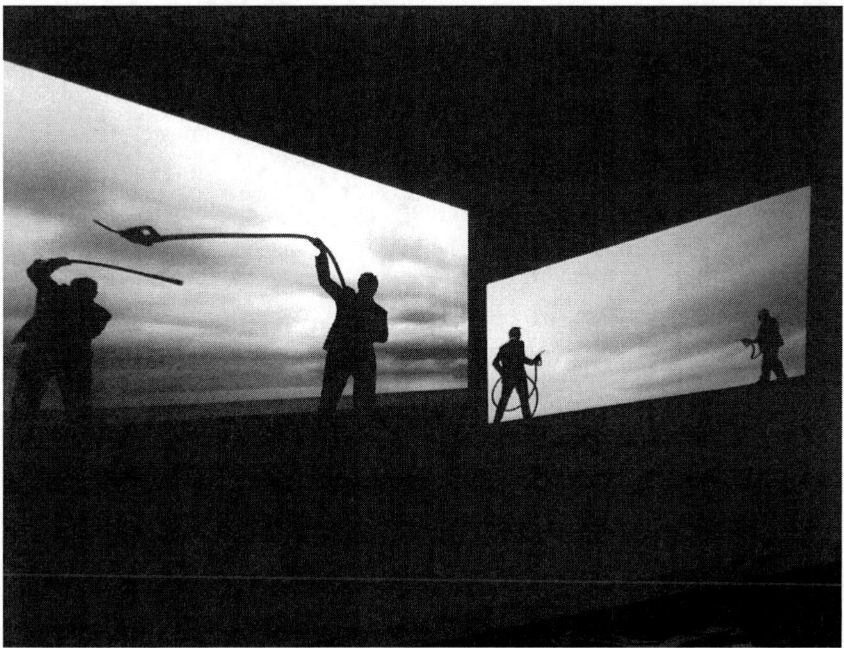

Fig. 2.8. Still from *Gas Men*, 2014. Video installation by Christopher Cozier.

located in the greater concept of nation?"[64] Although I would not dismiss the nation as a productive lens, Awai's, Chang's, Chen's, and Cozier's works demonstrate that Chineseness moves in, around, and outside such a framing. Indeed, the circulations of Chineseness in the Caribbean might be seen to anticipate and, partially, to constitute the neoliberal structures that facilitate the movement of Chinese labor today. While the older colonialist structures that engendered the traffic in people as productive units are not the same, one sees how the earlier profiteers of colonialist infrastructure (and a certain lack of regulation in respect to certain commercial practices within that system) have helped to set the conditions for our current reduction of people to fiscal embodiments. The Chinese Trinidadian iterations that at least partially comprise the art are figures in constant processes of incorporate-ing: continually disappearing, yet reemerging in some relation to the circulation of capital on the island.

All of the artworks I have discussed, but particularly those of Cozier, suggest an assemblage of elements. This assemblage is not so much an assemblage art, because usually the works have remained in the same medium, whether that be sandstone, metal, paint, or ink. Instead, each work incorporates into a more or less singular medium an assortment of visual elements to inspire thinking about a given totality inflected by particular themes. For example, quite disparate images signify Chineseness in each work: dragons, film stars, labels. And each also conjures different contexts for the articulation of this term: Awai's allusions to oil and the history of resource extraction on the island, Chang's Trinidadian nation, Chen's milieu of corporate finance, Cozier's references to commodity circulation. Following this disambiguation of the four artists from one another, we might say that they mark Chineseness at different if sometimes overlapping scales. Awai's is insular (a specific oil-field) and regional; Chan's work is at once municipal and national. Chen's sculpture in the national bank implies a unit of analysis even as finances-capes constantly intersect but also transcend such a framework. Cozier juxtaposes local signifiers with a wide range of referents that extend across many parts of the globe.

How do these different assemblages produce meaning? I have argued that they all, to some degree, incorporate Chinese bodies into figures of finance, literally evacuating Chinese bodies of individualized signification.[65] This assertion follows the critical maneuvers of scholars like Édouard Glissant and Lisa Lowe in thinking through a relay between oppression and the means of its undoing or at least survival under advanced capitalism. In their various articulations of, respectively, relation and intimacy, they offer ways to think about insurgent practices and unexpected collectivities that work to transform how we envision a particular worldview. Each model also imagines in distinct ways how one might think about not only the challenge to dominance but also a refiguration of the dominant.

I have insistently argued that Chineseness can signify simultaneously both dominance and oppression (indeed, this is also true of terms like *black* when understood in Caribbean as opposed to US-based contexts). But considerations of China and Chineseness force us to consider different scales in relation to Trinidad, the Caribbean, and globalization. Even as Chineseness is repeatedly incorporated into one scale of analysis, it can also be disarticulated, refigured, and made to force a rearticulation of the dominant. In Trinidad, multiple travelers—human agents, physical objects, and digital images—move through different waves, jostling one another. In the case of the Trinidadian works I have analyzed, Chineseness becomes and also generates the totality that we are capable of imagining.

NOTES

1. Nicole Awai, personal communication, November 14, 2018.

2. Michelle Stephens, "Oozing between Dimensions: Multiple Perspectives on the Real in the Works of Nicole Awai," *small axe* 52 (March 2017): 56.

3. I use Trinidad as the touchstone in the chapter as opposed to Trinidad and Tobago because Tobago still registers largely as a leisure space in the national imaginary. Most of the population lives on Trinidad, and Chinese investments are centered there as opposed to on its sister island.

4. Cecilia Chen, "Mapping Waters: Thinking with Watery Places," in *Thinking with Water*, eds. Cecilia Chen, Janine MacLeod, and Astrida Neimanis (Montreal: McGill-Queen's University Press, 2013), 277.

5. Lisa Lowe, *The Intimacies of Four Continents* (Durham: Duke University Press), 15–16.

6. Lowe, *Intimacies*, 24.

7. Moon-Ho Jung, *Coolies and Cane: Race, Labor, and Sugar in the Age of Emancipation* (Baltimore: The Johns Hopkins University Press, 2006). Lisa Yun, *The Coolie Speaks: Chinese Indentured Laborers and African Slaves in Cuba* (Philadelphia: Temple University Press, 2008).

8. Walton Look Lai, *The Chinese in the West Indies, 1806–1995: A Documentary History* (Kingston: The University of the West Indies Press, 1998), 6.

9. This is, of course, the title for Part VIII of Karl Marx, *Capital: A Critique of Political Economy, Volume I* (Chicago: Charles H. Kerr & Company, 1932).

10. Lowe, *Intimacies*, 164.

11. C. L. R. James, *Beyond a Boundary* (Durham: Duke University Press, 1993), 196.

12. James, *Boundary*, 197.

13. Eric Hayot, *The Hypothetical Mandarin: Sympathy, Modernity, and Chinese Pain* (Oxford: Oxford University Press, 2009), 140.

14. For an overview of this complicated history, see Look Lai, *The Chinese in the West Indies*.

15. Marx, *Capital*, 823.

16. Karl Marx, *Das Kapital: Kritik der Politischen Ökonomie*, 851. http://www.arbeiterpolitik.de/Texte/Kapital/KAPITAL1.pdf.

17. See the translation by Fredric Jameson, *Representing Capital: A Commentary on Volume One* (New York: Verso, 2011), 79. "Battlefield" is also the translation used in the Penguin Classics edition: Karl Marx, *Capital: A Critique of Political Economy Volume I*. Trans. Ben Fowkes (New York: Penguin Books, 1990), 915.

18. Jameson, *Capital*, 73.

19. Marx, *Capital*, 825.

20. Here, I have in mind a parallel to Avery Gordon's notion of haunting as signifying unresolved social conflicts. See Avery Gordon, *Ghostly Matters: Haunting and the Sociological Imagination* (Minneapolis: University of Minnesota Press, 1997).

21. http://www.thegstt.com/education/history-of-trinidads-oil/, accessed March 8, 2017.

22. Anne Hilton, "John Lee Lum," *Trinidad and Tobago Newsday*, Sept 17, 2006, http://www.newsday.co.tt/news/0,44441.html.

23. Ministry of Energy and Energy Affairs, *100 Years of Oil Production in Trinidad and Tobago (The Early Days)*, https://www.youtube.com/watch?v=Ucyt52-mo2o.

24. See W. Richard Jacobs, "The Politics of Protest in Trinidad: The Strikes and Disturbances of 1937," *Caribbean Studies* 17, nos. 1–2 (April–July 1977): 5–54.

25. Harvey R. Neptune, *Caliban and the Yankees: Trinidad and the United States Occupation* (Chapel Hill: University of North Carolina Press, 2007), chapter 5.

26. Elizabeth E. Sine, "The Radical Vision of Si-lan Chen: The Politics of Dance in an Age of Global Crisis," *small axe* 20, no. 2 (July 2016): 28–43.

27. http://ngc.co.tt/wp-content/uploads/pdf/publications/energy-map-of-tnt-2015 -ed.pdf.

28. Sean Metzger, Francisco-J. Hernández Adrián, and Michaeline Crichlow, "Introduction: Islands, Images, Imaginaries," *Third Text* 28, nos. 4–5 (2014): 335.

29. See the cover story of the *Trinidad and Tobago Guardian* business section on February 20, 2014: "InvesTT leads 35-member contingent in mission to China." Then-president Racquel Moses hoped to attract "US $1.8 billion in new investment" (BG4). To give context, Trinidad and Tobago's GDP was US $26.18 billion in 2014, so the potential deal was worth nearly 7 percent of Trinidad and Tobago's GDP.

30. Quoted in Sue-Ann Wayow, "Chinese Weekly Now Bilingual," *Trinidad Express*, July 21, 2010, accessed Oct. 3, 2010, http://www.trinidadexpress.com /business-magazine/98900394.html.

31. This information is taken from the website of S. C. G. (Caribbean) Group Limited, an overseas subsidiary of Shanghai Construction Group (which registered in Trinidad and Tobago in 2005). See http://www.scgcaribbean.com/Details-of-the-article?article _id=540, March 6, 2017.

32. Camille Clark, "Works Employees Put Chinese on the Run," *The Trinidad and Tobago Guardian*, May 21, 2010, accessed July 6, 2011, http://test.guardian.co.tt/?q=news /general/2010/05/21/works-employees-put-chinese-run.

33. Maraj, Lieselle, "500 Chinese Help Build TT," *Trinidad and Tobago Newsday*, July 15, 2007, accessed Oct. 3, 2010, http://www.newsday.co.tt/news/0,60612.html.

34. For an overview of this issue, see Aisha Khan, *Callaloo Nation: Metaphors of Race and Religious Identity among South Asians in Trinidad* (Durham, NC: Duke University Press, 2004).

35. Derek Walcott, *The Journeyman Years, Occasional Prose 1957–1974. Volume 1: Culture, Society, Literature, and Art*, ed. Gordon Collier (New York: Rodopi, 2013), 63. Of course, Chinese Trinidadians have also participated in Carnival, which I do not discuss here. On that issue, see Carlisle Chang, "Chinese in Trinidad Carnival," *TDR* 42, no. 3 (Autumn 1998): 213–219. More recent activities include the annual dragon boat races that I have witnessed in Chagville.

36. Printex is a gray building, about one quarter of a square block, containing Willi Chen's studio, residence, study, his son Jason's auto shop, and a menagerie of pets: eight dogs, seven cats, and four birds.

37. I have in mind Kim Johnson, *Descendants of the Dragon: The Chinese in Trinidad 1806–2006* (Kingston and Miami: Ian Randle, 2006), which, as the title reveals, celebrates the bicentennial of organized Chinese migration. But other works also engage in this celebratory mode to different degrees. See Trevor Millet, *The Chinese in Trinidad* (Port of Spain: Inprint Caribbean Limited, 1993) and Winston Hayden Chang, Jr., *The Legacy of the Hakka Shopkeepers of the West Indies* (St. Catherines, Ontario: Wanata Enterprises, 2004).

38. Michaeline Crichlow with Patricia Northover, *Globalization and the Post-Creole Imagination: Notes on Fleeing the Plantation* (Durham, NC: Duke University Press, 2009), xiv.

39. Crichlow, *Globalization*, 10.

40. See Steve Harney, "Willi Chen and Carnival Nationalism in Trinidad," *Journal of Commonwealth Literature* (1990): 120–131; Shin Yamamoto, "Swaying in Time and Space: The Chinese Diaspora in the Caribbean and Its Literary Perspectives," *Asian Ethnicity* 9, no. 3 (2008). Both of these articles focus on Chen's first volume of short stories, *King of the Carnival and Other Stories* (London: Hansib, 1988).

41. Kamau Brathwaite, *Roots* (Ann Arbor: University of Michigan Press, 1993), 42.

42. Eric Hayot, Haun Saussy, and Steven G. Yao, eds., *Sinographies: Writing China* (Minneapolis: University of Minnesota Press, 2008), xii.

43. Willi Chen, *Crossbones and Other Stories* (London: Hansib, 2009), 13.

44. Yamamoto, "Swaying," 175.

45. Chen, *Crossbones*, 13.

46. Chen, *Crossbones*, 14.

47. Chen, *Crossbones*, 13.

48. Chen, *Crossbones*, 16.

49. Sean Metzger, "Incorporating: Chineseness in Chen's Trinidad," *The Global South* 6, no. 1 (2012): 98–113.

50. Selwyn D. Ryan, *Race and Nationalism in Trinidad and Tobago* (Toronto: University of Toronto Press, 1972), 23–24.

51. Indeed, I argue this is true in all of the short stories that feature Chinese characters in *Crossbones*. See Metzger, "Incorporating."

52. Ewart S. Williams, "Foreword," in *The Story of Our Nation: An Exhibition of Selected Pieces of the Bank's Art Collection* (Port of Spain: The Central Bank of Trinidad and Tobago, 2007).

53. Geoffrey MacLean, "Introduction," in *The Story of Our Nation*.

54. The more abstract assemblage of geometric shapes of Chang's *Cosmic Event*, a mural in Independence Square, also suggests a parallel to the individual components of Chen's work, but I highlight the dragon here to indicate a consistency between the two artists in overall representational form.

55. Walcott lists several of the sources and materials. Walcott, *The Journeyman Years*, 446.

56. Alexandra Chang, *Circles and Circuits: Chinese Caribbean Art* (Los Angeles: Chinese American Museum, 2018), and Geoffrey MacLean, *Exhibition of Chinese Artists in Trinidad and Tobago* (Port of Spain: Geoffrey MacLean, 2006).

57. Leonard Folgarait writes that mural art demands a "constituency, full of awareness of their structural awareness to the government" (Leonard Folgarait, *Mural Painting and Social Revolution in Mexico, 1920–1940* [Cambridge: Cambridge University Press, 1998], 6).

58. Carlisle Chang, interview with Trinidad and Tobago Society of Architects, *Environs*, March 1977, accessed June 14, 2010, http://artsocietytt.org/1977-CarlisleChang -1977-interviewonarchitecture.pdf, 4.

59. Walcott, *Journeyman*, 406.

60. http://www.cnc3.co.tt/news/napa-shut-down-over-safety-report. NAPA has since reopened.

61. http://www.clarks.com/about-us.html.

62. Michael Fried, *Objecthood*, 154.

63. Sean Metzger, *Chinese Looks: Fashion, Performance Race* (Bloomington and Indianapolis: Indiana University Press, 2014), chapter 4.

64. Anne-Marie Lee-Loy, *Searching for Mr. Chin: Constructions of Nation and the Chinese in West Indian Literature* (Philadelphia: Temple University Press, 2010), 2.

65. In this sense, they play on a kind of racializing assemblage. Alexander G. Weheliye, *Habeas Viscus: Racializing Assemblages, Biopolitics, and Black Feminist Theories of the Human* (Durham: Duke University Press, 2014), 6.

3 — FLOWING

Widely deployed as a metaphor for describing transnational processes, *flows* name a seemingly self-evident linkage of seascapes and globalization. Commentators in popular media frequently use *flows* to describe the movement of beliefs, goods, information, people, and technologies across national and other territorial boundaries in order to demonstrate evidence of increasing interconnectivity on a planetary scale. In this chapter, flowing draws attention to the *action* of creating such connections by emphasizing embodied activities that facilitate the creation of ostensibly Chinese networks, in this case on the Caribbean island of Martinique. I highlight the corporeal practice of tai chi, a transliteration of taijiquan (literally meaning "supreme ultimate fist," or boxing). The form involves the slow, sustained, sequential, and, for me, ethereal movement of bodies. I investigate largely non-Asian bodies involved in such Chinese calisthenics as a living seascape in a seaside capital—a port city being transformed by Chinese migrant bodies feverishly engaged in urban shopkeeping and food service. This commotion that forms the background to the seascape of interest to me has, as its primary goal, the accumulation of wealth to facilitate the flow of these Chinese merchants from island to metropole.

Because of the stress on embodiment as an epistemology, this chapter places greater emphasis on explicating methodology as well as object of study. I have suggested throughout the book that visual seascapes of different kinds—paintings (introduction), documentary films (chap. 1), structural murals and other art intended for exhibition in public spaces (chap. 2)—may produce haptic and other sensory engagements. Such representations and the acts they engender push toward understanding globalization as a theatrical experience. Here, I elaborate that contention in a particular manner. In what way might the seascape translate into a corporeal form? How might non-Chinese individuals consciously enact global Chinese circulations through the body? The path to these queries involves my own research experiences as well as engagements with a number of people who construct Chineseness in particular ways. For these reasons, I engage to a much greater degree in this chapter of the book with discourses of Orientalism. However, given the breadth of scholarship in that area, I develop a specific framework, "Oriental sensitivity," that I deploy as a way to track the current and historical constructions of tai chi in a Francophone context.

Although I started my research with a general hypothesis about what Chinese flows—in terms of commerce and migrants—I would find in the Francophone Caribbean, I found that my encounters in Martinique compelled my consideration of the spirit and the flesh in ways that I had not previously experienced. This chapter moves through that process. First, I establish the contexts that informed my choice and knowledge of tai chi as well as the Chinese circulations in Martinique that contextualize it. Then I turn to Francophone commentaries on tai chi that grounded my initial engagements with practitioners on the island. This section demonstrates something I take to be characteristic of the surface encounters produced by globalization: An individual assimilates new spectacles into existing schema with which one is familiar. In my case, I arrived with many thoughts about, if very limited experience with, tai chi. The commentaries that I cite have an Orientalist valence, and I spend some time theorizing a methodology that acknowledges this continuing structure of knowledge production and attempts to move through rather than beyond or outside of it. I turn from these more intellectual frameworks to the materiality of researching bodies; these experiences altered the course of my research in unanticipated ways. I conclude with the implications of what it might mean to consider live seascapes, enacted in an everyday practice.

LOCATING A DISCIPLINE

Because of my longstanding interest in Caribbean intellectual history—from the works of writer and politician Aimé Césaire to those of surrealist and poet Suzanne Césaire, author and philosopher Édouard Glissant, filmmaker Euzhan Palcy, novelist Raphaël Confiant, and, especially, psychologist and revolutionary Frantz Fanon—I knew of Martinique's historical waves of Chinese immigration. Initially, I planned a study of holdings in the library established in 1883 by the antislavery activist and statesman Victor Schoelcher that might put into relief some of my work on Trinidad. In other words, I sought a comparative postcolonial context that would enable the examination of the British and French imperial legacies. As part of my preliminary research, I typed *Martinique chinois* in various search engines and media-sharing platforms, including YouTube. I had been looking for clips from a recent documentary on the subject of Chinese immigrants in Guyane and Martinique. One of the first hits intrigued me: a business focused on maintaining an ostensibly Chinese movement practice led by a black Martinican man. What is his place in the stream of discourse produced by Martinique's artistic and intellectual traditions?

During my later field research, I would eventually learn that this martial arts master, Michel Assouvie (b. 1962), had been practicing for over thirty years. Yet his desire to express respect for what he saw as Chinese culture has been mitigated by the migrant Chinese population itself. Indeed, many of Assouvie's participants describe the Chinese community on Martinique (estimated at less than one thousand people, or a quarter of 1 percent of the island's populace) as closed, even though the Chinese entrepreneurs often described themselves as integrated. What accounts for these apparent contradictions? Although I first sought answers in the library, the archive contained sparse material on Chinese migration to or cultural production on the island. Therefore, I ended up taking a very different methodological approach in which tai chi became the focal point of my research and conducted me not only to a new set of archival materials (in terms of newspaper articles and the tai chi club's own website) but also to the perspectives offered by local businesspeople, teachers, executives of large corporations, tai chi practitioners, and, as it turns out, a few health professionals. Many of these individuals I met through Assouvie's introduction; others I encountered wandering through the various businesses in the capital of Fort-de-France. Personal difficulties during my research brought me into contact with a network of doctors and nurses.

Tai chi may seem a highly unlikely form to express the contradictions of globalization in Martinique, because the isle's own cultural exports have been most influential in the domains of literature and music. As evidenced in these media, Chineseness has not, for the most part, factored as a major element in processes of creolization on the island (Confiant's novel *Case à Chine* is a notable exception). In the music industry, which has dominated the Caribbean's cultural production on the international stage, specifically French Antillean traditions converge with Chinese elements infrequently. For example, Edwin C. Hill has traced a history of the tam through a genealogy of French imperialism that includes the Caribbean and China.[1] Zouk, a major Francophone musical form, also has not intersected Chineseness very much, although songs like G. Gertrude and Wen Chun Tang's "Cha-Cha I Want to Dance with You (*ChaCha xiang gen ni tiao zhi wu*)" indicate sonic amalgamations taking shape through transnational soundscapes. My turn to a physical discipline like tai chi to investigate Chineseness illuminates a visible repertoire (in Diana Taylor's understanding of that word) of ostensibly Chinese cultural circulation on the island; this corporeal practice foregrounds bodies but delinks them from ideas of belonging based in family or genetics even as it suggests somatic connections. Put otherwise, my study of tai chi moves away from the forms of belonging that suffused the documentaries discussed in chapter 1 by revealing how groups of non-Chinese Martinicans learn a foreign movement practice.

This embodied rehearsal of movement is theatrical insofar as the corporeal training mimics the character of a Chinese cultural tradition. Dance scholar Yutian Wong has argued that purportedly national and ethnic dance traditions frequently impart a sense of authenticity, so that the choreography serves as a vehicle for ostensibly accessing some kind of cultural essence.[2] As will become evident in this chapter, Assouvie's club does not always replicate the form of tai chi with complete fidelity, and the small improvisations facilitate the fulfillment of certain expectations set by those who have joined the group for fitness. Meeting those expectations has a commercial value and enables him to sustain the tai chi club as a business. At the same time, the rhetoric mobilized by club members and Assouvie himself sometimes reinforces the idea that tai chi connects one to Chineseness—whatever that might mean for the individual. The diffusion of tai chi in Martinique reveals not only the global circulation of an ostensibly Chinese physical and spiritual practice but also the ways that disciplining body and mind through Assouvie's teachings engages local and transnational ways of moving through and understanding culture.

The references for Chinese culture specifically on Martinique thus emerge from both domestic and foreign sources. In terms of a more insular understanding of Chineseness, distinctions between Trinidad's and Martinique's respective immigration patterns help to illuminate the different ways in which waves of Chinese folks have shaped each island's image. Unlike Trinidad, which has a considerable history of Chinese Trinidadian artists working to articulate a national vision, Martinique's comparatively smaller Chinese migrant population has centered itself almost entirely in commerce. In part, this may have to do with the fact that few people from the initial groups of nineteenth-century imported workers survived and, of those who remained, many seem to have assimilated into the French imperial structure.[3] Most of this last group died without offspring, repatriated, or lost readily apparent Chinese connections through intermarriage. The 1930s witnessed a second wave of Chinese laborers to the Francophone island, including the arrival of one Mr. Ho Hio Hen, whose descendants continue to run one of Martinique's largest companies, named after the patriarch himself. These Chinese Martinican amalgams in business persist today in various forms, but they generally register as local; this commercial scene is one of the few sectors where Chineseness plays visibly into the dynamics of creolization.

In contrast, the latest wave of immigrants (from 1995 onward) seems to be generating new crosscurrents. According to scholar Isabelle Dubost, "Chinese denotes a complexity . . . it covers the status of foreigner, origin, phenotype, and social status."[4] Dubost argues that for Martinicans of non-Chinese descent, the terms denotes phenotype (*un sens phénotypique*) that corresponds to what she calls the Asian world (*monde asiatique*). She notes that in creole, one frequently hears *Mwen ka alé kay chinwa-a* ("I am going to a Chinese place"). This fits into the cultural nomenclature of Martinique more generally, where "one speaks of 'Syrians,' 'Chinese,' 'Coolies' (Indians), 'Metropolitans' [people from France] . . . but also of 'Blacks,' 'Whites,' 'chaben' (metis with light skin and light frizzy hair), 'milat' (mulattos) . . . the negative valence of these nominative categories varies according to periods and events."[5] In the postmillennial era, *Chinois* frequently connotes an identifiable group of working-class migrants in Fort-de-France. My contacts often described newer arrivals as focused on wage labor.

In contrast, tai chi suggests a greater investment in cultural refinement for those in the club. Probably not as well known on the island as other globalized forms of movement like ballet or yoga, tai chi seems comparatively more esoteric. In other words, the tai chi practitioners on Martinique recognize it as a means of exercise but also as part of a specific and decidedly nonlocal cultural tradition. The contexts for such tradition are provided by Assouvie himself during his teaching sessions as well as media that display other Chinese martial arts. In this vein, many of the club members had at least heard of *gong fu* (kung fu), which owes its wide dissemination to the film industry. When Martinicans do tai chi, therefore, they participate in a larger network of embodied movements and cultural mélanges that Asian film industries both enact and inspire across wide and sometimes unexpected geographies.

Cultural studies theorist Meaghan Morris has written of the importance of certain corporeal cinematic traditions to global articulations of Chineseness. Morris notes that "Hong Kong cinema since the 1960s has played a significant role in shaping what is now one of the world's most widely distributed popular cultural genres: action cinema."[6] From Hollywood to Wakaliwood (Uganda's fledgling film industry), *wuxia* films have morphed in an often unexpected manner, reflecting and shaping global connections. Such fusion filmmaking has proliferated Asian Westerns, often categorically labeled as the latest alimentary delicacy: the kimchi Western, the pad thai Western. The martial arts emphasis continues across other national borders and generic classifications. For example, Apichatpong Weerasethakul and Michael Shaowanasai's *The Adventures of Iron Pussy* (2003), a Thai film about a transvestite secret agent, melds Southeast Asian film genres with blaxploitation (which, of course, owes a debt to Hong Kong cinema) producing a mix of trash talking, hand-to-hand combat, and musical numbers. That film circulated through lesbian and gay film festivals much like Ekachai Uekrongtham's biopic *Beautiful Boxer* (2003), which features the story of Parinya Charoenphol, a transgender muay thai champion. As performance studies scholars May Joseph and Emily Roxworthy have argued respectively regarding the impact of gong fu cinema on Tanzanian youth culture and sumo demonstrations for Commodore Perry, the live exhibition of martial arts has played an important role in fostering cultural contacts; indeed, the presentational aspect as well as the many legends of its origin point to its theatrical display.[7] Richard Nichols has specifically observed that tai chi and aikido became standard components of many Western acting training programs beginning in the 1970s.[8] This genealogy suggests that tai chi functions as one form in a larger constellation of Asian martial arts traditions that have connected China, among other locations in the Pacific Rim, to the Atlantic world and its cultural production.

Cinema and other commercial industries have further helped to codify what people know about practices like tai chi. In an example such as Keanu Reeves's directorial debut *Man of Tai Chi* (2013), the narrative shows the official martial arts competitions that legitimize certain moves over others even as it participates in furthering myths of superhuman abilities gained through continuous study. Tai chi's history, like that of many spiritual/physical disciplines, remains as much reiterated fable as fact, which may explain some practitioners' sustained beliefs in its capacity to connect them to ancient China. The legendary progenitor of tai chi, Zhang Sanfeng, has been repeatedly depicted in films such as *Tai Chi Master* (directed by Yuen Woo-Ping, 1993; the Chinese title actually includes his name: *taiji zhang sanfeng*). Although much disagreement remains about his origins and life span, most adherents to the folklore concur that he lived for some time in the Wudang Mountains, a tale that lends mystique to this region even today. These oral narratives further recount a battle between a serpent and a bird that Zhang witnessed; the former animal owed its victory to its circular, supple movement and slow rhythms. In this myth, tai chi follows the principles embodied in the snake.[9]

Documented history, however, locates the beginning of tai chi in a more androcentric setting: Chen Village, Henan Province. This town lies in the Yellow River Valley and thus connotes associations with one of the cradles of civilization. Both the mythological and the empirical versions of this story, then, conjure links to the distant past. Moreover, because tai chi's spiritual dimensions draw on Daoism, its philosophical orientation also directs practitioners to Chinese antiquity. Such linkages, however, remain distinct from practices that might otherwise seem parallel. For example, the cosmology of *falun dafa* (falun gong) involves a comparatively greater amount of mythic elements and an organizational structure much more cultish in terms of revolving around the particular personality of Master Li Hongzhi. Yoga has a far longer history of historical documentation and, in the last few decades, stronger associations with commodification most obviously materialized by corporations such as lululemon.

Despite the vexed accounts of its origins, the majority of tai chi masters today recognize five styles, of which the Yang family (*yangshi*) style is the most common; it has a decidedly modern history. Yang Luchan (1799–1872) trained with the earliest documented master of tai chi and subsequently received a summons to the capital based on reports of his skills. Yang journeyed to Beijing to work with the Manchu elite. The dissemination of his teachings through his kin and students proved far reaching. Michel Assouvie teaches the Yang style in Martinique today.

Tai chi emerged in the context of cultural conflict and exchange. According to scholar Douglas Wile, "militia training" encouraged by the unstable political situation in the late Qing Dynasty facilitated the development of tai chi.[10] He links this physical and mental regimen to the self-strengthening movement as well as other (perhaps) coincidental phenomena in nineteenth-century China: tensions between Daoist and Confucian philosophies; demographic transitions that produced a preponderance of young men in the northern region from which the form springs; internal conflicts within the Middle Kingdom, such as the Nian Rebellion that encouraged people to learn self-defense; and larger geopolitical restructuring occurring through events such as the Opium Wars. For my purposes, the issue is not whether Wiles has written the correct history of tai chi (again, the authenticity of these tales is not the point). His conclusions either overlap with or inform many of the understandings of the martial art that continue to circulate outside of China.

The importance of tai chi's origin stories for my analysis of its Martinican enthusiasts is manifold, but not in terms of the narrative details. Rather, the historical information in all its variants connects tai chi to a notion of Chineseness that moves back several centuries—that is, before the industrialization of China. Much of the information about Chinese martial arts has paradoxically surfaced through the capitalist machinery of the film industry. The desire to access these kinds of cultural lineages does not necessarily intersect with a desire to meet one's newly arrived Chinese neighbors in Fort-de-France, whose lives tai chi club members frequently described as being concerned with financial success and sometimes as parsimonious. These interpretations, of course, involved a great deal of suppositions, because many of the Chinese small-business owners spoke French haltingly, and none of the score or so of tai chi club members I met during my visits to Martinique spoke any Sinitic languages (although a few, including Assouvie, were taking classes). Thus Chineseness registered for tai chi club members through bodily as opposed to verbal forms of communication and meaning making. Tai chi then promised access to an embodied form of cultural understanding.

TAI CHI AU MONDE DE LA FRANCOPHONIE

Tai chi has spread around the world; its particular uptake in Martinique stems largely from the efforts of Assouvie. Although born in Fort-de-France, he moved to Paris, where many young people from the overseas department pursue higher education and seek employment. In France, Assouvie began studies in judo and *Việt Võ Đạo* (Vietnamese martial arts). He became affiliated with what eventually evolved into the Fédération Française de Karaté et Disciplines Associées, an organization through which he won many competitive titles. During his training, one of his teacher's wives introduced him to tai chi. He developed an increasing attraction to that form after a sojourn in China. Returning to Martinique in 2003, he launched the tai chi club in 2007, which takes place in several locations across the island.[11] Besides regular classes, the club also offers occasional public performances as well as a group trip to China.

As Assouvie's own narrative illustrates, China often features prominently in people's impressions of tai chi. That claim might seem obvious, but why should this corporeal practice lead back to China? The import of such a question might be clarified through a roughly equivalent one: Would one expect those who practice yoga to wish to travel to India? Dance scholar Sansan Kwan argues, following Henri Lefebvre, that "space is experienced and constituted through the body."[12] Her spin on Lefebvre reorients his spatial theory to account for the construction of specifically Chinese urban spaces. Such work inspires my own thinking about tai chi as a movement vocabulary that renders visible a recognizable form of Chineseness. That form is exportable, subject to improvisatory modifications, and, paradoxically, imagined as a channel to some kind of cultural connection that might be authenticated in China.

This phenomenon undoubtedly has something to do with the masses of practitioners occupying parks and other public spaces throughout the country. Indeed, I continue to associate such physical activity and spectacle with Beijing parks at dawn, when I first encountered silent crowds in slow motion during my first Chinese study abroad experience. Tai chi interrupts the normative din and rush of urban Chinese life. Those first experiences continue to influence my thoughts about what tai chi does to create new spaces of cooperative possibility that forestalls, if it does not completely negate, the barking of street vendors and the chaotic onslaught of bodies surging from place to place. However, that lingering memory reflects not only my individual nostalgia but also imagery circulated through mass media. As one notable instance, Michelangelo Antonioni's documentary film *Chung Kuo* (1972) captures similar scenes, and the reference appears in many other descriptions of cultural encounter that have remained with me over the years, including Roland Barthes's *Travels in China*.

Given my own training in French literature and philosophy, the representations of tai chi in that intellectual tradition established one point of comparison for some of the interlocutors I would eventually encounter in Martinique. Certainly, I have long thought about the Orientalist valence of these descriptions, marveling at how similar experiences can lead to such entirely opposing viewpoints. For example, Roland Barthes's notebooks detail his 1974 visit to China with other editors of the journal *Tel Quel* after the group declared its support for Maoism. In his characteristically wry prose, Barthes's descriptions of tai chi prompt bizarre non sequiturs; the first in his travelogue offers a quick assessment that he then drops: "A guy taking his time doing his solitary gymnastics: no muscles, no bones either—what? 'Loosening up' his body? Dao?"[13] Barthes's observations flag his confusion and his Orientalist vision of Chinese flexibility as a corporeal mass that flows according to a philosophical concept he does not understand. Later in his journey, he recounts watching the elderly exercising (he contrasts this sight with more youthful groups participating in the regimented morning exercises popularized during the communist era and drawing on Mao's writings about physical education). Barthes writes, "Older people do Chinese gymnastics, slower more supple, more mysterious: individual gymnastics, as opposed to collective gymnastics."[14] These thoughts, written in response to what he witnessed outside his bus, compel his reflection on a proverb about exercise cultivating the physique and the mind. Barthes counters the adage, announcing that he prefers a dull mind in a slutty body.[15] As happens occasionally in his desultory musings, Barthes's ruminations drift to a different kind of flow.

Barthes is not the only person affiliated with *Tel Quel* to be moved by tai chi. A young Julia Kristeva wrote of the "precise suppleness of Chinese gymnastics" that one can see "at dawn or dusk along the banks of the Huangpu" in the published record of her China tour.[16] Like Barthes, she also finds that "neither muscular tension nor skeletal support" seems to enable movement; rather, "the rhythm . . . flows (*s'écouler*) with the blood."[17] Kristeva's interest in tai chi emerges from the fact that she could see women, previously (according to her account) barred from participation, practicing quite publicly. Part of her fascination seems to lie in the potential mobilization of corporeal bodies to shift the political one. Like the rest of *Des Chinoises*, this passage suggests a means of using the figure of China to critique France. What is interesting about such a formulation, to extend scholar Eric Hayot's assessment, is that such "Chinese strangeness does not, for Kristeva, arise from some ancient culture, but rather comes out of a modern society that steps into the same ontological and political space as Europe and the West."[18] Notwithstanding the fact that Kristeva also Orientalizes Chinese women (for which she has received strong critique), she suggests in a manner different from Barthes's a way of women acting that enacts politics in the form of creating spaces of liberatory possibility: for Kristeva, a tai chi–staged feminism. For my purposes, she began to illustrate how tai chi might offer an embodied response to homogenizing forces of the dominant: an iteration of the theatricality of globalization in which Western women might mimic the movements toward liberation that Kristeva sees in her Chinese counterparts.

ORIENTAL SENSITIVITY

The European visions that see bodies engaged in tai chi movements as continual flow but that alternately dismiss or celebrate such projects in different kinds of Orientalist discourse mark a perplexing beginning to my knowledge of tai chi. However, they also explicitly stage issues that attend the tracking of cultural currents in a world saturated with media representations of encounters with otherness. I am not invested in adjudicating whether my own perceptions are more accurate than those of someone like Barthes or Kristeva. As much as I might like to separate my own knowledge based on claims of Chinese cultural affiliation and study from these Europeans, I have never attempted tai chi for more than one or two sessions in a week. Nor have I acquired the physical or the spiritual discipline. The sequences of movement prove difficult. Because I do not possess muscle memory of the form, I find the concentration required taxing. I continue to think of what I have seen in the parks of Shanghai and Beijing, cities in which I have briefly lived, as properly performed tai chi notwithstanding that the professional school for which I work mandates that all first-year students take tai chi for at least one term demonstrating that the form might be "properly" practiced elsewhere. Notwithstanding this fact, the group of late teens stumbling around the UCLA School of Theater, Film, and Television seems like an exhibition of unsuccessful cultural collision and causes me a bit of embarrassment whenever I happen on that scene. However, the two French philosophers, the students, and I do not necessarily differ in our relatively superficial engagements with the lifelong practice that is tai chi. As observers or dilettantes, we reveal highly mediated embodiments of Chineseness, surface engagements produced through global circulations of a Chinese movement practice.

Rather than various discourses of cultural competence or navigation, I would like to transition to one of cultural unease, one that I would call, with well-meaning irony, Oriental sensitivity. I have arrived at this conception after some reflection about my own position as researcher and those of the individuals who served as my informants. I cannot subscribe to the self-Orientalizing discourse of native informant, and indeed my position either in Martinique or in China renders me anything but that. The groups of mostly Afro, but also Creole and white Martinican tai chi practitioners I met also could not claim native (Chinese?) knowledge of the physical practice in which they had invested time and money.

Most of the people with whom I have spoken in Martinique, including Assouvie, have discussed at length the limits of their knowledge of China, so it would also be difficult to ascribe to these speakers a sense of Afro Orientalism. Indeed, even if that term suggests "an entire range of black imaginings of Asia that are in fact negotiations with the limits and disappointments of black citizenship," the reported reasons for interest in tai chi most often had

to do with the need for exercise (although there were some interesting excep-
tions, as I will later reveal).[19] My interlocutors in the tai chi club discussed
China in complicated ways: a nation-state with a strong platform for pro-
moting national culture, a civilization with a venerable history, and a place
that had produced tremendous inequity, as evidenced by recent streams
of immigrants throughout the Caribbean. Asking about China and Chinese people, products, and aesthetics in Martinique elicited contradictory
responses that sometimes generalized *Chinese* in the most Orientalist fashion, much like Barthes's and Kristeva's perpetuating the idea of supple Asian
bodies. Yet I also heard recounted the material observations of folks who
had traveled to China with the club: comments about ubiquitous smog, and
diverse foods and culture from different regions. Several Martinicans offered
nuanced descriptions, sensitive to the fact that news reports and other media
frequently describe China in monolithic terms. Such play between one's
acquired knowledge and recognition of the limits of that knowledge (including the scaffolding of information through Orientalist structures) constitutes part of my definition of Oriental sensitivity.

To recognize that Orientalism exists does not negate the fact of my own
(conscious) immersion in those discursive formations. Certainly, I frequently
relied on a hackneyed assertion of Chinese kinship in order to initiate conversations, particularly when I interrupted Chinese folks working in their
shops. In fact, when I spoke to people of Chinese descent, I almost always had
conversations about family, a tactical move I thought might counteract the
impression that I might have been sent to check for papers. People in general
seemed comfortable with the idea that my interest in the Chinese folks on
the island stemmed from a broad extension of kinship relations. The tai chi
practitioners also probed my intentions. Because the relationship between tai
chi and globalization seems tenuous without quite a lot of explication, kinship became shorthand for me to mark my investments. My research examines culture and Asian immigration in the United States, I would frequently
explain, so I have been looking at Chinese immigration in the Caribbean.
Extensive explanation of my research in French would necessitate translating
many terms that would themselves require lengthy asides, since categories
of racial identification differ in the United States and Martinique. Often,
my brief research pitch would elicit a response requesting justification, so
family again served as an easy way to signal my investment in the topic. At

that point in the conversation, I tended to hear some variant of, "Now that you say it, I can see it." My *l'air Chinois* was often retrospectively affirmed by my interlocutors' mentions of physical characteristics: my eyes; sometimes my hair. I imagine my interviewees meant to establish a rapport with me in terms of recognizing some intrinsic connection between the professor and his subject matter. I also concede that I may well have set the conditions for my interview subjects to frame me in Orientalist terms. To explore the flowing energy that is tai chi in the space of Martinique involved layers of Oriental sensitivity that I simply did not obtain in my other research sites because of the ways in which bodies engaged in a corporeal practice laden with Chinese cultural connotations.

Jose Muñoz has offered cultural theorists the useful term *disidentification* as a way to mark a "positionality that has been rendered unthinkable by the dominant culture"; he emphasizes the partiality and paradoxes of identificatory processes.[20] His theory describes how minoritarian subjects, primarily within the context of the United States, enact politics and envision futures using the material resources of the present, but in appropriative fashion. I intend something different with Oriental sensitivity, although I perhaps overlap with Muñoz in putting my French theories to rather different purposes than that for which they were written.

In Martinique, I witnessed competing cultural frameworks (mostly French and Chinese but also American insofar as people referenced Hollywood cinema or read me as a tourist from a very powerful nearby nation-state); my interlocutors referred to the American, the Chinese, and the French as dominant in relation to culture depending on the context of the discussion. For example, when people discussed the influence of films, they frequently acknowledged the force of American mass culture. Discussions of migration and political power involved decisions made in France. Such power dynamics did not necessarily mitigate the strength of an Antillean or Martinican identification, especially when people referred to the recent working-class Chinese migrants. In other words, *"la culture Chinoise"* demanded respect for its many contributions to the world, but the latest wave of migrants sometimes elicited less appreciative remarks characterizing them as opportunists who did not integrate into Martinican society. Such continual fluctuations as to what constituted the dominant in any given context mitigated the utility of disidentification. Oriental sensitivity intends to address the complexities of power by thinking about the perspectives that might render one cultural framework dominant in a particular instance (for example, I often listened to individuals assert the relative value of Chinese versus French culture).

As I began to perceive varying understandings of dominance from local perspectives, my sense of appropriate interview questions also began shifting. For example, I had wondered what role Chinese merchants had in the 2009 general strike in the Francophone Caribbean, and on Martinique specifically. People politely avoided answering my queries in that regard. I learned to be careful of fantasies of postcolonial solidarity animating my own vision, something I perhaps had internalized from years of reading Fanon. In a 1960 essay republished in *Toward the African Revolution*, he celebrated Martinican resistance to French rule, marking a link between the Algerian war and the contemporary bloodshed on his native soil.[21] Insofar as I elaborated from Fanon, my own hypotheses about how the presence of Chinese migrant entrepreneurs might matter on the island often proved incorrect.

How do people engage a discipline like tai chi to navigate through but also access systems of power? This question became increasingly relevant during the course of my research. Rey Chow has coined the term *coercive mimeticism* in order to think about the ways in which minority subjects do not necessarily mimic the colonizer but rather the ideal image of the ethnic constructed through the colonizer–colonized relation.[22] I wondered frequently what this ideal in Martinique might be and what happens when the ethnic fails to embody that image. The answer to all of my inquiries depended on my access to what any individual might say to a researcher and tourist, notwithstanding my repeated visits there. The material realities of Chinese migration to the island and the cultural form I had somewhat inadvertently come to study required, on the one hand, far more mediation than some of my engagements with other Chinese cultural circulations that I address in this book. On the other, tai chi promised a more direct channel to see Chinese movement practice instantiated in individual bodies.

For me, bodies in motion promised to reveal something about how Chinese circulations produced visceral sensations in Martinique. Such a study of perception does have an antecedent in Fanon, who concerned himself with the "violent confrontation between the colonized and the colonial system" in Algeria; he contended that it produced what he called a "sensitivity," which he then articulated as the mental disorders produced because of occupation.[23]

However, tai chi generates a wide range of possibilities in terms of cultural contact, and the dissemination of ostensibly Chinese practices cannot be reduced to violence or another order of oppression. My extension and appropriation of Fanon's thoughts on French imperialism, therefore, also shape my notion of Oriental sensitivity to mark tactical identifications and disidentifications with various cultural flows as they materialize or otherwise manifest through corporeal engagement.

During my research, my own somatic experiences reminded me that bodies do not only register cultural phenomena. The flesh can misbehave, reacting to known or unknown stimuli in sometimes uncomfortable ways. In my case, such an incident also resulted in my temporary connections to various machines and material therapies that provide a counterpoint to my investigation of physical circulations of Chineseness. Globalization's material enactments take different forms, and my experiences in Martinique encouraged me to pause before critiquing all such manifestations.

METHODOLOGICAL PROBLEMS

"Je n'arrive pas." As I uttered this to the doctor, I found myself thinking about the many different times I had heard this phrase during my initial visit to Martinique. Earlier in the morning, a member of the tai chi club, exasperated with the movement sequence, chanted a dirge, "Je n'arrive pas," before relinquishing his body to stasis. The tai chi master, Michel Assouvie, had lamented the same as we drove to his Mandarin class in the city of Lamentin. Was he improving in his skill level, I had queried? "Je n'arrive pas." The phrase generally means "I cannot (do something)." Literally, it states, "I do not arrive," or "I am not arriving." The sound "rive" recalls the French word for bank (of a river). I registered the word, thinking it might prove useful in furthering the discursive element of my research on seascapes. In this case, however, I had offered the sentence in response to a question about my bowel movements: "Je n'arrive pas."

I discuss a blockage in a chapter otherwise concerned with flowing because the former condition raises a hyperawareness of the latter when discussing one's own body. After a week in Fort-de-France, I had developed increasing abdominal pain, combined with significant swelling in the scrotum. Although I had hoped that this discomfort would disappear, one of the servers at the previous day's breakfast (on a Sunday) looked me up and down and announced, "Vous souffrez." That an Afro Martinican serveuse offered this assessment to me in a hotel called L'impératrice (the Empress) struck me as ironic, and also uncomfortably intimate. The waitress knew something about my interest in Chinese immigrants in the island's capital, as I had begun conversations with whomever I could after I arrived, wondering if any impromptu discussions might yield some productive insights regarding the many apparently Chinese-run "snacks" (fast food counters) and bazaars in downtown Fort-de-France. I hoped to ascertain what non-Chinese locals thought about their Asian neighbors. I had wondered if indeed people felt like they suffered as new waves of migrants streamed into the small businesses.

The suffering to which she gestured in my person was, of course, less existential in nature. Attention to my body had, for me, shifted my perspective—from considering my role as observing relations in town to thinking about the way I physically inhabited the space of my observation; it generated awareness that people noticed me as much as I watched them. As the distinction between my public and private personas began to erode, I experienced what Laurent Berlant has called "mobile processes of attachment."[24] This brief, intimate encounter resulted, I suspected, from a woman's reading my corporeal condition as an index (in the semiotic sense), registering symptoms like my awkward gait and otherwise tortured movement as a manifestation of a cause-and-effect relation in my body. Her inquiry into my well-being suggested, however fleetingly, a desire to recognize me, a kind of affective connection initiated through my physical state.

Given that my deteriorating health had become so obvious, I finally mustered the resolve to ask for a ride to a doctor's office from Assouvie. He had facilitated my initial research on Martinique, introducing me (and sometimes himself) to a number of diverse figures, many of whose thoughts shape this chapter. As Assouvie put it, I offered him a reason to speak with Martinicans whom he knew but with whom he had little contact; his hope was that introducing a scholar to these individuals might grant him some access to the Chinese community with which he had little success in creating dialogue, despite his own investments in a Chinese cultural form. I watched his tai chi session before we drove to meet his Chinese tutor, by which time I began to feel rather faint. I had, of course, rehearsed the description of various body parts and processes in French, words not in my everyday vocabulary. At the local clinic, Assouvie advised me to stay quiet as he guided me past a half a dozen mothers and their children waiting outside. He told them an American professor needed to see the doctor urgently (not completely untrue). Pain got the better of my desire not to display my own bourgeois privilege. As always, my interview began with questions about what I was doing in Martinique. And, as always, my answer describing a research project to investigate representations of Chinese people and practices on the island piqued my listener's interest. At the very least, the discussion gave me something to think about as the doctor probed my body. That encounter concluded with me receiving a directive to head immediately to the hospital; my initial exam suggested the possibility of *une torsion du testicule* (a term I had admittedly not practiced, so thank goodness for cognates). I carried a sealed letter to my next physician.

At the hospital, I presented my secret missive; a nurse escorted me straight back to an examination room, where I repeated my interview about Chinese folks in Martinique as the nurse inserted an IV into my arm. Naked and alone (sometimes the cliché works), I contemplated the possibility of having a major operation and wondered how long and where I would recover. A technician took a sonogram of my testicle and then wheeled me back into the examination room to wait for the doctor. As my anxiety got the best of me, I pondered the headlines in Martinique: US professor dies of testicular inflammation. That is not really how I imagined my passing, but I knew that death on small islands is often an event, given the relative infrequency of its occurrence. To frame this matter in a perhaps unusual perspective, I would like to suggest that even relatively mundane events on small islands may quickly become theatrical as journalists and gossips seek the stories of the day.

I offer an explicit description of my own embodied experience because it produces for me a visceral sense of unease, one that we might extend to surface encounters with the other, whether that be environmental conditions of a place to which one's body is unaccustomed or meetings among different people (so I reiterate in a more specific fashion Oriental sensitivity in the sense of being both participant and spectator in my research on corporeal experiences of Chineseness on the isle). This tale also reveals the unexpected intimacies I experienced with complete strangers as I pursued this research project on globalization, Chineseness, and representation. My diagnosis and treatment demonstrated the precarity of human bodies in transit even as it exposed me to the vast circulation of medical technologies and pharmaceuticals. I met a cross section of health professionals with whom, in all likelihood, I would not have otherwise had the opportunity to speak. Overall, the interruption to my research process helped clarify the stakes of different sorts of cultural exchange. Such exchanges also involved further evidence of globalization, but of qualitatively different kinds, such as the circulation of medical technologies. Far from the archival study I initially imagined I would be doing, I found myself focusing on how the body can become a global interface in conjunction with both the technological apparatuses to which I was attached and to the cultural practices that I had come to study.

Oh, and the cause of my memorable ailment? The doctor could only offer, "Je n'arrive pas la trouver."

LIVING SEASCAPE

Taking a Friday ferry from Anse a l'Ane across the Bay of Fort-de-France, I spotted in the distance a group of people seemingly suspended in motion. Disembarking, I walked toward the foot of Fort St. Louis, on the eastern end of the *malecon*, catty-corner from La Savane. The image became increasingly clear and increasingly animated. This time the assemblage numbered sixteen, split into two groups according to level of ability, with the instructor in front. The most advanced group distinguished itself not only through the fluidity of motion—with deft transitions from a push to a whip to cloud hands—but also through its sartorial appearance. Several of the more proficient individuals wore a loose-fitting silk pant and shirt ensemble in white. The obvious coach in this scene sported a bright yellow version of the same pattern, which shined in the remaining shards of twilight as he jogged back and forth between the clusters of his pupils. Most of the rest of the troop wore black sweats and white T-shirts. Together, they created an ethereal spectacle of moving bodies by the side of the sea, largely illuminated by the glow of the garrison wall.

I had arrived toward the end of a two-hour session of Martinique's tai chi club. Having participated earlier in the week, I recognized the awkward stumbling of those, like me, who were unsure of the sequence of movement. And when, during a brief pause, Assouvie handed out a series of fans, I knew to expect the increase in pace that would elevate the heart rates of everyone, producing sweat and the endorphin-induced satisfaction of having exercised. This conclusion was Assouvie's innovation; he recognized that his students

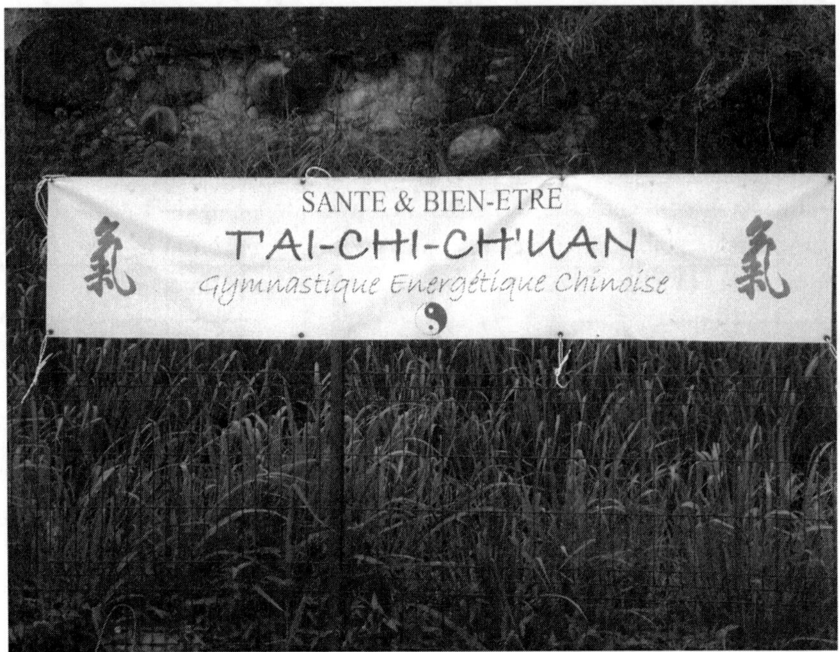

Fig. 3.1. Martinique's tai chi club announces itself in public space.
Photo by Sean Metzger.

wanted to feel physical exertion in exchange for the euros they had spent to join him for the evening. This last succession of gestures and stances also marketed the club, as the noise and display of the flicking fans attracted attention from passersby.

Although the outdoor sessions by the seashore have now been discontinued, the club's weekly visits to the site of the long-standing colonial battlements comprised perhaps the most sustained public exhibition of Chinese expressive culture anywhere on Martinique. What interests me about the routinized performances is that no ostensible Chinese subjects were involved. Indeed, since Assouvie began the club in 2007, on returning from a decade in the metropole, almost no people of Chinese descent have participated. On this particular evening, however, the island's major constituent demographics were represented: white Europeans, Creoles, black Martinicans. But the absence of any Chinese participants was noticeable, because there has been a significant increase in Martinique's Chinese population,

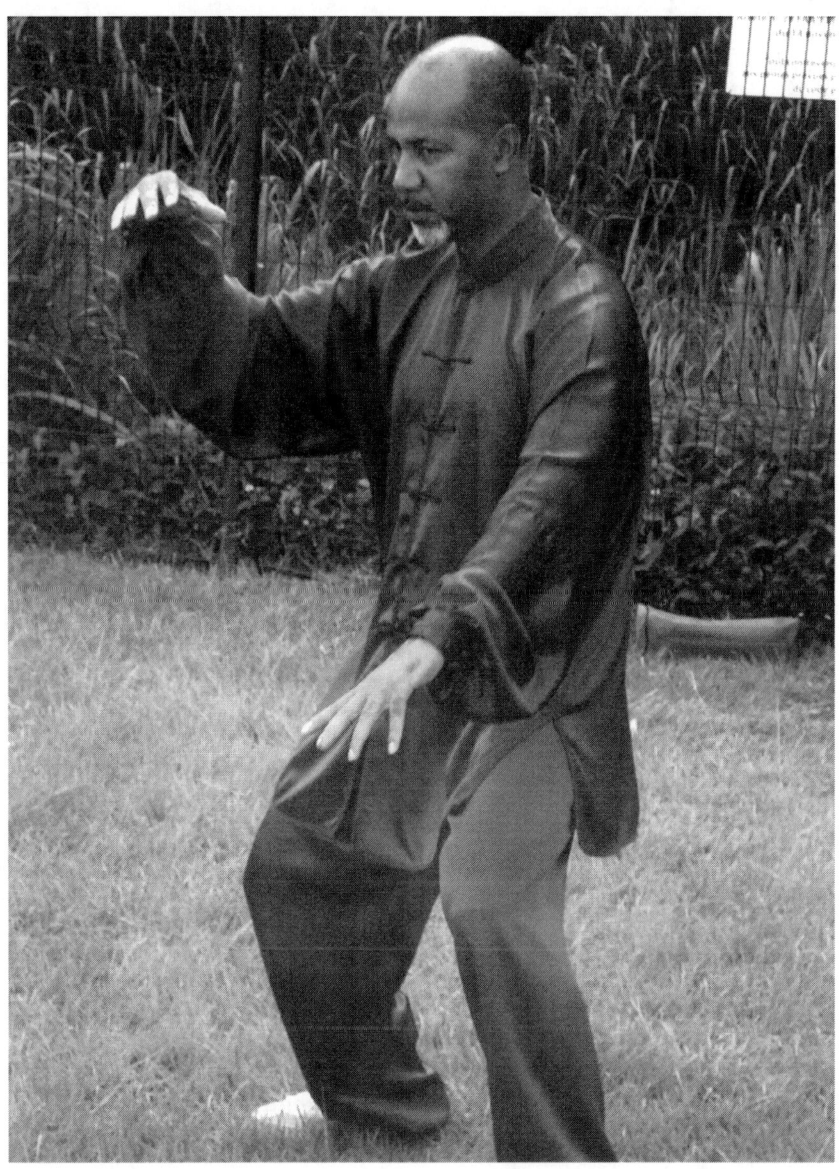

Fig. 3.2. Michel Assouvie does a demonstration for his students.
Photo by Sean Metzger.

centered in Fort-de-France and nearby Lamentin.[25] Earlier in the week, for example, I had observed a trio of women chatting in Mandarin as they walked around La Savane without acknowledging Assouvie's group.

David Ho, the leader of the recently formed Chinese community organization in Martinique, estimated the population at close to one thousand of the more than four hundred thousand island inhabitants. If this number seems miniscule as an overall percentage, a half kilometer stroll into downtown brings the sight of restaurants, snacks, and bazaars adorned with red lanterns, Chinese characters, and *maneki-neko* (an appropriation of Japanese kitsch) that dot the area. This is a town where the look of the urban landscape is in flux. The long-term residents often say that as soon as a local (Martinican) closes shop, a Chinese immigrant will claim the space. Such processes of change register in the seascape adjacent to the center of the city. Some of the tai chi students are engaged in language study; all of them are cognizant of the growing influence China is exerting in the overseas department and the world. A tension emerges between the increasingly felt presence of Chinese immigrants on Martinique and the feeling of Chineseness tapped by the tai chi club. As I have suggested, several of the participants reflected that their exercise routine drew on an illustrious Chinese cultural heritage, which the recent laborers who migrated to the island either had no time to study or no interest in engaging.

The very naming and identification of the Chinese community as such is interesting in this context. Again, this recent wave of immigrants was being perceived by many islanders as qualitatively different from the earlier waves of Chinese migrants, the traces of which are easy enough to find in the city. I have already mentioned that the Schoelcher library across La Savane contains several records documenting the nineteenth-century coolie traffic that carried the initial Chinese population to Martinique's shores. On a visit to Ho Hio Hen, I met an employee, a member of the Ho family, who told me that they had helped people who had arrived from China. How exactly this person did not want to say, but certainly, the Ho Hio Hen group, which runs a large grocery conglomerate across the Francophone Caribbean, has the resources to facilitate immigration for Chinese migrants. I had heard from another informant, a creperie owner whom I had met serendipitously when looking for lunch in town, that many of the newer Chinese migrants moved from Guyane, where entry seemed to be less monitored, to Martinique or

Guadeloupe. As the creperie owner explained to me, residence in France or its overseas departments for five years earns one the right to apply for French citizenship. With that status comes a high degree of mobility across the European Union. Therefore, claiming affiliations with potential sponsors at Ho Hio Hen would potentially facilitate a person's transition from Chinese migrant to French citizen. Whether or not this informant had accurate knowledge of other Chinese folks working in the neighborhood, the perception that the new "community" is actually a transitional group complicates the ways in which people identify and understand Chineseness in Martinique.

The changing feelings about Chinese people and things, I would argue, can be analyzed in the live seascape at the foot of Fort St. Louis. The tai chi club generally acknowledged the practice as a sign of Chinese cultural heritage, even as they questioned in various ways the expanding power of the Chinese government at the time. What factors, then, explain the participants' attachment to a particular form of Chineseness as an unchanging aesthetic form? In part, such distinctions seemed to involve differentiating between culture and economics. Such a divide—no matter how artificial—enabled categorization of tai chi practitioners as preserving the best of Chinese culture against the image of markedly different corporeal behaviors of new Chinese entrepreneurs often described with the terms *le niveau de base* ("the lowest level"). At stake here is what performing Chineseness means in different contexts. Such performances transform or otherwise impact on the idea of the local as Martinique becomes a relay station for a certain group of entrepreneurially minded migrants on their way to the metropole. This kind of movement seems to strike some of the island's population as exploitative even when the precarious conditions of those who have migrated might also be acknowledged. Claims to Chineseness are thus contingent and rewrite the place of Martinique, the French overseas departments, and the Caribbean archipelago of which they form a part as nodes in a global network where individuals might imagine and shape new trajectories for work and life. At the same time, tai chi club members who seek a corporeal connection to Chineseness for reasons of physical development or spiritual enlightenment see corporeal practice as a form of cultural affinity that produces better health and/or a larger worldview. What does this new geography (writing of place) tell us about new flows of capital and people from China or elsewhere?

Each participant in the club has a unique answer to this question. One of my informants tells me she has pursued tai chi because she has always felt Chinese, although she was born and continues to live in Martinique. She materializes this feeling of attachment through the physical discipline of tai chi. This movement practice entails moving energy (qi) around and between us. We may remember that Jean-Luc Nancy has elaborated being singular plural as circulation, as everything that *"se passe"* between us.[26] Tai chi is an interesting phenomenon in this regard because it is movement that does not go anywhere (there is no teleology), but this movement nevertheless brings an awareness of and creates connection. In this vein, the practitioner of tai chi does not move in place so much as move, creating place. In tai chi, one recognizes one's body as part of a system of energy, so individual and community do not necessarily indicate binary oppositions, but rather, something more like a process of articulation that one realizes through the flowing energy that exists in and around us. With this formulation in mind, I would ask again what it might mean for a black Martinican woman to feel Chinese. What might we learn if we think about place, movement, identification, and belonging as an ensemble in relation to what would often be held up as an Orientalist construction?

Certainly, not all responses to Chinese folks setting up shop in Fort-de-France expressed appreciation of the changing surface image of the urban seascape. I had seen the young Afro Martinican comedian called Bobi perform as the opening act to Pascal Légitimus's *Alone Man Show* on June 2, 2012, at the National Stage (Le CMAC [Centre Martiniquais d'Action Culturelle]—Scène Nationale de Martinique) in the city. Légitimus's solo performance largely concerns his background as the son of an Armenian costumière and an Antillean actor. The humor and pathos of the show turn on cultural misunderstanding and reconciliation. As a kind of introduction to these issues, Bobi offered a series of vignettes that commented on facets of everyday island life, including the emigration of young intellectuals to the metropole and the changing look of downtown. For me, this section proved frustrating, as he presented much of the skit in Antillean Creole. Despite my lack of comprehension at the linguistic level, the sequence clearly exploited for laughs the crossed signals between Chinese shopkeepers and their clientele. The gestural vocabulary participated in a long and transnational tradition of yellowface performances, complete with exaggerated accents, expressions, and movements. Despite my requesting a script and/ or an interview, I ultimately could produce no more information about this act (his online vignettes do not include this bit). Nevertheless, Bobi's playing Chinese threw into relief the actions of the tai chi club, who also engaged an ostensible tradition of Chinese physicality but in a markedly different manner.

Bobi and certain members of the tai chi club mimic movements that they recognize as Chinese; this construction of Chineseness is theatrical in the sense that the individuals imagine on some level becoming something else through a set of embodied practices. The motivations fueling such embodiments would seem to stem from quite distinct desires: for Bobi, a means to generate laughter in an audience, perhaps at the expense of those being impersonated on stage; for some tai chi members, a way to connect to a cultural world beyond the shores of Martinique. Both performances register Chinese flows, but they emphasize different elements of such circulation and express divergent feelings about the manners in which Chineseness manifests as a global phenomenon. In spite of such discrepancies, they both draw on certain assumptions about learned behaviors in relation to forms of embodiment that I have described as Oriental sensitivity.

To reiterate, Oriental sensitivity is a corporeal manifestation of unease produced through an acknowledgment of cultural knowledge and the limits of that knowledge specifically in the wake of Chinese cultural flows. In Bobi's performance, it manifested as a burlesque of Chinese life in response to changing economic realities on Martinique. For me, Oriental sensitivity names several layers of identification and disidentification such as my own claims of kinship to express affiliation (avowedly stretched) to build rapport with my Chinese interview subjects on the island. I became aware of them looking at me as much as I studied them. Oriental sensitivity also recalled the French texts that provided the scaffolding for my knowledge of tai chi in the first place; such Orientalist works I criticized even as I invented my own constructions of the embodied practice based on my anecdotal observations, which were also always partial. Finally, Oriental sensitivity indicated for me a kind of corporeal intelligence demonstrated in, for example, differing competency in the Chinese movement sequences performed by myself and tai chi club members. In other words, Oriental sensitivity named physical attachments to and enactments of Chineseness.

My point here is not to reproach myself, Bobi, or the tai chi club for these constructions. Instead, I have tried to suggest that such impressions are an inevitable consequence of the surface encounters produced through processes of globalization. Moreover, such encounters produce multiple possibilities of relating to another through sometimes unexpected types of identification and also through more familiar strategies of stereotyping. When the seascape becomes an everyday practice of intercultural articulation, the potential exists to harness energies that might bring people together or split them apart. In Martinique, tai chi showcases a sustained effort to form relations beyond one's self along the shoreline where cultures meet.

NOTES

1. Edwin C. Hill, *Black Soundscape, White Stages: The Meaning of Francophone Sound in the Black Atlantic* (Baltimore: The Johns Hopkins University Press, 2013), 99–104.

2. Yutian Wong, "Introductions: Issues in Asian American Dance Studies," in *Contemporary Directions in Asian American Dance*, ed. Yutian Wong (Madison: The University of Wisconsin Press, 2016), 16.

3. Jean Luc Cardin and Denys Cuche, "Chinese Immigration in the French West Indies: Focus on Martinique," in *Essays on the Chinese Diaspora in the Caribbean*, ed. Walton Look Lai (St. Augustine: University of the West Indies, 2006) 172–191. Jean Luc Cardin, *Martinique "Chine-Chine": L'Immigration Chinoise à la Martinique* (Paris: Éditions L'Harmattan, 1990).

4. "En fait, ce terme de "Chinois" dénote une complexité de sens. Il recouvre à la fois le statut de l'étranger, son origine, sone phénotype et son statut social." Dubost, "Au delà de l'ethnicité: les 'Chinois' à la Martinique." Andre Calmont and Cedric Audebert, *Dynamiques Migratoires de la Caraibe*, GEODE: Terres d'Amerique (Paris: Karthala, 2007), 243.

5. Dubost, "L'ethnicité," 243–244.

6. Meaghan Morris, "Introduction: Hong Kong Connections," in *Hong Kong Connections: Transnational Imagination in Action Cinema*, eds. Meaghan Morris, Siu Leung Li, and Stephen Chan Ching-kiu (Hong Kong: Hong Kong University Press, 2005), 1.

7. May Joseph, *Nomadic Identities: The Performance of Citizenship* (Minneapolis: University of Minnesota Press, 1999). Emily Roxworthy, *The Spectacle of Japanese American Trauma: Racial Performativity and WWII* (Honolulu: University of Hawaii Press, 2008).

8. Richard Nichols, "A 'Way' for Actors: Asian Martial Arts," *Theatre Topics* 1, no. 1 (March 1991): 43–60.

9. This story was recounted by Michel Assouvie. See A. Céphise, "Michel Assouvie, créateur de l'association tai-chi Martinique: 'Permettre à tous les Martiniquais de pratiquer cette discipline,'" *France-Antilles*, Sept. 28, 2015.

10. Douglas Wiles, *Lost T'ai-Chi Classics from the Late Ch'ing Dynasty* (Albany: State University of New York Press, 1996), 7.

11. Céphise, "Michel Assouvie"; Michel Assouvie repeated this information in conversations with me.

12. Sansan Kwan, *Kinesthetic City: Dance and Movement in Chinese Urban Spaces* (Oxford: Oxford University Press, 2013), 17.

13. Roland Barthes, *Travels in China* (Malden, MA: Polity, 2012), 21.

14. Barthes, *Travels*, 97.

15. Barthes, *Travels*, 98.

16. Julia Kristeva, *Des Chinoises* (Paris: Editions de Femmes, 1974), 107 (my translation).

17. Kristeva, *Chinoises*, 108 (my translation).

18. Eric Hayot, *Chinese Dreams: Pound, Brecht, Tel Quel* (Ann Arbor: The University of Michigan Press, 2003), 105.

19. Helen H. Jun, "Black Orientalism: Nineteenth-Century Narratives of Race and U.S. Citizenship," *American Quarterly* 58, no. 4 (2006): 1050.

20. José Muñoz, *Disidentification: Queers of Color and the Performance of Politics* (Minneapolis: University of Minnesota Press, 1999), 31.

21. See "Blood Flows in the Antilles under French Domination," Frantz Fanon, *Toward the African Revolution*, trans. Haakon Chevalier (New York: Gove, 1964), 167–169.

22. Rey Chow, *The Protestant Ethnic and the Spirit of Capitalism* (New York: Columbia University Press, 2002), chapter 3.

23. I use my own translation here of Frantz Fanon, *Les Damnés de la Terre* (Paris: Gallimard, 1991),300. Richard Philcox translates *sensitivité* as "sensibility." Frantz Fanon, *The Wretched of the Earth*, trans Richard Philcox (New York: Grove, 2004), 182.

24. Lauren Berlant, "Intimacy: A Special Issue," *Critical Inquiry* 24, no. 2 (1998): 284.

25. Dubost, "L'ethnicité."

26. Jean-Luc Nancy, *Being Singular Plural*, trans. Robert D. Richardson and Anne E. O'Byrne (Palo Alto: Stanford University Press, 2000).

4 ~ EBBING

Given the environmental crisis and economic upheaval that attend China's rapid development, the ocean beckons with opportunity even as it threatens to engulf those who might engage in precarious migrations from one place to another. On February 5, 2004, twenty-three Fujianese migrant workers drowned on the coast of England, in Morecambe Bay, where the rising tide overwhelmed them. These workers had survived arduous journeys from China, although the details of how each one had arrived on the English shoreline remain submerged in an unrecoverable past. Nevertheless, certain moments of these lives registered in historical record, particularly instances involving contact with the overseas laborers' kin. Although the group ultimately perished as the tide surrounded and swallowed it, several of the individuals used their cell phones to inform relatives of the impending doom. Technology facilitated a kind of tidalectics that involved both the mediated preservation of aspects of personhood (such as the sound or transcription of a voice) and speculation about the furtive activities in which each migrant had engaged since departure from China to death in the sea.

Film director and documentarian Nick Broomfield and filmmaker/installation artist Isaac Julien created screen seascapes that address this event; both refract the perilous experiences of the now-deceased Chinese cockle pickers, mostly from Fujian province, in the larger contexts of migration and labor. The motion pictures counter the stillness of death even as they capture some of the ways in which the victims' images and personal stories have circulated posthumously. Broomfield and Julien's respective artistic projects converge in citing the Morecambe Bay incident as inspiration and in expressing the desire to reframe knowledge about these migrants. In so doing, they facilitate for audiences an immersive process, what gender and cultural studies scholar Astrida Neimanis has called, in the broader context of the Anthropocene, "learn[ing] to read in watery archives the politics of erasure."[1] The projects of Broomfield and Julien themselves reflect and require from viewers an engagement with material conditions as well as imagination. Like many of the artistic projects I have discussed in this book, these works materialize tidalectics in this manner as well as in terms of a fluidity of time. The deaths of the Chinese workers in Morecambe Bay focalize this chapter by providing an inquiry into the artists' configuration of and engagement with this event as opposed to journalistic and institutionalized human rights discourse that, as I will argue, attempts to fashion more of an empirical view, one that ultimately limits human agency and subjectivity. Instead of verification of what happened, the screens of both Broomfield and Julien explore conditions of possibility for representation and, in Broomfield's case, action.

Seascapes thus offer an alternative to an impasse of empirical knowledge when information cannot be verified and when certain frames, like governmental policies regarding human rights, emphasize not subjects' lives so much as the abuses of power that circumscribe them. As Michaeline Crichlow suggests, art might be the best vehicle to apprehend the process of human trafficking, since it can capture the rich dimensionality of this phenomenon.[2] Whereas journalistic coverage might emphasize economic determinism and the inequities of human rights in terms of both definition and distribution, art foregrounds representation and the conditions, which enable intelligibility. How do media forms shift the capacity to recollect the experience and very material mechanics of trafficking? What circuits of power and technologies of visibility enable us to see what are often invisible currents of both documented and undocumented human labor? What sorts of fantasy projection do the dissemination of media networks across the globe enable? What possibilities, not only for communication but also for identification and production of agency (and subjectivity), become available through such networks?

Discourses of human trafficking frequently refer to push and pull factors such as lack of resources at home and perceived economic opportunity abroad that prompt individuals or groups to move under these conditions; this metaphor might productively be cast in relation to the ocean—more specifically the tides and changes in sea level that result from gravitational pull on a planetary scale. Placing migration's push and pull in relation to briny ebb and flow facilitates commentary on the figuration of human trafficking. To demonstrate the assumptions embedded in this discourse as promulgated by the United Nations and, in turn, many of its constituent members, an inquiry into representation is critical. For example, the UN's 2016 *Global Report on Trafficking in Persons* continues to divide participants into two categories, which suggests one possesses agency (the trafficker) or one does not (the victim). Rife with statistics of one horror after another, this field of study and intervention nevertheless posits the unknowable facets of human trafficking, including the reliability of numbers themselves. Moreover, the attempts to define this form of human movement yield vexing questions about when and how migrants and/or victims might express agency. Indeed, any mention of willful acts by trafficked people tends to recede amid the focus on the monitoring and policing of this experience.

People who traverse networks of human trafficking engage in various forms of theatricality. Individuals conceal, impersonate, and pretend in order to circumvent law enforcement and other forms of regulation. Focusing on theatricality in relation to human trafficking thus returns attention to bodies and the ways they might exhibit various forms of agency at various nodal points in the trafficking circuit. Broomfield and Julien's reconstructions of trafficked people's potential experiences and/or the politics of representation around them adds further depths to the ways in which theatricality can be understood vis-à-vis the case of the Chinese cockle pickers.

I specifically elaborate theatricality in the case of the cockle pickers through ebbing, another logic of the seascape that, in this instance, brings into relief the subjectivity of trafficked persons and highlights the ways in which informal, sometimes illegal, and often out-of-sight streams of labor help produce something we might call the Chinese Atlantic. The ebbing of the tide at Morecambe Bay literally revealed the bodies of the dead. Ebbing further illuminates the ways in which we discern human trafficking and offers a means through which to consider the ethics of representation in relation to this practice. Both cinematic seascapes that I investigate in this chapter work through immersive theatrical practices. The techniques deployed differently by the artists ultimately enable a consideration of what happens after the conclusion of an engagement with a world (or large network) of trafficking.

To begin this investigation, I revisit the metaphor of push and pull. The global becomes visible when situated within the context of tidal movement, for tides move according to the alignment of celestial bodies: physics working on a worldwide scale. However, the impetuses for human traffic do not align with such a "tidy" explanation (here the etymology of tidy becomes relevant, since that word is linked to time, specifically what is seasonal and, hence, predictable and orderly). To render, for example, the human trafficking of Chinese people (once themselves described as "Celestials" in English-language discourse) as subject to systemic pushes and pulls belies the choices exercised by individuals and groups during the course of a life trajectory and the calculated risks taken during that time. Rhacel Parreñas has therefore argued that "indentured mobility" might better name certain flows of human labor.[3] I remain with human trafficking discourse in order to discuss specifically how such rhetoric performs and to imagine how artistic practices open questions that move through but also beyond linguistic terms and the ostensibly bounded geographies of sending and receiving countries. Again, the play between human trafficking discourse and the imaginative reconstructions used to represent the Morecambe Bay incident exhibit a tidalectics. Such tensions recall instances in this book where material reality and artistic invention elicit different ways of seeing, as is the case, for example, with chapter one's elaboration of documentary films. Here, my focus on Fujianese migrants in England reveals how news outlets frequently collapse differences between terms like *human smuggling* (usually understood to involve volitional participation by all parties) and *trafficking*.[4]

Push and pull, ebb and flow: A dialectic tension between consent and coercion continues to impel migration. I argued, in relation to one of the earliest documentations of Chinese overseas labor, the *Cuba Commission Report* of 1876, that several Chinese workers sent to the New World were "held in thrall even when documented evidence would suggest the opposite," and that these workers finally "refused all of the possibilities for becoming subjects" within the terms of the Enlightenment through coordinated suicides.[5] Taking one's own life refused the terms of subjectivity offered through the idea of toiling until one became economically and therefore legally self-sufficient, a status continually deferred through what Lisa Yun has called "contract technology."[6]

This historical antecedent suggests a lineage of trafficked Chinese labor in the development of transnational capitalism within the Atlantic world, but the mechanisms for and pace of migrant workers in and out of China has also shifted significantly since the nineteenth century. In terms of passage to Western Europe, for example, the creation and eventual disaggregation of the former Soviet Union has opened new pathways for travel, licit or otherwise, by which Chinese laborers might seek employment in a place like England. According to at least one multiauthored study, Fujianese migrants in Europe constitute "one of the most visible results of . . . Chinese globalization."[7] The authors theorize that Chinese globalization is a series of open-ended processes that circulate and presumably help produce "Chinese versions and visions of modernity, parochialism, and cosmopolitanism" across transnational social spaces.[8] On the one hand, then, Chinese globalization would seem to name ostensible new ways in which China interacts with and helps shape the world stage (and here I note that the authors carefully point out the multiplicity contained in the term *Chinese*). On the other hand, the structure of these migrations recalls those questions of agency that have repeatedly arisen in relation to individual enterprise and exploitation over the last hundred and fifty years.

As social scientists David Kyle and Rey Koslowski write, "Many contemporary slaves know that they will be smuggled illegally across borders to work, and they sometimes know the nature of the work—what they often do not know is the terms of the 'contract.'"[9] Kyle and Koslowski argue that Fujianese migration in particular, and Chinese migration in general, brought renewed attention to the issue of global human smuggling around the millennium. They cite the grounding of the *Golden Venture* off the coast of New York in 1993; a series of events in 1998, including the release of Richard Donner's blockbuster, *Lethal Weapon 4*; and the death of fifty-eight Fujianese migrants inside a truck in Dover, England, in 2000.[10] The precariat (anthropologist Anne Allison's term, which I adopt here) of Chinese irregular laborers in transit connects the three examples.[11] News reports in the cases of physical migration suggest that individuals have fled post-Mao China in the wake of its capitalist transformation, the guarantees of the socialist state to work and livelihood now lost.

In their larger argument, Kyle and Koslowski attempt to differentiate between smuggling and trafficking based on evidence of coercion.[12] "Many human smuggling operations around the world are more analogous to travel agencies than to the infamous slave traders of the past," they write.[13] The emphasis on coercion in human traffic discourse forestalls efforts to draw parallels between a labor contract and the larger social contract, so central to a tradition of liberalism and post-Enlightenment discourses of subjectivity and human rights. Such rhetoric usually presumes a social benefit to those who subordinate some of their individual interests to the state and larger structures of governance. Given the ways that corporations have taken over many of the state's previous functions, from economic security to defense, the social contract frequently fails nowadays. How and for whom is agency and accountability produced through contractual matrices? The seascape of Morecambe Bay, replete with undocumented Chinese laborers washed ashore, foregrounds related quandaries. Is there subjectivity outside of a contractual relation, whether between employer and worker or worker and state?

Legal discourses of human traffic tend not to dwell on the latter of these questions. Legally, an agent exists within the parameters of a contractual arrangement, and to imagine otherwise might be to venture away from the language of law in a productive manner. The peculiar alignment of visibility with *victims* of human traffic attributes responsibility to the exceptional case of organized crime rather than the mundane phenomena of hoping and suffering under neoliberal capitalism. Agency in the discourse of human trafficking tends to reside in the hands of the snakehead (or *shetou*, a term that has come into English translation to refer to an individual who takes money to facilitate undocumented human migration from one country to another). In this vein, the Palermo Protocols addressing this matter and issued by the United Nations in 2000 (effective in 2003) requires subjects to perform victimhood in order to seek legal redress:

> "Trafficking in persons" shall mean the recruitment, transportation, transfer, harbouring or receipt of persons, by means of the threat or use of force or other forms of coercion, of abduction, of fraud, of deception, of the abuse of power or of a position of vulnerability or of the giving or receiving of payments or benefits to achieve the consent of a person having control over another person, for the purpose of exploitation. Exploitation shall include, at a

minimum, the exploitation of the prostitution of others or other forms of sexual exploitation, forced labour or services, slavery or practices similar to slavery, servitude or the removal of organs.[14]

To be recognized as a subject in this discourse depends on victimhood. In other words, the subject must dispossess someone or be the dispossessed. Much of the reporting on the cockle pickers has furthered this construction. A single moment of recognition, then, can direct how an audience might understand the entirety of someone's life. In this way, the human traffic protocols potentially screen out the very humanity they would seek to protect. For people entangled in human traffic, visibility and recognition come at a cost. Morecambe Bay constitutes one recently privileged site where we witness the failures of labor, technology, and, in the end, hope to yield a better life.

This chapter demonstrates how two specific artistic projects (Nick Broomfield's film *Ghosts* and Isaac Julien's installation *Ten Thousand Waves*) address the 2004 Morecambe Bay incident. Although Broomfield and Julien use different filmmaking and exhibition practices in an attempt to engage audiences with migrants' subjectivity, their works nevertheless produce different forms of identification for spectators through various processes of immersion in which the audience takes an active role in shaping the structure of or response to the events depicted. To various degrees, they also raise questions about the diffusion of Chineseness across space, the waning affect produced by spectacular displays of migrant mortality, and the capitalist pull away from an ethics of responsibility. Broomfield and Julien's projects further demonstrate relations between form and content by suggesting ways in which human traffic as transnational circuits of labor might be entangled with particular streams of globalized aesthetic production. Unlike the Martinican case of tai chi, in which the physical practice becomes a sign of health and leisure that signifies a kind of cultural capital that most of the immigrant laborers are not seen to possess (at least by the island's "local" population), the examples in this chapter complicate the relation of labor to aesthetics. They suggest that to understand human trafficking, one must approach it through various kinds of theatrical practice. *Ghosts* and *Ten Thousand Waves* imbricate the beholder as Chinese figures in these two pieces become no less than the litmus test for humanity, at once exploiter and exploited.

The particular seascapes by Broomfield and Julien illustrate processes of subjectification for people who have either chosen or have been forced into precarious overseas labor. The seascape, an ocean view, a perspective on the sea, serves as an epistemology. I use it to evoke Appadurai's notion of "scape" as vicissitudes of human experience within globalization but also to gesture to a genealogy of Chinese migration related to the development and acceleration of capitalism in its presumed cradle: the Atlantic. Both *Ghosts* and *Ten Thousand Waves* imaginatively extend the extant evidence of one recent crisis moment in this labor stream in order to surface subjects who otherwise might remain at the bottom of the ocean, below the threshold of representation. The pieces intensify the theatricality of cinematic seascapes by drawing on forms of immersive theater in their construction. In this manner, they offer something akin to yet different from the documentaries that hinge on reeling discussed in chapter 1. This phenomenon is in part because of the fact that all the ostensible subjects, the cockle pickers, rather suddenly perished and thus require a different relationship to evidence and ethics than those of the earlier films. With less of an available archive, the filmmakers imagine and invent their ostensible subjects.

WHEN GHOSTS SPEAK

A narrative feature with documentary characteristics, *Ghosts* is a precursor to the nine-screen installation, *Ten Thousand Waves,* first exhibited in 2010. Created under the auspices of England's Channel 4, a public service television channel that began in 1982 and has long been associated with arts and minorities in the UK (including the work of Julien), *Ghosts* premiered in 2006 at the San Sebastian film festival in Spain. It went on to Sundance in 2007 and has been screened publicly in locations from Singapore to Sweden. The film uses a variety of techniques—including handheld camera work and improvised dialogue (based on a script) spoken by a cast of nonprofessional actors—to bring a realist aesthetic to the phenomenon of human trafficking and its aftermath. Indeed, together with his lead actress Ai Qin Lin, the director engaged in a period of undercover journalism to reveal the precarious experiences that he wished to document. Broomfield met Lin through contacts at the Chinese church in King's Cross, London. Lin was herself a formerly undocumented Chinese migrant, whose actual experiences served as the basis for the migratory passage depicted in the film.[15] Her own life trajectory haunts the images, particularly at the conclusion, when she reunites after several years with her child, whom she sent back to China. For his research, Broomfield assumed the guise of an undocumented Afrikaner and picked spring onions and performed other low-wage labor with Lin. Such intimate engagements with his subjects rehearsed the reality that Broomfield wished to project on screen.

Broomfield's work is precisely a projection, because, as sociologists have suggested, "we actually know very little about trafficking as a social problem."[16] The deaths of the Chinese cockle pickers prompted their movement into public visibility; the reconstruction of how each of those individuals arrived on the muddy flats in England is largely a matter of conjecture. The absence or invisibility of these human migration stories leads me to emphasize the conditions of possibility for seeing trafficked individuals and the fantasies reflected through and created by art. Put otherwise, I am invested in traffic as a problem of visual and theatrical epistemology limned by the seascape rather than in trying to intervene in empirical debates and policies about smuggling, trafficking, and circulations of workers. Pertinent to my efforts, Broomfield's film attempts to reenact on film some of the nodal points in the journey of a trafficked Fujianese laborer. Whatever other status it might hold, *Ghosts* is an aesthetic production invested in a realist narrative, bookended by a scene of peril taking place at a disappearing shoreline.

The central visual motif within *Ghosts* is the seascape of Morecambe Bay. In an interview for *Indie Film Nation*, Broomfield stated, "I wanted to use the real locations, and use the real people, use Morecambe Bay, for example, which is where the tragedy happened, which has its own character and . . . danger about it."[17] Broomfield established his foreboding atmosphere by opening the film with a black screen; the audience hears a consistent but indeterminate noise on the soundtrack, which the visuals eventually show emanating from a van's tires rolling across the soggy earth. The title appears in English and Chinese (respectively, *Ghosts* and *Guilao*, which means both "ghost" and "foreigner/Westerner"). The title sequence continues with a pair of informational epigraphs: first, "The film is based on real events which took place in 2004," and then, "The 3 million migrant workers in the UK are the backbone of the food supply system, the construction, hospitality and health industries."[18] This contextual device introducing the narrative reminds the viewer of contemporary politics before the film cuts to a long shot of a single white passenger van on the mudflats. A superimposed title locates the film: "Morecambe Bay, England, February 5th 2004."

The length of the shot, together with the informational titles, establishes a pseudo-objective authority for the viewer. Such an establishing sequence sets up a clinical analysis of worker exploitation and injustice by aligning the spectator with the political perspective of the filmmaker before the film shifts the audience into a more subjective mode by cutting to another point of view shot through the passenger windshield. The film has visually constructed the isolation of these workers by showing the vehicle alone, cruising through a downpour on the silty ground. The two men in the front of the van discuss, in Chinese, their situation: "Ghosts won't come out when it's like this. That's good for us, though." That line provides dramatic irony and indicates how goals for realism work in tandem with a constructed narrative.

The first four minutes of the film reveal the frightening character of the sea. Although the group has apparently escaped the immediate physical violence suggested by shots of beaten faces in the interior of the van, the pilgrimage to the empty beach becomes the group's undoing. As the scene progresses, the film cuts to the rising tide. The Chinese workers comb through the sludge, seeking small shellfish. At the same time, water flows around the van, as if the sea would willfully engulf the workers spread across the saturated shoreline. Shots of the oceanic flow recur as the light dims. Time-lapse photography indicates the passage from day to night. A lighthouse battles the twilight and ensuing obscurity. A camera at water level pans to the van, now with five individuals huddled on the roof in the dark, the waves having reached almost to the top of the car windows. Discussing options, some decide to swim into the darkness. Others place the cell phone calls for which this event became so well known. In these moments, Ai Qin Lin appears on the car to ask her mother if she is behind on her payments. An abrupt jump cut takes the viewer to Lin biking on a rural road.

This film attributes migrant precarity to structural inequities. The China sequence shows Lin's labor in the fields before cutting to a simple white-tiled and cluttered kitchen. The protagonist decides she must seek work abroad despite the protestations of her parents. The reason? Cut to a close-up of Lin's baby in a crib. The child's future depends on Mom's sacrifice. And that sacrifice involves her seeking out a *shetou* ("snakehead") for a grueling passage. But before this happens, the film displays a tearful goodbye at the bus station and a passage through picturesque terraced rice fields. These images reinforce a clear message: Ai Qin Lin left because she had no other options.

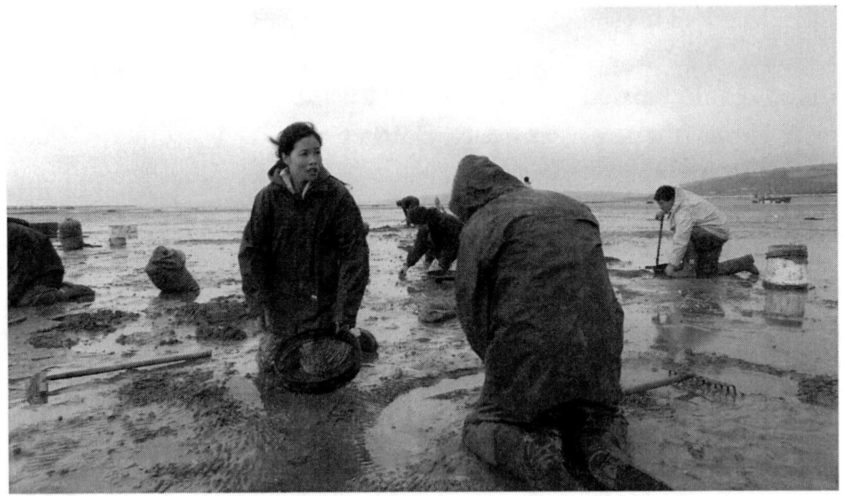

Fig. 4.1. The protagonist works the mudflats in the center of the frame. Still from *Ghosts* by Nick Broomfield.

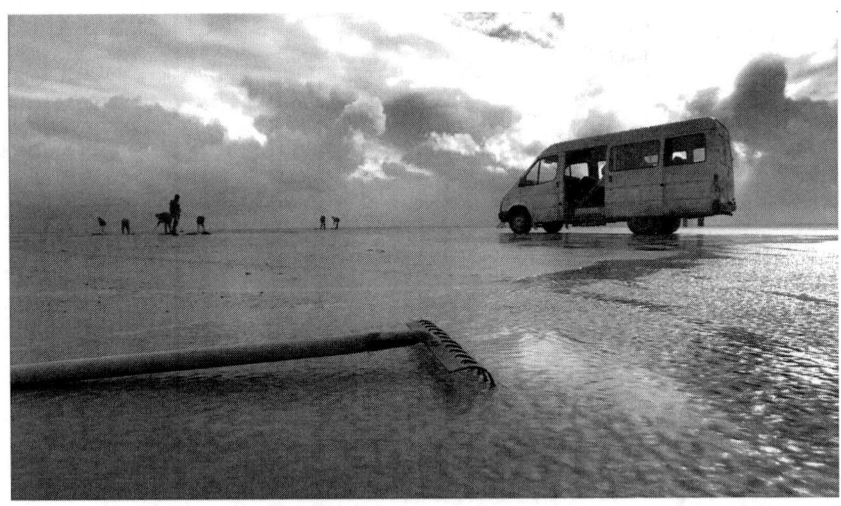

Fig. 4.2. The sea threatens to engulf the shore. Still from *Ghosts* by Nick Broomfield.

The migration sequence comes next and takes a full five minutes of the film. After showing Lin on the bus gazing at the Chinese countryside, the film cuts to a map of China. Fuzhou appears prominently, and a red line actively traces a route through southern China into western Xinjiang province, southern Kyrgyzstan, eastern Uzbekistan, Kazakhstan, and finally to Russia. The soundtrack shifts from an instrumental accompaniment to the song "When Flowers Are in Bloom." The allusion may refer to Wong Kar Wai's *In the Mood for Love*, a film that expresses nostalgia for 1960s Hong Kong and the pleasures of cultural migration in terms of people and products of that era. The map reappears, and the red line heads south to Ukraine. Superimposed images show people, including Lin, walking through Romania. A shot of misty mountains cuts to a semi-trailer truck. A title announces the group's arrival in Belgrade, where a garage door opens and people load into the empty cargo space. The emphasis here is on a dark interior save for Lin's illuminated face. The film transports the viewer to a parking lot in Calais. Lin boards a smaller truck and is sealed into a coffin-like compartment. Cut to an image of the prow of a ship cutting through water. The camera tilts upward to reveal a freighter named *Riverdance* carrying shipping containers. The passage ends with Lin landing in England; a title reads, "Entire journey 6 months."

This elaborate sequence visually constructs and condenses the narrative of migration. Lin encounters mostly male contacts that broker her arduous travel. They form a staggeringly large transnational network involving multiple agents in several countries. The alternation between graphics and close-ups analogizes a kind of social scientific methodology; the film provides data about migrant travel through semiotic indexicality (the red line produced by a particular trajectory of traffic) and renders this objective fact human with a case study displayed through the affective responses of Lin and her fellow travelers. This sequence of migration helps the spectator interpret retroactively *Ghosts'* opening sequence on the tideland and the scene's recurrence at the end of the film. Lin, subjected to the will of others in various ways throughout the narrative, becomes the central point of identification within the film's diegesis and for its extradiegetic spectators. At the same time, most of those who broker sections of the journey remain nameless and appear only briefly. Their momentary presence points to a massive network of unidentified intermediaries who facilitate migration but whose investments and profits remain out of the frame. They constitute part of a trafficking ring that curtails the agency of individuals who, for whatever reason, have entered or been forced into this web of perilous transit.

Cultural studies scholar Roger Bromley interprets *Ghosts* in terms of Agamben's notion of bare life.[19] In Agamben's framework, bare life (bodies subjected to biopolitics) opposes the sovereign (a figure who exists both within and outside the law, since that person has the power to suspend it). Such a notion places particular emphasis on the state, broadly configured. In the case of the cockle pickers who died, this formulation might make sense because, for example, neither China nor England would pay for the bodies to be shipped back to the families of the deceased. Moreover, the unrecognized labor of these largely unrecognized people in the film produces the foodstuff that sustains the English population, as evidenced in work at a poultry plant and an onion farm.

Bromley's theorization via Agamben, however, tends to obscure the agency of stateless individuals. Bare life assumes perhaps too quickly that state or other dominant power constrains subjectivity. In contrast, Broomfield insists on showing pleasure and the unlikely relations that emerge within the margins of the sociopolitical order, relations that might only emerge within such spaces. For example, the difficult work at a poultry factory enables an opportunity for connection as a white worker and Lin share family photographs during a break. The film invests in a specific humanism that attempts to demonstrate the volitional agency of Lin and the ways that agency becomes circumscribed differently at various points in her trajectory of traffic.

According to the film, whatever agency the character expresses has much to do with gender, understood from a Chinese perspective in theatrical terms. Mandarin denotes sex work in theatrical language. *Chutai* refers to those who entertain clients on site (literally "on stage"); *zuotai* refers to those who go "off stage" with their clients (usually to hotel rooms and the like). Sex work in this lexicon suggests one plays a role. Lin's earliest work opportunity is massage. She turns down the job and with it a salary of some two hundred and fifty pounds a week, intimating that she refuses a path toward prostitution. This scene highlights the risks of falling into sex trafficking; in tension with this construction, at least one major study indicates that Chinese female migrants understand sex work as a possible means of overseas employment prior to their departure.[20] This possibility of sex work heightens the theatricality of the protagonist in several ways. It suggests that the protagonist plays roles within the diegetic world. Whether this moment in the film reflects part of Lin's actual experience or is a complete invention of the filmmaker, the narrative sequencing constructs her other employment opportunities as alternatives to selling her body. These choices in turn become signs of her agency. This scene, then, demonstrates one way in which the filmmaker deploys gender as a sign signifying vulnerability (most of the cockle pickers who drowned in the bay were men, so showing a woman's experiences accentuates particular dangers to which a man may or may not be subject). The female protagonist in this story contextualizes trafficking as an intersectional issue that forces the staging of women's sexuality: their availability, their chastity, or other forms of desire or attachment. In the diegetic world, human trafficking heightens the quotidian sensation that one continually plays an often quite specifically gendered and sexed role. The unrelenting threat of discovery that one is pretending—to have a marriage, to have papers, to belong—reveals the status of those trafficked to be a theatrical one.

To illustrate further this point, the most hopeful moment in the film involves Lin's day labor at an apple orchard. The outdoor light brightens the overall look of the film, and the soundtrack features Teresa Teng's 1970s hit "Moon Represents My Heart" (*yueliang daibiao wo de xin*), which begins, "You ask me how I deeply I love you" (*ni wen wo ai ni you duo shen*). This song became popular at the moment when socialist realism's hold waned and an increasing number of foreign influences once again started to circulate in China. This scene thus implies parallel moments when cultural migrations might offer neither suffering nor terror but joy and love. The scene suggests that Lin's otherwise oppressive conditions provide material experiences of a potential future that might prove satisfying and sustainable for the protagonist.

We might wish to shy away from this idealism, but the film finally maps Lin's personal story onto the cockle pickers. She miraculously survives the sea and reunites with her son. This ending contradicts the decidedly gloomy demise of those who drowned. In *Ghosts*, the migrant laborer's future is her offspring, from whom travels have separated her. The ostensible happy conclusion elides the issues of financial insecurity that prompted the migration in the first place. The push and pull of the sea finally offers both calamity but also, in terms of narrative sequencing, a paradoxical hope, which may be ful-filled by the film's final plea to donate to the Morecambe Bay Victims Fund.

Broomfield's methodology immersed him in the world of undocumented labor slogging in England. The final appeal to take action in the form of finan-cial support for the Chinese workers' families asks that individuals assume the care that neither China nor England agreed to provide. Although such a suppliant message might seem to use a cinematic form of Brechtian address, the screen finally throws responsibility onto private philanthropy. I do not condemn such an entreaty but instead point out that *Ghosts* somewhat unex-pectedly accepts the ebbing of state social support that its commentary on neoliberal restructuring of labor would otherwise seem to critique. Immers-ing oneself within the world of human trafficking and labor would seem, however uncomfortably, to reinscribe the state's reluctance to value human life.

The different types of immersion for filmmaker and the audience also extend Samuel Weber's ideas about globalization and theatricality, with which I began this book. As I have suggested, the world of human trafficking we see through Broomfield's *Ghosts* is theatrical in the sense that migrants performing irregular labor act or otherwise pretend to circumvent various forms of surveillance, but the film also provides a totalizing perspective, that is, the viewer sees various parts of a network imagined as a whole: an appa-ratus that moves people from China to England. In the extradiegetic world, in order to be recognized within human traffic discourse, subjects must per-form victimhood. For those seeking livelihood in England, such actions may yield benefits; indeed, several migrants sought legal recognition in the past by performing as asylum seekers. The film demonstrates how different sorts of performance animate all aspects of the trafficking experience represented.

The film's status as an aesthetic object further complicates the ways in which the experiences of and discourses about human traffic produce forms of theatricality. Within the world of the film, signs of human trafficking structure the narrative: cramped quarters, the looming possibility of sex work, visualized physical violence, labor undertaken without adequate safety precautions. These scenes in the film evoke clichés as much as they might also derive from empirical realities by drawing on an archive of imagery and narratives frequently used to establish human trafficking in popular media. Although such devices ultimately elicit sympathy for figures like Lin, they function by offering supposed mimetic equivalencies between the constructed scenes and the actual situations of those trafficked. Notwithstanding the filmmaker's desire to recreate for the audience a realistic vision of human trafficking, *Ghosts* reenacts scenarios that one might *imagine* the now deceased cockle pickers to have experienced. Such reenactments include significant investment (in terms of production value), such as staging a slowly flooding van. Obviously, these actors, whether professional or not, remained alive at the end of the shoot. All of the sequences of exploitation aim to produce an affective reaction in order to encourage viewers to decide what to do next: donate to the fund, recommend the screening, or find some other means of acting on behalf of those whose lives have now passed.

The film's lingering provocation to act leads to the logic of ebbing, despite the fact that my discussion to this point has highlighted immersing the filmmaker and viewer into the sphere of human trafficking. *Ghosts* revolves around the conundrum of what should happen once the media fury and the cry of public outrage softens to inaudibility.[21] The film forcefully scripts the past in order to imagine an alternative future. To what degree might art not only continue a cultural discourse but also foster new forms of social connection and commitment? Broomfield's call to action echoes (and it is worth remembering that echoes are ebbing sounds that are not localizable) as it helps viewers imagine subjects beyond the victimhood on which human traffic discourse insists. Yet this very recuperative act is itself caught in a dilemma of how one might ethically represent a heartbreaking catastrophe that resulted in the loss of particular lives, reanimated for the camera.

MEDIATING MIGRANTS' MORTALITY

Julien has explicitly stated that he took his inspiration for *Ten Thousand Waves* from the Morecambe Bay incident.[22] His artistic response to the event immerses the spectator in a heterochronic temporality that, in part, continues the technological afterlife of those who perished. The installation juxtaposes scenes including 1930s Shanghai, found footage from Maoist China, mythic visions of a flying woman (actress Maggie Cheung) across various backgrounds, a green screen showing the physical construction of the shots with Cheung, a calligrapher painting the installation's title, and images of the ocean. Whereas Broomfield reconstructs and reenacts a more or less linear pathway for his protagonist, notwithstanding the bookending of the principal narrative with shots of Morecambe Bay, Julian scrambles both place and time. Despite these differences, both Broomfield's and Julien's uses of technology offer what might be understood as extensions of the mediated presence of the cockle pickers that have continued long after their passing.

On February 5, 2004, the families of several cockle pickers working in Morecambe Bay heard from their loved ones for the last time. The cell phone calls they placed demonstrate how even those individuals subject to human trafficking engage technology that alter quotidian experience, transforming, for example, even the temporality of death. Rather than a mere post-mortem record, these phone calls capture the time immediately prior to loss of life. The disembodied sounds of the victims' voices continue to echo beyond their watery graves. They begin a process that rescripts human subjectivity for those whose conditions of existence have largely rendered them exploited objects in a migrant labor force. The phone calls reverberate with these workers' experiences and generate public interest in the life stories of people otherwise unseen in their English worksite, people who were scarcely recognized as such by British and Chinese authorities alike until their bodies washed ashore.

This situation resonates strongly with Rey Chow's elaboration of Walter Benjamin's writings on the age of mechanical reproduction: "Rather than reality being caught in the sense of being contained, detained, or retained in the copy-image (understood as a repository), it is now the machinic act or event of capture, with its capacity for further partitioning (that is, for generating additional copies and images ad infinitum), that sets reality in motion, that invents or makes reality, as it were."[23] The mediated conversations of the imperiled cockle pickers both testify to their existence and activate processes that restore these individuals' humanity to previously unconcerned publics. In the wake of the news reporting, Broomsfield's film, and Julien's more abstract response to the Morecambe Bay drownings, the victims' life narratives have been reconstructed and circulated to the extent that each individual has achieved far more human recognition after death. People with access to technology around the world might achieve a certain digital afterlife given everyday exposure on various media platforms. What is interesting about this particular case—and human trafficking in general—is that the circuit of traffic enables visualization of the points at which people become visible and invisible in their life trajectories and the public audiences to whom such visibility might matter at any given moment.

As a riposte to a reductive discourse that would have audiences imagine the cockle pickers as continually subjected to the wills of others, *Ten Thousand Waves* immerses the spectator in an artistic reflection on media, time, phenomenology, and death. Julien's installation brings together folk tales, found footage, reconstructions of Chinese film, and poetry. These convergences, constructed through a specific architectural design, transform how viewers understand migrant experience. The form of the installation captures some of the fractured experience of migrancy even as it combines several disparate technologies by means of which stories about migration circulate.

Julien's nine-screen work has been altered to fit the places of its exhibition. The most ambitious display to date took place at New York's Museum of Modern Art (MOMA). Museum curators Sabine Breitwieser and Martin Hartung showed *Ten Thousand Waves* in the Donald B. and Catherine C. Marron Atrium, a sixty-foot-high space that can be viewed from a number of angles. The double-sided screens were suspended at different levels above a floor covered in blue carpet on which sat four amoeba-shaped chaises and five large, circular ottomans. The film ran on a loop of approximately fifty minutes. In order to see the exhibition from several vantage points, I visited the museum four times in the course of a week in January of 2014. Repeated visits also enabled me to see different audiences engage the work; these spectators included individuals who would lounge on the furniture in order to observe a full cycle of screening and as well as those who passed by or through the installation en route to another gallery. Given the entry price of twenty-five dollars and the number of activities that compete with the museum in New York (not to mention the number of exhibitions on display in the museum itself), many visitors saw the actual installation only once, and only in segments. However, the exhibition includes a placard about the museum videotaping and/or live-streaming the program during its opening hours. To watch this spectacle is to consent to being recorded as part of it. Even as the screens themselves reproduced images, the exhibition itself was multiplied both through MOMA's official videography and through the many photos and videos uploaded by museum visitors to various social media sites. In this continual process of reproducing screen images, the installation works within the atrium's architectural specificity even as it constantly transcends it.

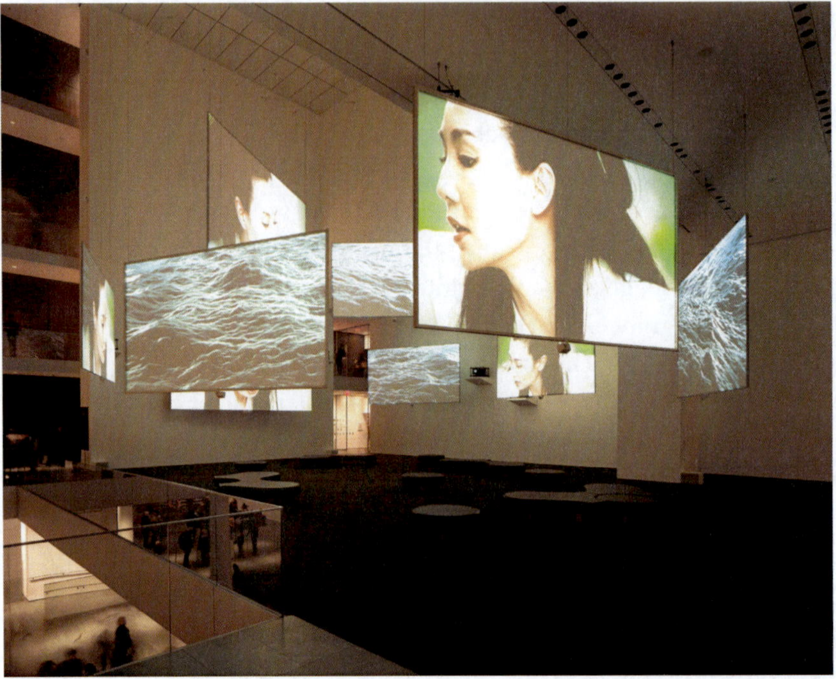

Fig. 4.3. Images of Maggie Cheung as Mazu are juxtaposed against shots of the sea in the atrium of New York's Museum of Modern Art. Isaac Julien, *Ten Thousand Waves*, 2010. Nine-screen installation, 35 mm film transferred to high definition, 9.2 surround sound, 49′ 41″. Courtesy Isaac Julien, Metro Pictures Gallery (New-York) and Victoria Miro Gallery (London). Installation view, the Museum of Modern Art, New York, 2013. Photograph: Jonathan Muzikar.

Julien has expressed an interest in the mobile spectator, an idea he borrows from theater in the sense of wandering through a specific performance space, but he multiplies the potential effects of motion and circulation. Again, the audience immerses itself among a physical set of double-sided screens, even as this set of participant–spectators might themselves be projected on someone else's online social media network. By looking at Julien's installation, one potentially becomes both an image and image-maker. This facet of the installation materializes Julien's long-standing desire to make "an intervention into the museum and the gallery, an intervention with the moving image."[24] Rather than a rarified repository of masterpieces of modern art (MOMA overwhelmingly displays European and American male artists from its permanent collection), this museum exhibit supports individuals who actively or passively partake in the process of *moving* images, of contextualizing Julien's own piece and the sections of MOMA in which it is located in idiosyncratic ways through new placements across various media.

Julien's mobile spectator perambulates through a particular place but potentially circulates as her or his digital likeness. This sort of immersion integrates the viewer into the ever-expanding art piece. On an affective level, the spectator also functions as a copy image to move others, eliciting emotional responses from onlookers far removed from the site of the installation itself. Julien's form of immersive art corporeally engages and also captures and extends his viewer.

Such sharing of art also offers implicit commentary on visuality itself. Images create different meanings depending on the framing and circumstances of their display. To attempt to document, in some pseudo-objective manner, the deaths of cockle pickers for the consumption of tourists and art aficionados in New York at twenty-five dollars a head seems crass. To project spaces of reconstruction and reflection that the audience might augment through their own devices would seem a decidedly more thought-provoking and probably more ethical project. However, screens may conceal as much as they reveal.

Unlike Broomfield's film, Julien's installation does not address the material conditions for victims' families produced in the wake of the incident at Morecambe Bay. For example, a complicated informal system of debt and credit structures the experiences of the families of the cockle pickers.[25] Certainly, Julien is quite conscious of the expenses and profit generated by filmmaking and multiscreen format cinematic experiences designed for prestigious art institutions. (Witness his recent work *PLAYTIME*, 2013–14.) But if a critique of art's imbrication with capitalism appears through *Ten Thousand Waves*, it emerges only obliquely. Information pertaining to how Julien's work trades on the misfortune of others and questions about ownership, profit, and responsibility never appear on screen. The very presence of so many projection panels, however, urges audiences to consider what is and is not visible in the juxtaposed elements that assemble its loose and ambivalent narrative structure.

This reflection on absence and what remains unseen constitutes part of the logic of ebbing. Julien's installation would seem to enjoin museum visitors to consider what comes into relief after immersion in all those screens. Given the looped film and the seating arrangement as well as the tendency of museumgoers to move rather than stay in place, the experience of engaging the piece is likely to have been radically different for each person. For example, seeing only the 1930s reconstruction or the calligraphy sequence would obscure the installation's associations with mortality. The durational piece works quite differently for those who have the patience and time to sit through a complete screening. What endures from the drowned individuals is also highly individual depending on one's knowledge of the cockle pickers, the continued struggles of their families, and the media representation around the deaths. Such a range of impacts finally also comments on mediation itself to the extent that the arguable subject of *Ten Thousand Waves* and the subjects for whom it might provide some kind of elaboration can only emerge through sustained attention. The complicated routes of trafficking require work on the part of anyone who desires to understand, much less to attempt to redress, the trafficking case that inspired Julien's installation.

GENEALOGIES OF FORM IN JULIEN'S OEUVRE

To understand Julien's own political investments in this installation requires some contextualization of his larger oeuvre. A variety of factors contributed to the aesthetic development of *Ten Thousand Waves*. English national cinema and queer cinema offer useful contexts for engaging Julien's work and also demonstrate some of the political stakes that have informed and continue to animate his artistic projects. Indeed, the continual return to the politics of screening as a mode of capture, exhibition, and profitmaking constitutes part of Julien's creative signature.

Antecedents for Julien's new media projects might be located within the late 1950s/early 1960s New Wave in England. Building on the movement known as the Free Cinema, the British New Wave brought a realist aesthetic to the patriotic masculinities celebrated in WWII that were encouraged, during the war years, by the Ministry of Information's Films Division. To be sure, New Wave films articulated their own sexism and machismo, but they also placed the spotlight on the workers and the social conditions throughout England that produced disenfranchisement. These films projected stories that reflected and shaped contemporary English life, anticipating Julien's focus on the stream of labor, albeit a Chinese immigrant one in this case, that inspired *Ten Thousand Waves.*

The decidedly English valence of these midcentury films belies the enormous international investment in English cinematic production from as far back as the 1920s. It is worth noting, for example, that in 1969, "90 percent of the investment in British cinema came from America."[26] Such investment helped to launch the cinematic career of one the most enduring Cold War figures, James Bond. By the early 1980s, there was a resurgence of films that returned to the specific landscape of England, especially to the plight of the disenfranchised.

During the 1980s, Channel 4 (particularly its Multicultural Department) and the British Film Institute funded low-budget productions.[27] These monetary sources, along with workshop programs targeting ethnic minorities and the protests against such programs (for tokenism), facilitated the formation of several artist collectives. These included the Black Audio Film Collective and Sankofa, with which Julien was associated. Whereas the former group mainly produced documentaries, Sankofa often worked in the genre of the art film.[28] The legacy of this kind of work—smaller, independent pictures—successfully brought the margins to the center, so that British cinema soon became largely defined, in an international context, by those filmmakers who either emerged or were particularly active during this period: Derek Jarman, Neil Jordan, Sally Potter, Peter Greenaway, and Isaac Julien, to name a few. Sankofa depended on streams of public funding. The waning of government support for the arts led many artists to consider more seriously the ways in which they might address a commercialized arts sector. One venue for patronage came in the form of commissions from museums, which arrived, as Julien notes, coeval with pronouncements of the death of cinema.[29]

Rather than subscribe to a hypothesis about the end of cinema, I find it useful to situate Julien within genealogies of cinema that anticipated the form's transformation. Here Julien's work fits within another such genealogy: queer cinema. The phrase "new queer cinema" was coined in the early 1990s to describe a body of largely American but also some British films that explicitly addressed the subject of sexuality through formal innovations that resisted conventional narrative structures. Queer cinema attempted to debunk the official stories propagated by oppressive governmental regimes. The 1980s, after all, had been the decade of new conservatism, of Reagan and Thatcher, and of the AIDS pandemic. Julien's films from this period of the late twentieth century register concerns over the policing of racialized bodies that were and are always also sexualized.

In such a context, Julien's codirected *The Passion of Remembrance* (1986) and his meditation on Langston Hughes, entitled *Looking for Langston* (1989), use pastiche—found objects, old newsreels, stills, experimental fiction, etc.—to index black queer cultural formations across time and space. Such formations counter the official histories promoted by the US and UK governments at the time. They question the legitimacy of the nation as the defining rubric under which we talk about culture in general and cinema in particular. In other words, Julien's films raise the issue of local racial formation within the national space of England while they interrogate that frame. Such querying operates across the filmmakers I have described in this book. However, Julien's films in particular work as a kind of call and response—what I term an antiphonal aesthetic—that constructs the black, gay British subject at the same time it deconstructs the assumptions that render the articulation of a black, gay Englishman possible. Such antiphonal aesthetics continue in works like *Young Soul Rebels* (1991) and *The Attendant* (1993), which also underscore the role of music in filmmaking and its importance to black expressive culture more generally. The latter film also initiated his sustained interrogation of what is possible in the space of the museum. Julien's work within the tradition of queer cinema, finally, is to interrogate form by playing with structures of desire.

Insofar as a queer sensibility informs *Ten Thousand Waves*, Julien would seem to play with screen icons and the mechanisms of their production. Julien juxtaposes seemingly apolitical scenes of the creation of star discourse with footage that renders quotidian life spectacular. The cockle pickers posthumously became characters in larger narratives about human rights violations. The migrant workers became, for a while, if not household names, at least media spectacles in which their demise prompted news coverage. The quick passage from obscurity to celebrity overlaps with the sorts of historical projects about minoritarian populations that have interested Julien.

The interest in sound and the documentation of aural phenomena that are not, strictly speaking, tangible shapes some of Julien's choices in documentary film production.[30] Both *The Darker Side of Black* (1994) and *BaadAsssss Cinema* (2002) address music and soundscapes as much as they address modes of production largely controlled by black people. This emphasis on sound, the ways in which echoes from the past can haunt the present, seems directly linked to Julien's investigation of the voices accompanying the blurred images of Morecambe Bay in *Ten Thousand Waves*. For example, instead of using aerial (in this case, from a helicopter) shots that would have provided a bird's-eye view and an accompanying sense of visual control, the piece uses the movement of the camera and a tone of desperation captured in the soundtrack to convey the Chinese laborers' precarious plight. Although it is not always clear who is speaking, the exhibition catalogue attributes the voices to "the woman responsible for the cockle pickers . . . and the rescue workers."[31] Whereas the voiceover is often used to establish narrative authority, Julien deploys it in *Ten Thousand Waves* to quite the opposite effect. Although sound often provides a mood for the images throughout this work, it does little to render a coherent narrative.

Unlike the conditions of many film screenings, the continual traffic through and around the exhibition space of *Ten Thousand Waves* further fragments a viewer's experience of narrative. Multiple sounds and sights competed for the attention of MOMA's visitors. Although similar situations might structure spectatorship in relation to many of Julien's museum installations, the acoustics and sight lines in the atrium intensified the ambient noise and the other components of visual and sensory ambiance that museumgoers experience. This sensorial immersion provides an aesthetic analogue to the situation of being caught in a physical environment (noting, of course, that the cockle pickers' situation is not an all equivalent to some elective participation in an artistic construction). Nevertheless, the attempt to find various scales of comparison to the events at Morecambe Bay drove Julien to seek various ways of allegorizing them not only through the content of *Ten Thousand Waves* but also through its form.

These efforts recall Julien's previous screen installations for gallery and museum spaces. Giuliana Bruno has written in detail about the methods that Julien employs, especially in the installations *Vagabondia* (2000) and *Baltimore* (2003), to choreograph memory "with a network of performative voices and sounds as well as movements."[32] According to Bruno, these pieces fold different temporalities in relation to one another and in relation to a set of subjects and objects that creates surfaces of contemplation and encounter. Particular processes of black recollection interrogate archives as acts of remembering and as spatial configurations. In her analysis, Julien's artworks posit pure "–scapes" through "folds of future mnemonic projection."[33] Bruno does not spend much time pursuing the full implications of this statement; she mentions –scapes particularly in relation to the "total light space" created by sheets of ice in Julien's installation *True North* and links it tentatively to *Ten Thousand Waves.*[34]

Nevertheless, Bruno's insistence that Julien spatializes memory (consistent with her citation of the English historian Frances Yates) and disrupts linear time through a folding operation recalls Arjun Appadurai's book *Modernity at Large*. Appadurai is also interested in –scapes and time, although his emphasis is less on aesthetics and subjectivity than Bruno's. He elaborates the suffix "–scape" in order to describe a metaphorical landscape of "global cultural flows."[35] However, Bruno's and Appadurai's different scholarship might intersect in thinking through the ways in which a kind of folding temporality helps bring into relief cultural scenes otherwise rendered opaque in dominant discourses. Following Appadurai, –scapes might further designate "deeply perspectival constructs, inflected by the historical, linguistic, and political situatedness of different sorts of actors."[36] He deemphasizes the individual, who creates and is enmeshed in "larger formations," including "nation-states, multinationals, diasporic communities, as well as subnational groupings and movements (whether religious, political, or economic), and even intimate face-to-face groups, such as villages, neighborhoods, and families."[37] But the folding of which Bruno writes enables shifts in scale as part of the aesthetic operations of Julien's screen technologies. Appadurai's research offers a means to clarify how the idea of –scape as an aesthetic might also fold in the empirical evidence of Chinese laborers in England.

The resonances of –scape with the action of "escape" gestures to the ways in which individuals might try to shift their livelihoods and the conditions of possibility for representation. The seascape is particularly relevant to the situation of the cockle pickers, since their representation as subjects in popular media has everything to do with oceanic perils. Thinking through the entangled discourses and images of overseas migrants has a noteworthy precedent in Julien's *Western Union: Small Boats* (2007), a three-screen installation that draws some inspiration from film (Luchino Viconti's *The Leopard,*

1963). *Western Union* focuses on Sicily to investigate often-clandestine human movement from various parts of Africa to Europe. For example, the dance sequences on the screen suggest a choreography of bodies moving through space; the volition and care behind such motion throws into relief the often more serendipitous actions that structure human migration. Moreover, the radical disjuncture between figures passing through the opulent interiors of the Palazzo Gangi and bodies strewn on the beach force into consciousness vast class inequities. Ultimately, Julien asks, for whom and to what ends are human migrations that frequently result in death representable? As I have noted, Julien mutes this rather explicit query in *Ten Thousand Waves*. Still, the aquatic submersion of the Chinese individuals paradoxically rendered them hypervisible—too late to render their lives meaningful to the press beyond their positions as victims. Building on Bruno and Appadurai, I argue that Julien's *Ten Thousand Waves* folds together a particularly Chinese Atlantic seascape, one structured by a particular logic of return and refraction that I designate with the word *ebbing*.

In part, *ebbing* designates the actual physical engagement with Julien's installation at MOMA. To see the exhibition required repeatedly turning one's body and adjusting one's orientation to view the circle of screens, sometimes selectively illuminated with images that occasionally ran across several panels (e.g., a car moving across one screen and onto another). This sort of movement is literally a process of re-turn (that is, "turning again"), but I qualify such action with the word *ebbing* because the film's different scenes advance and transition at a regular and relaxed tempo. Unlike, say, one of the action films for which the film's featured star, Maggie Cheung, is known, the editing in Julien's installation generally does not create suspense or elicit a sensation of extremely rapid movement. The transitions from one sequence to the next allow spectators enough time to shift position at a tranquil pace. But the installation nevertheless obliges a spectator to reposition, if not relocate, her or his body, as no vantage point could afford a full view of the entirety of the film. At the same time, because of the length of the piece, a continual ebb and flow of arrival and departure characterizes the audience as a whole. This phenomenon is in part because a spectator's interest might wane (or ebb). Again, the structure of Julien's installation demands that the spectator will always miss something in any given viewing. This resistance to a complete or totalizing account counters Broomfield's *Ghosts*; for Julien, ebbing moves beyond affect to include physicality and a struggle with narrative closure.

The physical conditions of the installation draw the visitor into a consideration of the more metaphorical aspects of the exhibition generated by its visual and aural content. The allusion to the Morecambe Bay incident encourages reflection on what follows in the wake of drowning. In other words, what happens to this labor stream with the ebbing of the tides? Following Bruno's logic, the imagery folds the spectator into interconnecting, perhaps collapsing, time and space. However, the exhibition is quite specific in terms of what sorts of materials it folds together. The fold has been productively elaborated in the scholarship of Olivia Khoo and my own ensuing writing.[38] Both of us investigate the fold to think through traveling forms of Asianness. Khoo theorizes the fold as part of a formation she calls the Chinese exotic, which "permits certain images and representations of diasporic Chinese femininity to circulate and become globally visible."[39] The Chinese exotic structures the legibility of Chinese diasporic femininity and also the experience of that category. As one expression of the Chinese exotic, Khoo looks at a character played by Maggie Cheung, Julien's featured star in *Ten Thousand Waves* (her screen time is comparatively greater than that of Zhao Tao, who plays a ghostly version of Ruan Lingyu, one of China's most celebrated early celebrities).[40] Extending Khoo's Chinese exotic in relation to Julien's film helps parse the particularity of his depiction of female Chinese screen icons and may also help parse the on-location filming in China and the variety of other Chinese semiological signs in the installation.

GENEALOGIES OF TRANSNATIONAL ASIAN FORMS

Julien's work draws heavily on Chinese iconography from the urban—including the contemporary Shanghai skyline and reconstructions of a 1930s Shanghai cityscape—to the rural and from linguistic signs rendered in calligraphy (*shufa*) to fantastic embodiments of Chinese mythology. Rather than only revealing the postmodern pastiche of late capitalism, these different components in the show articulate potential agency and the limits to such agency. In this vein, the congeries of Chinese references elaborate what Appadurai refers to as the "imagination as a social practice."[41] In my view, such practice pushes spectators to think differently about the material circumstances for Chinese laborers. Rather than framing the Morecambe Bay incident as a series of human rights abuses, *Ten Thousand Waves* shifts discussion to other factors motivating migration.

According to the press release for the show, the juxtaposition of elements comments on modernization through a specifically Chinese cosmology: "Following ideas surrounding death, spiritual displacement, and the uniquely Chinese connection with 'ghosts' or 'lost souls,' the film links the Shanghai of the past and present, symbolising the Chinese transition towards modernity, aspiration and affluence. Here, Julien employs the visual language of ghost stories, with recurrent figures and images appearing and disappearing."[42] This construction of Shanghai is obviously quite specific, ignoring moments in Shanghai's past when the city did not serve as a beacon of China's capitalist development. Moreover, the exact relationship remains unclear between Shanghai and emigration patterns out of Fujian, where most of the cockle pickers trace their roots.

But perhaps this lack of clarity is the point, since ghosts represent a problem in terms of visuality (Jacques Derrida argued this point in relation to the revenant, a spectral figure that begins by coming back; however, the principal ghost in *Ten Thousand Waves* functions in a slightly different fashion, as I will argue).[43] In *Ten Thousand Waves*, the main character is Mazu (Maggie Cheung), a deity thought to exist apart from the dead she calls back. Worshipped widely throughout Greater China and the diaspora, Mazu connotes safe passage for fishermen both in the past and today. However, across various time periods and geographical areas, the particular associations of the goddess have varied.[44] Because she traverses diverse territories, often appearing only briefly before disappearing, she is less a figure that comes back (which often applies attachment to a specific place) than one who manifests as need arises. The desire for safe travel, then, correlates as often to a movement toward a new place as a return to one already known. Julie Y. Chu has described the appeal of Mazu as involving a "politics of destination."[45] This issue of destination raises the question of why people engage in precarious journeys in the first place. Unlike most human traffic discourse, however, a politics of destination does not necessarily attribute the motivation for travel to the horrible conditions of home, to the imagined opportunities for something better, or to forced migration. Following this politics of destination, the subjective desires of the cockle pickers cannot be reduced to a formula in which they only seek financial opportunity or have been exploited by a snakehead.

Such caveats might well inform how one understands Isaac Julien's Mazu, shown on screen as a retrospective guide. Her appearance follows the death of the cockle pickers, whom she would seem to escort back to China. Her all-white costume, a color traditionally worn for mourning, seems to reinforce this idea. This section of the film ostensibly draws on a folktale from Fujian about Yishan Island, a safe haven to which the deity ushered several sailors in danger of being swallowed by a storm. After returning to their homes, the mariners could never again locate their insular refuge. Obviously, the cockle pickers found themselves with less fortune on their side, and, insofar as the film relates Mazu to their actual experience, she provides a place to harbor their spirits after the end of their mortal lives. This manifestation of Mazu correlates with Avery Gordon's writing about ghosts as embodiments of unresolved social conflicts. Exactly which social conflicts (e.g., economic exploitation, human trafficking, or precarious labor) Mazu might represent remains somewhat ambiguous in Julien's piece. Certainly, one might read nostalgia in the implicit return of seafarers to China's shores. Flying over China's rural landscape of picturesque mountains and rivers, Mazu provides a romanticized homecoming to China's scenic beauty.

But Mazu also appears in Julien's film flying through Shanghai's postmillennial skyline. This placement of the screen goddess conjures the sorts of phrases that have been used to describe the city in recent years, including the tagline for the Shanghai World Expo in 2010, "Better City, Better Life." What role does the working class have in such a vision? What role does faith? Is spirituality waning under advanced capitalism or merely changing forms? Julien does not answer these questions, but his visual juxtapositions raise them. The film folds such queries together in provocative ways, specifically using the allure of the movie star. Perhaps most notably, several sequences depict Cheung in a harness being pulled by assistants across a green screen. Here, we might ask: what happens when a society worships screen goddesses whose cosmopolitan mobility is enabled by the labor of usually unseen workers? What is at stake in not seeing the everyday toil that renders the urban environment livable and even enchanting? Exactly how and for whom does a city generate a better life?

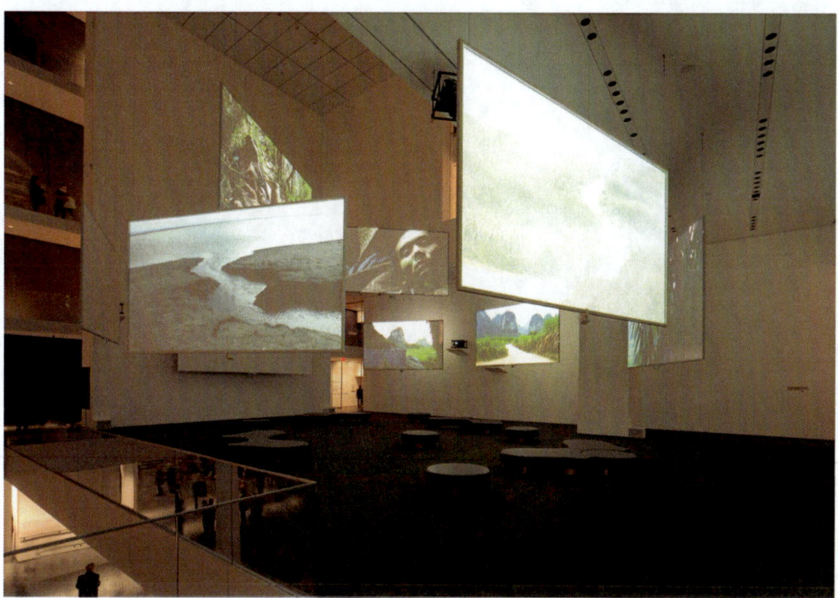

Fig. 4.4. The installation places corpses of the sailors within scenes of China's scenic beauty and interconnected waterways. Isaac Julien, *Ten Thousand Waves*, 2010. Nine-screen installation, 35 mm film transferred to high definition, 9.2 surround sound, 49' 41". Courtesy Isaac Julien, Metro Pictures Gallery (New York) and Victoria Miro Gallery (London). Installation view, the Museum of Modern Art, New York, 2013. Photograph: Jonathan Muzikar.

The film continually evokes the tensions between pushing and pulling, ebbing and flowing. These dynamics are in turn expressed as shifting between ostensible traditions and signifiers of modernity. For example, even the calligraphy sequences depict the flow of energy through the hands of a master, Gong Fagen, to create Chinese characters (*fantizi*) on a clear surface. The ink from the written words 萬重浪 (*wan zhong lang,* or "ten thousand waves") drips down the transparent screen until being wiped clean by a set of anonymous assistants. An aesthetic project, Julien continually reminds the viewer, requires work. Put differently, labor and aesthetics are entwined, folded together in ways that sometimes produce, for example, visions of the Chinese exotic. But such exoticism is often predicated on the disavowal of the blood, sweat, and tears that helped to fashion it.

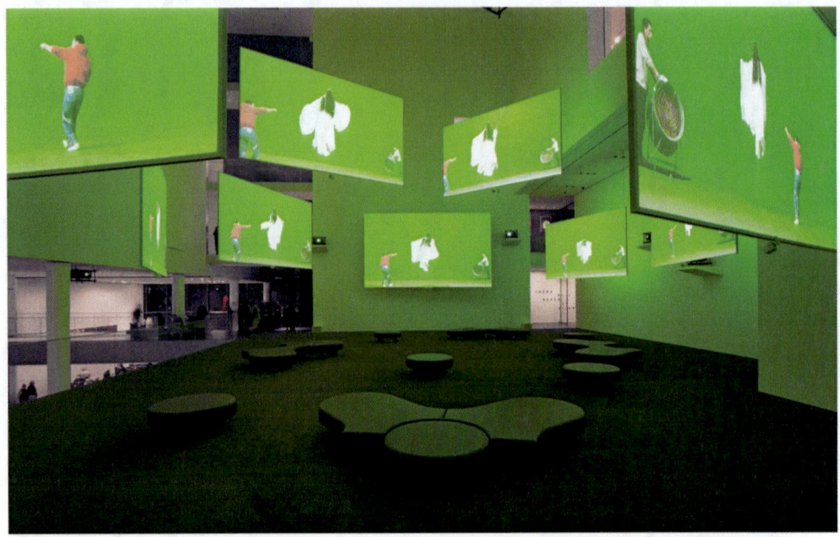

Fig. 4.5. The usually concealed labor of creating the film is demonstrated in the green screen sequences. Isaac Julien, *Ten Thousand Waves*, 2010. Nine-screen installation, 35 mm film transferred to high definition, 9.2 surround sound, 49′ 41″. Courtesy Isaac Julien, Metro Pictures Gallery (New York) and Victoria Miro Gallery (London). Installation view, the Museum of Modern Art, New York, 2013. Photograph: Jonathan Muzikar.

Following this line of argument, the scenes of 1930s Shanghai play on the seen and unseen. Julien himself has noted the remarkable efficiency of Chinese crews who built for him reconstructions of 1930s Shanghai, complete with a trolley. The actress who plays Ruan Lingyu, Zhao Tao, has starred in many of Jia Zhangke's films, works that have frequently depicted the nightmarish aspects of China's modernization projects. Certainly, the allusion in *Ten Thousand Waves* to Ruan Lingyu's film *The Goddess* and the reference to the screen icon of the 1930s suggest the high cost that urban life can exact on people, particularly women (*The Goddess* depicts a woman who prostitutes herself to provide for herself and her child; Ruan committed suicide at the age of twenty-four). Zhao Tao's temporal placement in this earlier moment of China's cinematic history thus interrogates a lineage of Chinese capitalism. In other words, the star discourse around Zhao Tao suggests one future for 1930s Shanghai: a booming yet in many ways dystopian China.

In these depictions of Shanghai and the layering of Chinese female stars, *Ten Thousand Waves* seems to have moved far from the ostensible event that inspired it. Whither does the installation drive audiences to Morecambe Bay? As much as the screens facilitate a consideration of the seen and unseen, the sound design for the show plays with the heard and unheard. In my own case, the direct allusions to the Morecambe Bay incident that punctuated the soundtrack often eluded me. After each visit to MOMA, I found myself contemplating the scale of images, the vastness of projected and actual space. Such considerations of the spectacle, of the immersion in the scene, often inhibited my ability to recollect, for example, narrative sequence or the aural experience of the installation. As I have mentioned, the latter phenomenon also involved the ambient soundscape of the museum itself. In any case, although my research had informed me to expect poetry about Morecambe Bay, I did not process that auditory aspect of the show until months after visiting it. Yet that element is one of the most explicit linkages to the historical event of 2004 and to the subjects of human traffic.

THE EBBING OF NOTORIETY

Isaac Julien's *Ten Thousand Waves* was in many ways a collaborative endeavor. His work gestures to other forms of cultural production: the films of its lead actresses, calligraphy, and the recontextualization of the installation on various social media sites. In this spirit, I eventually read what I believed I had missed in the exhibition in terms of the literary aspect; this retrospective reflection on the literary is, I argue, part of and a counterpoint to the sonic component of the installation, and it continues Julien's intermedial engagement. Sound carries in the form of waves that vary not only in amplitude and frequency but also in the ecology of transmission (open air versus populated space, etc.). Although Julien's work could not saturate his live spectators with water, it certainly does immerse them in sound, if we understand sound "as an ever-present vibratory field . . . a constant flux of resonances and oscillations that are felt in the body as well as heard by the ear."[46] As with the visual aspects of the screens, *Ten Thousand Waves* produces a phenomenological experience of sound that is fragmentary, its partiality contingent on individual desire (what one desires to hear or concentrates on) as well as the particular circumstances of exhibition in a museum or gallery space at a given time. The acoustic atmosphere, then, helps create an embodied experience for the visitor, one that aesthetically analogizes submersion in a screen environment to that in an aqueous one.

The dramatic monologues written by Chinese/American writer Wang Ping further an alignment among installation viewers and the Chinese cockle pickers. The poet labels each of the nineteen dramatic monologues that constitute her work, "Ten Thousand Waves," as a voice (or, in three cases, as voices) of the deceased. In other words, these names correlate with the Chinese laborers who drowned in Morecambe Bay. Although she penned most of the poems in an individual persona, she marks two as couples. The series ends with a "Chorus from All Ghosts."[47] As a group, the poems subordinate the details of the human trafficking that preoccupy much of the journalistic coverage and emphasize the subjectivities of the individuals who died.

For example, the first of the nineteen individual poems comprising the series opens with the purported voice of Xie Xiao Wen, a forty-one-year-old man who perished in Morecambe Bay. The first verse situates the cockle pickers in place and time: "On the night of the Lantern Festival/ We streamed into the sea."[48] In China, the lantern festival (*yuanxiaojie*) typically ends the festivities of *chunjie* ("spring festival" or "lunar new year festival"), which is generally a time of family reunification. The date of the calamity corresponds to the conclusion of festivities in China and amplifies Xie Xiao Wen's yearning for home, which this speaker and those of later monologues construct as China. The dramatic monologue marks the precarity of their situation as the workers attempt to stand "cockling/In the sand of the distant North Wales Sea."[49] To cockle, to oscillate unsteadily as if standing in a rowboat, is to upset balance. In this case, the imperiled laborers pay with their lives for seeking fortune in the mudflats; the second poem, attributed to thirty-four-year-old Wu Hong Kang, summarizes this state of affairs in its penultimate line: "How empty is desire."[50] Both of the initial poems use the first person plural and speak of collective actions and sentiments.

Migratory displacement marks the poem cycle as a whole. Over half of the individual poems end with some mention of the North Wales Sea. As the verses reach conclusion, the oceanic referent becomes the Yellow Sea and the East China Sea. The content of the poems enacts a geographic movement that reflects Julien's use of Mazu as leading the cockle pickers from Morecambe Bay back to China. However, the *form* of these verses complicates the assertion of a linear passage home. Often thought to have reached its nadir in Victorian England, the dramatic monologue potentially connotes English-ness even as it is linked to a wide range of generic precedents.[51] The speakers also express themselves primarily in English, a language that seems unusual for recent immigrants sharing their innermost thoughts. However, this linguistic choice enables English speakers to enter into the imagined subjective worlds of the Chinese laborers, and it eventually produces sympathy for their plight. Wang Ping renders the experience of displacement cross-cultural as she enables English-only readers to engage the constructed sentiments of the drowned Chinese workers.

This solicitation of the reader's affective response to the conditions expressed by the cycle's various speakers works through conventions of a poetic form that has often been evaluated precisely on the basis of its rhetorical efficacy.[52] One of the genre's most influential commentators, Robert Langbaum, wrote of the ways in which dramatic monologue produces identification: "Not only can the speaker of the dramatic monologue dramatize a position to which the poet is not ready to commit himself intellectually, but sympathy which we give the speaker for the sake of the poem and apart from judgment makes it possible for the reader to participate in a position, to see what it feels like to believe that way, without having finally to agree."[53] The structure of the dramatic monologue shares some commonality with the seascape in the sense of asserting a perspective. In demanding that the reader take the position of the poem's speaker, the dramatic monologue constructs a kind of theatrical impersonation through which the reader attempts to inhabit the speaker's subjective viewpoint.

Perhaps in the strictest of terms, Wang Ping's "Ten Thousand Waves" does not quite qualify as a series of dramatic monologues, since three of the constituent poems involve multiple speakers (although these voices enunciate in unison). However, I am less interested in whether the work adheres to a genre than the ways in which that genre might assist in elucidating the verses. The poet plunges her reader into the realm of the dead, constructing echoes as a way to iterate or reflect the cockle pickers' outlooks on their lives and employment. Each monologue is relatively brief (all but two of the poems consist of thirteen lines or less; the longest is the chorus, which runs twenty lines). The reader-speaker relationship emerges through the collective testimonies and observations offered in the individual poems. In this case, the dramatic monologue elicits less a relationship of reader to a specific speaker than to a group of speakers, who ostensibly share certain characteristics.

This effect occurs because of several elements in the *Ten Thousand Waves* cycle. The progression of the individual verses to a chorus suggests that the voices work as an ensemble, finally producing a collective account of their experience. To take the roles of the cockle pickers is, therefore, to join this imagined collectivity. Several thematic features also recur. For example, four of the poems use Asian trees (longyan, or longan, and lychee) as ways of marking time and place; these organic references might contrast the reader's experience encountering the posthumous technological circulation of the cockle pickers' voices and images across several platforms. The trees also encourage a consideration of kinship explicitly marked in nine of the poems in laments about lovers, wives, mothers, daughters, and sons left in China to fend for themselves. This emphasis on the impossibility of family and things growing together in the wake of the Morecambe Bay incident suggests the loss of a heteronormative (and also Confucian) ideal. To read the poems is to enter a structure in which home equals the site of biological kin; recognizing the loss of those connections constructs certain forms of identification between reader and speakers.

Lin Guo Gang speaks the ninth poem, and here, Wang Ping introduces Chinese text in the cycle. A thrice-repeated line, "*Fumu zai, bu yuan you,*" precedes a possible translation: "When father and mother are around/ The son does not wander far from home."[54] The English adds specific mention of a boy, but the Chinese renders the subject a bit more ambiguous in terms of gender. The action concluding the second half of the line, *you*, contrasts with *zai*, meaning "to be at a place." *You* is the word for swim as well as to wander or roam. Delivered as a truncated Confucian proverb (usually understood as "Do not travel far while your parents are alive"), the poem intimates filial piety. Placing these words in the mouth of Lin may lead to the aftermath of the incident, during which Lin's wife "managed to pay off half the debt of 200,000 yuan (£20,000) left by her husband (the remainder was paid by donations from the UK)."[55] These are the only Chinese words in the cycle, and they are repeated after poem eighteen as a concrete poem in the shape of a cross. The reiterated statement memorializes the demonstrated survival of a family in crisis.

Aside from the naturalizing of certain forms of kinship, the cycle offers two poems in its second half that enlarge the context for all of the voices. Lin

Zhi Fang (one of the youngest to succumb to the waves) and Yu Hui recite a litany of "the tolls": the numbers of Chinese people who have died as a result of precarious migrations. They specifically list, among other sites, Rockaway, New York (the Golden Venture incident), and Dover, England. The claiming of these trafficking episodes reinforces another quality that Langbaum has associated with dramatic monologue insofar as "there is at work in it a consciousness, whether intellectual or historical, beyond what the speaker can lay claim to."[56] The historical consciousness evoked in "Ten Thousand Waves" links disparate instances of human trafficking as a continuing phenomenon. Although the details may differ, the fate of migrating subjects is, according to the poem, potentially the same. As the pair of drowned subjects laments, "starved, raped, dehydrated, drowned, suffocated, homesick, heartsick, worked to death, working to death/ We know we may end up in the same boat."[57]

This insistent "we" recasts the mention of an ocean craft earlier in the cycle in the voice of a Chen Ai Qin, identified in news reports as a thirty-nine-year-old woman (one of the three females who lost their lives). Her verse elaborates this rudimentary description, albeit only slightly. Chen crafts a paper boat "full of bleeding hearts" that ache "to be called home again."[58] Desire and creativity enhance the portrait of someone known primarily by her age and gender in the press. However fleeting, these efforts would seem to attempt to restore some humanity to people only known in the media as human trafficking victims. Reading across the poems also demonstrates how aspirational hope yields to anxious pessimism. Pangs of nostalgia to cruise home in the earlier poem transform into the foreboding sense that a boat might serve as one's coffin.

Ultimately, the poems work in multiple ways to produce meaning around an event that is, in Julien's larger installation, largely unknowable and accessible primarily through devices like mythmaking and historical juxtaposition. As performatives, the voices testify to lives otherwise submerged in the currents of history. The naming of individuals in this case marks those who might otherwise remain anonymous. As assemblages of words that elicit an affective response, the verses produce sympathy through heteronormative structures of identification. As monologues, the poetry immerses the reader in the subjective position of another, fostering a kind of theatrical impersonation. All of these different elements in Wang Ping's poetry work through textual seascapes, providing a particular perspective on the lives of those who drowned.

This emphasis on marine views—twelve poems end with explicit mention of the North Wales Sea—becomes an anaphora that reminds the speaker and the readership of most of the cockle pickers' fates: seeking bounty in what became their aquatic tombs. Only when the water recedes do the bodies matter in public discourse. Invisible until dead, those who succumbed to the waves in Morecambe Bay in 2004 have departed, leaving gaps in the understanding of the final node of this circuit of human trafficking and of what might have led to this event. The poems ultimately stress the production of meaning through absence. The lingering words of the ghosts haunt us, like Wu Jia Zhen's, a cockle picker who died at the age of thirty-six, that Wang Ping ventriloquizes: "Tides ebb and flow with the moon/ Our house is empty, covered in tall weeds/ I walk on the sand, eyes on the sea/ Who can fill the hollow hearts/ In the bottomless North Wales Sea?"[59]

The repeated invocation of death returns me to various questions of theatricality with which I began. Certainly, Wang Ping's textual supplement to the installation, Isaac Julien's art piece as a whole, and Nick Broomfield's film all raise ethical questions about what it means to substitute various aesthetic forms for the actual lives of trafficked people. Such inquiries, however justified, participate in a long tradition of antitheatrical prejudice that challenges the stand-in (in this case, for a deceased Chinese cockle picker). The provocation of theatricality is that one might perform another without being that other and often without sharing the life experiences of that other. Yet I have tried to suggest that trafficking remains inextricable from representation.

Here, Joseph Roach's work on memory, performance, and substitution is instructive. Roach elaborates the term *surrogation* to describe the continual process by which communities attempt to fit satisfactory alternates into vacancies within the social fabric of what he calls the "Circum-Atlantic."[60] His emphasis on oral and corporeal retentions within specific communities correlate with specific functions of performance, particularly in London and New Orleans, although the implications of his scholarship extend well beyond those cities. This modality of Atlantic thought underscores uneven cultural transmission from one individual and/or communal body to another. In the wake of this influential theorization, we can see how certain aesthetic devices might articulate the vexing issue of trafficking: As particular people and their stories recede out of memory because of death or imprisonment, more generalized signs remain that indicate a structure of trafficking. Such signs approximate what institutions such as the UN have authorized as the experiences that define trafficking victims. If surrogation functions in the case of the Chinese cockle pickers, then it is to render them legible within human trafficking discourse.

In contrast, the logic of ebbing I have outlined here highlights processes of theatrical substitution when individuals no longer belong to any easily identifiable community or when communities outright reject former or potential members. Witness the cockle pickers claimed by neither England nor China. Ebbing enables us to imagine and to reanimate the scattered remains of the deceased to think again about the present and about what might be done in the future. If, as Roach reminds us, "cities of the dead are primarily for the living" to consider how the past continues to haunt the present, ebbing brings into view what remains now to enable us to think about what happens next.[61]

NOTES

1. Astrida Neimanis, "Water, a Queer Archive of Feeling," in *Tidalectics: Imagining an Oceanic Worldview through Art and Science*, ed. Stefanie Hessler (Cambridge, MA: The MIT Press, 2018), 196.

2. Michaeline A. Crichlow, "Human Traffic—Past and Present," *Cultural Dynamics* (2013) 25, no. 2: 123–140.

3. See Rhacel Parreñas, *Illicit Flirtations: Labor, Migration, and Sex Trafficking in Tokyo* (Palo Alto: Stanford University Press, 2011).

4. Here, I borrow one element of Xinyi Jiang's essay "Fujianese Migration and the British Press Coverage of the Dover Incident," in *Migrations and the Media*, eds. Kerry Moore, Bernhard Gross, and Terry Threadgold (New York: Peter Lang, 2012), 196–197.

5. Sean Metzger, "Ripples in the Seascape: The *Cuba Commission Report* and the Idea of Freedom," *Afro-Hispanic Review* 27, no. 1 (2008): 107 and 117.

6. Lisa Yun, *The Coolie Speaks: Chinese Indentured Laborers and African Slaves in Cuba* (Philadelphia: Temple University Press, 2008), 110.

7. Frank N. Pieke, Pál Nyíri, Mette Thunø, and Antonella Ceccagno, *Transnational Chinese: Fujianese Migrants in Europe* (Stanford: Stanford University Press, 2004), 12.

8. Pieke et al., *Transnational*, 15.

9. David Kyle and Rey Koslowski, *Global Human Smuggling: Comparative Perspectives* (Baltimore: The Johns Hopkins University Press, 2011) 10.

10. Kyle and Koslowski, *Smuggling*, 2–3.

11. Anne Allison, *Precarious Japan* (Durham: Duke University Press, 2013).

12. Kyle and Koslowski, *Smuggling*, 5.

13. Kyle and Koslowski, *Smuggling*, 3.

14. United Nations, Human Rights Office of the High Commissioner, *Protocol to Prevent, Suppress and Punish Trafficking in Persons Especially Women and Children, Supplementing the United Nations Convention Against Transnational Organized Crime* (New York: United Nations, 2000) 42.

15. See his interview at https://www.youtube.com/watch?v=CHlbMYbDbag, accessed April 23, 2016. For a brief overview of Ai Qin Lin's migration, see Hsiao-Hung Pai, "A Ghost No More," *The New Statesman*, Jan. 8, 2007.

16. Kimberly Kay Hoang and Rhacel Salazar Parreñas, *Human Traffic Reconsidered: Rethinking the Problem, Envisioning New Solutions* (New York: IDEBATE, 2014), 1.

17. Nick Broomfield, interview with Bruce Himmelblau, *Indie Film Nation*, June 29, 2009, https://www.youtube.com/watch?v=OgZE3GLJ6tU.

18. Obviously, this statement resonates differently given the shifts in immigration policy that may attend the wake of Brexit. Broomsfield's film now seems all the more relevant, yet the Blair administration from 1997 to 2007 also saw immigration as a central issue connected to both economic development and security.

19. Roger Bromley, "Undesirable and Placeless: Finding a Political Space for the Displaced in a Cinema of Destitution," *Interventions: International Journal of Postcolonial Studies* 14, no. 3 (2012): 341–360.

20. Ko-Lin Chin and James O. Finckenauer, *Selling Sex Overseas: Chinese Women and the Realities of Prostitution and Global Sex Trafficking* (New York: New York University Press, 2012), 56.

21. There were several reports on the deaths and the subsequent trial. For examples, see Joe Boyle, "Death in a Strange Cold Land," BBC News, March 24, 2006, http://news.bbc.co.uk/2/hi/uk_news/england/4582470.stm#map; and Jonathan Watts, "Going Under," *The Guardian*, June 20, 2007, accessed May 27, 2018, http://www.theguardian.com/uk/2007/jun/20/ukcrime.humanrights.

22. Isaac Julien and Cynthia Rose, *Isaac Julien: Riot* (New York: Artbook/ D.A.P., 2013), 193.

23. Rey Chow, *Entanglements: or Transmedial Thinking About Capture* (Durham: Duke University Press, 2012), 4.

24. Julien and Rose, *Riot*, 122.

25. This statement is derived from Jonathan Watts's "Going Under," accessed July 26, 2014, http://www.theguardian.com/uk/2007/jun/20/ukcrime.humanrights. In order to pay the snakeheads for transportation and other expenses (lodging, food, work documents), each worker borrowed several thousand RMB from relatives, fellow villagers, and other creditors. With interest rates at 10 percent or more, the accumulated debt for many families amounts to several hundred thousand yuan on salaries to be paid by households that earn monthly incomes in the triple digits.

26. Duncan J. Petrie, "British Cinema: The Search for Identity," in *The Oxford History of World Cinema*, ed. Geoffrey Nowell-Smith (Oxford: Oxford University Press, 1999), 609.

27. For an elaboration of this point, see Isaac Julien, "Burning Rubber's Perfume," in *Critical Cultural Policy Studies: A Reader*, eds. Justin Lewis and Toby Miller (Malden, MA: Blackwell, 2003).

28. Although I offer this schematic distinction, other scholarship has pointed to the Black Audio Film Collective's work "as an archaeological excavation into the limits of medial evolution and as a metamedial engagement with the epistemological conditions of the imperial archive"; K. Eshun, "Untimely Meditations: Reflections on the Black Audio Film Collective," *Nka: Journal of Contemporary African Art* (2004): 39.

29. Julien and Rose, *Riot*, 138.

30. J. Kahana in "Cinema and the Ethics of Listening: Isaac Julien's *Frantz Fanon*," *Film Quarterly* 59, no. 2: 19–31, offers a useful interrogation of sound in general in Isaac Julien's work, particularly in *Frantz Fanon: Black Skin, White Mask* (1996).

31. Julien and Rose, *Riot*, 204.

32. Giuliana Bruno, *Surfaces: Matters of Aesthetics, Materiality, and Media* (Chicago: University of Chicago Press, 2014), 169.

33. Bruno, *Surfaces*, 181.

34. Bruno, *Surfaces*, 181.

35. Arjun Appadurai, *Modernity at Large: Cultural Dimensions of Globalization* (Minneapolis: University of Minnesota Press, 1996), 33.

36. Appadurai, *Modernity*, 33.

37. Appadurai, *Modernity*, 33.

38. See Olivia Khoo, *The Chinese Exotic: Modern Diasporic Femininity* (Hong Kong: Hong Kong University Press, 2007), and Sean Metzger, "At the Vanishing Point: Theater and Asian/American Critique," *American Quarterly* 63 no. 2 (2011): 277–300.

39. Khoo, *Exotic*, 27.

40. Maggie Cheung previously played this role in the biopic *Center Stage* (Stanley Kwan, 1991). For spectators familiar with Cheung's career, this coincidence adds an element of spectrality to Cheung's ghostly character in *Ten Thousand Waves*. She continually returns through different screen embodiments.

41. Appadurai, *Modernity*, 31.

42. *Ten Thousand Waves* (London: Victoria Miro Gallery, 2010).

43. Jacques Derrida, *Specters of Marx: The State of Debt, the Work of Mourning and the New International*, trans. Peggy Kamuf (New York: Routledge, 1994).

44. For specifics, see Chee-Beng Tan, "Tianhou and the Chinese in Diaspora," in *Routledge Handbook of the Chinese Diaspora*, ed. Chee-Beng Tan (Routledge: New York, 2013).

45. Julie Y. Chu, *Cosmologies of Credit: Transnational Mobility and the Politics of Destination in China* (Durham: Duke University Press, 2010), 12.

46. William Moran Hutson, "Sonic Affects: Electronic Music in Sound Art, Cinema, and Performance," diss. (University of California, Los Angeles, 2015), 1.

47. Wang Ping, *Ten Thousand Waves: Poems* (San Antonio: Wings, 2014), 82.

48. Wang Ping, *Waves*, 74.

49. Wang Ping, *Waves*, 74.

50. Wang Ping, *Waves*, 75.

51. On this issue, see Robert Langbaum, *The Poetry of Experience: The Dramatic Monologue in Modern Literary Tradition* (New York: W.W. Norton & Company, Inc., 1957).

52. In this regard, I am thinking of scholarship on the dramatic monologue ranging from Langbaum's 1957 *The Poetry of Experience* to Cornelia D.J. Pearsall's "The Dramatic

Monologue," in *The Cambridge Companion to Victorian Poetry*, ed. Joseph Bristow (Cambridge: Cambridge University Press, 2000).

53. Langbaum, *Experience*, 105.

54. Wang Ping, *Waves*, 77.

55. Hsiao Hung Pai, "What Happened to the Families of the Drowned Cocklepickers of Morecambe Bay," *The Guardian*, Oct. 22, 2012, accessed Nov. 14, 2016, https://www .theguardian.com/world/2012/oct/22/drowned-chinese-cocklepickers-morecambe-bay.

56. Langbaum, *Experience*, 94.

57. Wang Ping, *Waves*, 79.

58. Wang Ping, *Waves*, 75.

59. Wang Ping, *Waves*, 77.

60. Joseph Roach, *Cities of the Dead: Circum-Atlantic Performance* (New York: Columbia University Press, 1996), 2.

61. Roach, *Cities*, xi.

5 ~ EDDYING

EDDYING INDICATES A SORT OF COUNTERCURRENT. THE SPIRALING water shifts orientation. In March of 2018, I once again encountered Isaac Julien's *Ten Thousand Waves*, but this time at the Zeitz Museum of Contemporary Art Africa (MOCAA) in Cape Town. My visit there also enabled me to see another screen installation: William Kentridge's *More Sweetly Play the Dance* (2015). I had first seen Kentridge's multiscreen project at the Eye Museum in Amsterdam, where it opened. The juxtaposition of the installations in the context of African art as well as the setting of the Cape Town harbor altered my impressions of the two artworks as individual pieces and in relation to one another. Such an experience complicated my ongoing research on seascapes in South Africa by two other artists, DALeast and Pieter-Dirk Uys, who articulate in different ways the pivotal role that the Western Cape plays in the Chinese Atlantic in terms of both generalizing about larger phenomena shaping Chinese-inflected globalization and specifying South Africa's particularity in such processes. *Eddying* in this case suggests a particular convergence of Chinese flows within a nation-state that has transformed tremendously in the last thirty years and the Dutch colonial legacies that have informed that space. Even as South Africa's colonial histories might remind one of the presence of the Dutch East India company with which I began this book, the rainbow nation's current relations with China serve as a kind of sextant that might suggest the course of Chinese-inflected globalization on the horizon, across different oceanic imaginaries.

ESTABLISHING COORDINATES

Postapartheid South Africa established formal diplomatic relations with China in 1998; by 2017, according to China's ambassador to the rainbow nation, Lin Songtian, South Africa had been China's "largest trading partner in Africa for eight consecutive years."[1] That trade amounts to several billion dollars annually and the presence of over one hundred Chinese companies of various sizes operating throughout South Africa.[2] Visible concentrations of Chinese traders can be seen in "China malls" around the country. Corresponding increases in tourism and overseas student opportunities moving in both directions have also occurred in this period. Over the last decade, five Confucius Institutes have been established at institutions of higher education: the University of Stellenbosch, Rhodes University, the University of Cape Town, Durban University of Technology, and the University of Johannesburg. Although estimates place the number of Chinese people in the country at three hundred fifty thousand to five hundred thousand, which is less than 1 percent of South Africa's total population, it remains the largest group of Chinese residents in terms of raw numbers of any country on the continent. Such developments have resulted in an increasing amount of artistic endeavors that help to express what Chineseness might mean in the new South Africa.

I examine an archive of seascapes in three very unlike formats: the two previously mentioned screen installations, a proscenium stage play, and the work of a street artist. Again, my turn to South Africa has much to do with China's investments there and specific seascapes that focalize empirical shifts and the fantasies that attend those changes. The first Forum on China–Africa Cooperation occurred in 2000. With its comparatively strong infrastructure, South Africa has served as a gateway and potential model for China's investments on the rest of the continent. In August 2010, South Africa and China signed a comprehensive strategic cooperation agreement during President Zuma's visit to Asia. How are different forms of Chineseness reconfiguring power on different scales? This question is particularly important because, unlike any other site in my study, South Africa had a significant influx of immigrants from Taiwan (as opposed to mainland China) from the late

1970s through the early 1990s. The shifting relationships with Chineseness calibrate with South Africa's role on the world stage.

Cape Town might seem like an unusual choice for a chapter that emphasizes Chinese circulations in South Africa. Although I attend to one artwork that signifies an unspecific geography, I highlight pieces connected to Cape Town because it has served and continues to function as a "relay or nodal point in multiple circuits of exchange," especially for "many of the earth's shipping lanes."[3] As anthropologist Anne-Maria Makhulu has pointed out, Cape Town also designates an area where squatter settlements continually foster spatial negotiations. What she terms the "struggle for a full life" manifests in quotidian claims to and acts of homemaking.[4] These continual home-ing processes (to borrow Michaeline Crichlow and Patricia Northover's phrase) manifest in all the artworks that I investigate. They call into question assumptions not just about landed property but also vistas of the ocean and access to areas for public use, such as beaches.

From certain perspectives, Johannesburg might initially seem a more likely candidate than Cape Town for an African nodal point in a study of the Chinese Atlantic; what Loren Kruger calls an "edgy city" manifests in the "improvised, performative quality of cosmopolitan agency, affiliation, or practices."[5] Her wide-ranging study of municipal history counters scholarly emphasis on the nation in the postapartheid period. Although she does not specifically address how flows of Chinese culture, finance, and people complicate the city's edginess, one could imagine an extension of her work focused on the physical site of Johannesburg's Chinatown or the establishment of its younger cousin in the suburb of Cyrildene. Such a framework might reference the Transvaal gold fields that resulted in the mass migration of Chinese workers to the country in the first decade of the twentieth century. It might also draw on the later stories of people like Ufrieda Ho's family, whose clandestine journey across the Indian Ocean to the Durban docks and then to Johannesburg suggests a different oceanic paradigm than the one I have been outlining in this book.[6] However, Cape Town, in contrast to Durban and Johannesburg, is situated on the Atlantic (the Indian and Atlantic oceans meet off Cape Agulhas, a couple of hundred kilometers east of Cape Town). Moreover, the capital of the Western Cape has become a site where the representation of Chinese flows through seascapes of various kinds has emerged with particular force, as evidenced, for example, in the simultaneous exhibitions of Julien's and Kentridge's respective installations.

Zeitz MOCAA occupies a prominent place in the Victoria and Alfred Waterfront, a commercial and tourist center inaugurated in 1988. Although the harbor had been developed for over a century prior to that time, in the last three decades, a shopping mall, aquarium, hotels, and residences have been added. Zeitz MOCAA opened in 2017 in the old grain silo complex, which had become defunct with the rise of container ships. Windows from various locations, and especially from the top floor restaurant and function room, provide ample views of the harbor and city. The area around the museum also contains the Robinson Dry Dock, the oldest of its kind in the world, operating since the nineteenth century. The museum provides vantage points inside the museum for seeing this facility. In sum, Zeitz MOCAA sits in an active port, leisure center, and tourist destination.

Because of Zeitz MOCAA's location, ships undergoing maintenance frequently shape part of the background of the museum. En route to the entrance, I saw the Yuh Mao No 106, a Taiwanese fishing vessel, being cleaned by its crew. The Taiwanese flag reminds one of how Chineseness has signified in South Africa over time. Although South Africa is a peninsula, it has been islanded at various moments in its history, notably during the later years of apartheid (1948–1991). After the UN shifted formal recognition of China away from Taiwan in 1971 and suspended dealings with South Africa in 1974, the two governments established mutually beneficial trade agreements that led to a dramatic uptick in South Africa–Taiwan relations. These connections reveal something of the logic of the eddy in terms of marking a certain surge in cultural exchanges that might include Taiwanese as much as Chinese (PRC) circulations in the Atlantic. To fathom flows of Chineseness is to consider seemingly unobstructed cultural and financial streams knowing that others (like Taiwan's) remain blocked or have ebbed over time.

The museum itself did little, if anything, to frame the Chinese circuits engaged by the installations of Julien and Kentridge. Information placards generally provided name, date, and country of the artist's birth; online descriptions added a bit more material. In the case of *Ten Thousand Waves*, the curious viewer learned about Julien's biography and that this particular piece "was shot in China and poetically weaves together stories linked to China's ancient past and present. The work explores the movement of people across countries and continents and mediates unfinished journeys."[7] Unlike the exhibition of *Ten Thousand Waves* at MOMA, where viewers obtained much more specific information about the content and form, Zeitz MOCAA provided less detail about the formal innovations and narrative components of Julien's work. In the absence of such information, the placement of this gallery installation among others within Zeitz MOCAA's network of contemporary art encouraged the viewer to explore Julien's work as a further meditation on postcolonial representation in a world saturated by mass media.

In this vein, several of the museum's other video installations intersected or otherwise resonated with Julien's. Two of these will serve as examples to illustrate these diverse convergences. First, Zeitz MOCAA included a video installation by Yinka Shonibare, MBE (RA), another artist based in London, who was raised in England and Nigeria. His *Addio del Passato* (2011) screened in the Dusthouse, one of the museum's campus buildings, accessible by skyway. The Dusthouse formerly filtered the air of the adjoining structures; for the exhibition, one entered onto a short platform to view a projection on the opposite wall of otherwise unadorned concrete, save for the translucent stained glass windows that filter light into the space. The relatively narrow building stands quite tall and functions as something of an echo chamber for the soundtrack. Notwithstanding the characteristics of its exhibition, *Addio del Passato* interrelates with Julien's *Ten Thousand Waves* in several ways. Both use explicitly theatrical enactments of well-known narratives. In Shonibare's case, he depicts a black opera singer adorned in silver wig and a Dutch wax print dress performing Violetta's aria from act three of Verdi's *La Traviata* (when the character realizes that she will soon die from tuberculosis). The song is repeated over the course of the film's approximately sixteen-minute duration. This diva simultaneously plays Frances Nisbet, the widow of British Naval Officer Lord Nelson. Nelson had a maritime career that helped to establish the British Empire across oceans; he met Nisbet on the Caribbean island of Nevis. She appears to have remained loyal to him despite their eventual estrangement.

The black singer playing Nesbit delivers her aria in a postcolonial context. Dutch wax print borrows from batik, an Indonesian process of wax-resist dyeing that enables the creation of elaborate patterns. The Dutch successfully marketed its fabricated goods in West Africa, where the material became a mainstay of quotidian dress. Bedecked in these garments, the black body in the setting of a European palace on screen also contrasts with the very industrial look of the Dusthouse itself. This contrast reminded the visitor of the stark juxtapositions of wealth across geographies. The song sung by a seemingly isolated soprano conjures death (the emphasis on sound in Shonibare's work further underscores the importance of soundtracks across the screen installations in the museum, as I will demonstrate shortly).[8] The installation asks in part how black life matters in the context of European imperialisms.

This expressive line intersects the kinds of questions that *Ten Thousand Waves* poses in relation to Chinese migrants, whose representations have also been shaped to a degree by legacies of colonialism. Because the exhibition of Julien's work in Cape Town did not provide explication of the Chinese figures visualized in the work, the audience might as easily think about Taiwanese fishermen as Fujianese cockle pickers, given the Taiwanese presence that might be working just outside the museum space. In fact, moving from one image of Dutch wax print to a display of unspecified Chinese bodies might, for some viewers, connect the disparate images by encouraging contemplation of how the Dutch colonial past haunts the present from places like Taiwan to South Africa.

An exhibition in the museum's Centre for the Moving Image housed *Penny Siopis, This Is a True Story: Six Films (1997–2017)*. A large, open room with several alcoves containing a number of screens, the space facilitated the showing of all six titles simultaneously. Although one could focus on an individual film, light emanating from the projections as well as sound from each narrative infused the room. Like that of Julien's work, although on a less concentrated scale, the curation of *Penny Siopis* created a sense of immersion among screens. The content of Siopis's films involved significant amounts of found footage (often of the somewhat grainy 8mm and 16mm variety) contextualized through a voice or musical motif that helped unify each individual work. The details of the films are not as relevant here so much as the idea that they frequently addressed quotidian life in South Africa, often dealing with older generations of the filmmaker's Greek family. As a counterpoint to Julien, this installation also addressed structures of memory, particularly demonstrating how the everyday becomes history. The presence of so many screens again emphasized the technologically mediated world and human experience therein.

These installations helped to reframe *Ten Thousand Waves*. Zeitz MOCAA arranged Julien's screens to fill the gallery space from nearly floor to ceiling. The much more compact spatial layout left a path for the spectator to walk past the screens to the door (on the same wall as the entrance) leading to the next exhibit. This meant that the peripatetic spectator followed a semicircular path from entrance to exit. Those who wished to find a place to watch the film at length either stood (usually by one of the screens to avoid foot traffic) or sat along the walls. As with MOMA, no vantage point allowed one to see all of the images. In order to maximize the viewing experience, the perambulating viewer had to double back. This eddying motion produced a self-reflexivity about the process of immersion itself in the sense of repeating movements to see the sequences of *Ten Thousand Waves*, described in detail in chapter 4. The structure of repetition reminded one of Shonibare's use of historical narratives and the repeated refrains embodied and sung by his lead actress. The structure also recalled Siopis's use of found footage; Julien also incorporates found footage in *Ten Thousand Waves*. Within these contexts of juxtaposed art exhibitions, Julien's work furthers an inquiry into structures of repetition. How, for example, do certain narratives and/or visual images gain traction? How and why do certain events register in private and public memory?

The most salient difference between the exhibition of *Ten Thousand Waves* in Cape Town versus New York was the soundtrack. Whereas MOMA's atrium diffused the sonic elements of the installation, Zeitz MOCAA's more compacted space created something akin to an echo chamber. One could distinctly hear the recitations of the poems and the sounds of the churning ocean. At times, the viewer's immersion in soundwaves analogized the visual representations on screen. Such an overlap created a comparatively stronger sense of submersion, of losing oneself among the sights and sounds of water. In the Zeitz MOCAA exhibition, the observer sometimes became part of the screened seascapes. If I hesitate in my celebration of this effect, it is because I also noticed during my viewings the image of a man floating upside down in the sea. I did not remember this sequence from my first encounters with the artwork in New York, although the film itself had not been altered for South Africa. In any case, the poetry cycle and immersive elements compelled me to interpret this image as that of a drowned man, provided without any context of the cockle picker deaths that inspired *Ten Thousand Waves* in the first place. I continue to ponder what it means to reproduce death in this manner. What are the ethics of representation concerning those involved in human traffic?

As I have suggested, the screen installations I have discussed implicitly and sometimes explicitly represent death. The literal and metaphorical reflections provided by the films spurred me to consider again Kentridge's *More Sweetly Play the Dance,* which is a kind of danse macabre, a genre of allegory popular during the Middle Ages that featured a variety of figures en route to the grave. In contrast to Julien's work, the tone of Kentridge's work seems to celebrate the passage to death in no small part because of the lively soundtrack. That said, neither *Ten Thousand Waves* nor *More Sweetly Play the Dance* engages a linear temporality. Both draw on myth, a kind of worldview that exists outside of a normative timeline. In the case of the former installation, the sailors' deaths do not end their journeys so much as initiate a return via the goddess Mazu (Maggie Cheung's character) to where they began. In a similar vein and despite the fact that Kentridge has organized his installation on a horizontal axis (in a manner consistent with danse macabre), Kentridge engages circular temporalities. If the movement of his progression of people and objects indeed pushes toward death (*More Sweetly Play the Dance* suggests this idea), the entire film nevertheless runs in a loop. Thus both installations engage a kind of circularity that might further describe the logic of eddying. This temporal circulation repeatedly suggests the afterlife of Chinese presence in the Atlantic world. Chinese figures in each work move back and forth across boundaries, and they also appear and disappear in an endless loop during the exhibitions.

MORE SWEETLY PLAY THE DANCE

South Africa's preeminent artist, William Kentridge, has exhibited *More Sweetly Play the Dance* in several Atlantic metropoles. I first saw the looped, fifteen-minute, eight-channel video installation with four megaphones in the EYE museum on the bank of Amsterdam's Ij River, which is connected to the North Sea canal.[9] Kentridge has long created intermedial work—operatic and theatrical performance, film, and other visual art—within and outside of the country. The EYE's curator, Jaap Guldemond, has described this particular installation as a "frieze" and a "band of moving images" that he links to Kentridge's earlier work of moving silhouettes entitled *Shadow Procession*

(1999).[10] The artist himself has cited Plato's "Allegory of the Cave" as intellectual context for this work, but it also productively links to the American artist Kara Walker's silhouette murals *Gone: An Historical Romance of a Civil War as It Occurred Between the Dusky Thighs of One Young Negress and Her Heart* (1994) and the subsequent work she has done with both cutouts and motion pictures in this vein. These varied antecedents provide a number of philosophical, art historical, and thematic perspectives from which to observe *More Sweetly Play the Dance.* Certainly, the work engages all of them, but commentators have missed the ways in which Kentridge also plays with seascapes in his work. Kentridge describes his creative process from drawing to animation as a continuum. His explanation of his technique correlates with my own emphasis on seascapes: "Drawing for me is about fluidity."[11] Kentridge's technique produces fluid-looking landscapes, which means, particularly in the case of *More Sweetly Play the Dance*, that it looks like a seascape.

The screen installation's location in a Dutch waterfront building conjured the earlier histories of sea traffic that brought Africa and China together through the Dutch Golden Age that I discussed in the introduction. The piece traveled (movement itself is of course a thematic in and a material practice that constitutes the work), but its exhibition at this particular site recalled legacies of Dutch colonialism and its intersection with the China trade. In this case, the artist, a Jewish man whose parents achieved notoriety defending victims of apartheid, took a new commission and combined it with another project dealing with China's Cultural Revolution.[12] Kentridge's earlier commission centered around the *yangbanxi,* or model operas, promulgated under the reign of Mao's wife, Jiang Qing. *Yangban* means template or model, and Kentridge seems to have adapted the silhouette as a vehicle for connecting a material template (the silhouette) and an ideological one (the opera). Like Julien's work, *More Sweetly Play the Dance* is a creative reenactment—to reiterate, one that depicts a procession of various figures in a medieval danse macabre but transformed under Kentridge's direction to become "part carnival, protest, and exodus."[13] The caravan includes the African Immanuel Essemblies Brass Band (which also provides the score), "skeletal silhouettes, robed figures, priests, anonymous carriers, fleeing refugees, itinerants carrying saints, stick fighters, the sick, miners performing spade dancers," and others.[14] The movement of onlookers within the museum

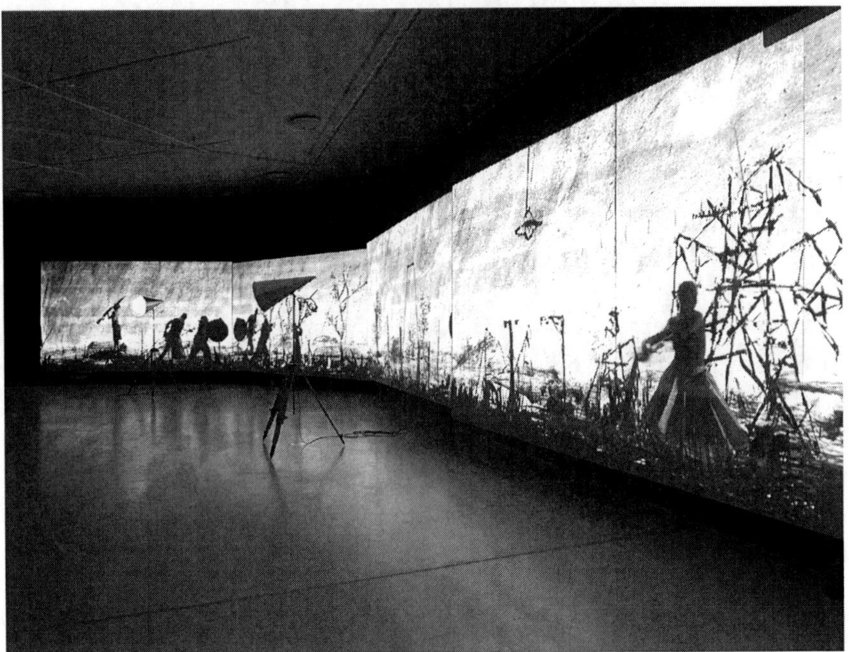

Fig. 5.1. *More Sweetly Play the Dance* is a screen installation of a processional
performance. *More Sweetly Play the Dance*, 2015. William Kentridge exhibition
If We Ever Get to Heaven, 2015, EYE Film Museum, Amsterdam.
Photograph: Studio Hans Wilschut.

space occasionally obscures the view, so the spectator becomes a part of the
procession at different moments as well.

One of the most astute commentators on parades as events and processes,
performance studies scholar Joseph Roach, has described the carnivalesque
marches of Mardi Gras as a "whirling maelstrom of intercultural surroga-
tions, condensed in space and time, each an eddy in the larger circum-Atlantic
vortex."[15] Although Roach's circum-Atlantic "insists on the centrality of
the diasporic and genocidal histories of Africa and the Americas" without
attending to China (or migration from anywhere in Asia), his attention to
how processionals generate meaning in the Atlantic world more generally
leads to a productive consideration of what *More Sweetly Play the Dance*
does.[16] For Roach, surrogation is an open-ended process of substitution that
attends performance, one that continually bodies something forth from the

past. These acts might reinscribe hegemonic histories, but they also facilitate counternarratives and embodied practices that contest the dominant narrative. Building here on Roach's work, I find that Kentridge's installation creates another eddy in the logic of Atlantic discourse, one that challenges many accounts of South African apartheid. Put otherwise, Kentridge moves beyond the frame that emphasizes South Africa's struggle as a black–white one.[17]

Historical icons are few and far between in *More Sweetly Play the Dance*, so the last figure in the procession draws special attention: "the final dance of Dada, on a trolley, *en pointe*, brandishing her Chinese carbine."[18] This image refers to communist-era China through its evocation of *The Red Detachment of Women* (1964), one of the model operas that combines Beijing opera (*jingju*), Western ballet, and Li folk dance from Hainan Island (the opera's source material is a 1961 film and the novel that inspired its creation). The story recounts the tales of a female Red Army unit formed in 1931. As US–China relations thawed during the end of the Mao years, the opera became famous as the cultural performance selected for Richard Nixon to see during his visit to Beijing. The single image of the rifle-toting dancer, therefore, condenses a number of historical referents. Kentridge's vague invocation of Hainan, despite its current reputation as a tourist destination (it is referred to as the Hawaii of China), suggests antipodal connections that work to sustain forms of militant, perhaps even feminist, revolution celebrated in a processional structure that envisions material concerns including housing and health care. The communist collectives bodied forth through the dancer Dada Masilo in the final moments ruptures the insistent linearity of the exhibition. Her slow rotation en pointe reiterates with a difference the robed figure whose whirling dance begins the procession. These spins that bookend the parade, together with the loop of the film itself, recall the logic of eddying in the form of the movement.

These eddies also function in a temporal register. The work plays with temporalities of capitalism and communism. During the 1960s, when *The Red Detachment of Women* premiered, South Africa's apartheid government moved away from mainland China in ideological terms. Indeed, South Africa positioned itself as staunchly anticommunist, which may be one reason the United States took so long to impose sanctions on the regime. The embrace of capitalism involved a turn back to China after that country's post-Mao

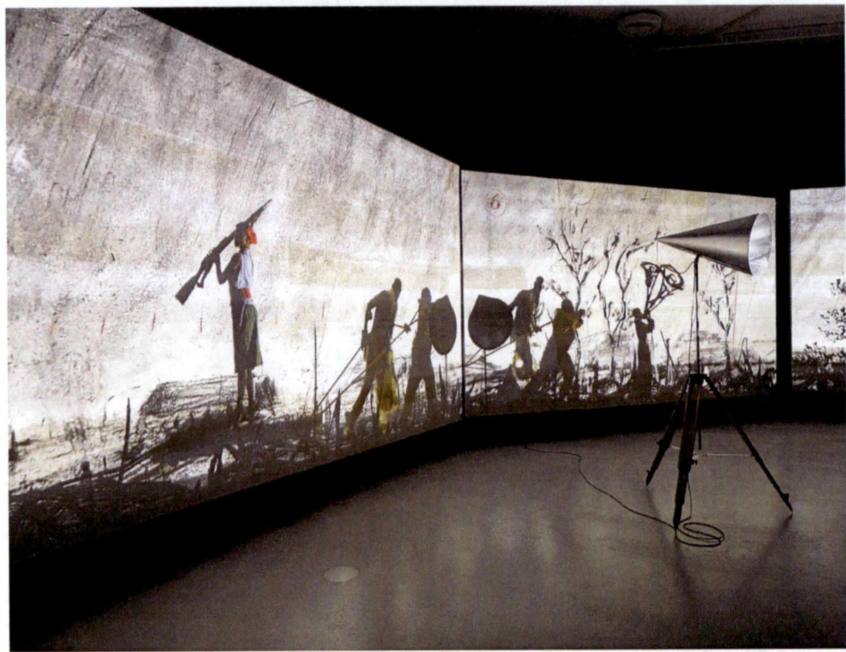

Fig. 5.2. Detail: Dada Masilo concludes the procession with rifle in hand. *More Sweetly Play the Dance,* 2015. William Kentridge exhibition *If We Ever Get to Heaven,* 2015, EYE Film Museum, Amsterdam. Photograph: Studio Hans Wilschut.

market reforms. In Kentridge's piece, the miners might also imply the rapid spread of Chinese investment in their industry across the African continent (e.g., chromium in South Africa, copper in Zambia, and uranium in Namibia). Chinese allusions provide one point of intersection for thinking about the diffusion of capitalism. Kentridge has also said that the 1929 Disney film *The Skeleton Dance* served as an inspiration for some of the sequences.[19] This citation connotes a history of transatlantic relations stretching back to Harold Shaw's direction of the first animated film in South Africa in 1915. Despite the emphasis on the procession of a line of bodies and images, *More Sweetly Play the Dance* does not present a clear position on the many references it amalgamates. Indeed, the very ground on which the figures walk constantly morphs during the course of the looping film.

Kentridge based the environments constructed through the image "on the mining landscapes around Johannesburg."[20] In this regard, they suggest accumulation through resource extraction and may ground postcolonial theorist Homi Bhabha's assertion that the installation presents us with a procession of the dispossessed. Bhabha describes the background as "the nonlandscape around Johannesburg"; I tend to agree with the first half of this assessment, although I do not think one could really locate any exact place in the expressionistic drawings.[21] For me, the suggested physical environment seems like a marsh or wetland, something between land and sea. Perhaps my impression also has to do with the fact that I first saw the installation in a museum that sits on reclaimed land (like so much of the Netherlands). In any case, such a viewing of the installation—as constructed through a seascape—pushes the installation's connotations of potentiality. As Roach has argued in relation to the jazz funeral procession, such events indicate transformation rather than death as finality. I have elsewhere argued that silhouettes (and there are many silhouettes in Kentridge's installation) indicate transitional forms that might be filled with detail in the future.[22] Moreover, the music in *More Sweetly Play the Dance* does not offer a dirge so much as a celebratory process of becoming.

This notion of potentiality occurs in several other ways. The revolutionary Dada signifies imminent change. Bhabha pushes the analysis of transition also in terms of time: "The work confronts us with the iterative rhythm of death/life—not its overcoming—with that which comes before normative politics, moving against the grain and temporality of normative ethics."[23] Put otherwise, this installation does not offer a public sphere or a framework through which acts might be adjudicated. Instead, the piece offers perpetual motion, movement without any clear teleology. Whither China and Chineseness here? Audiences can only imagine this condition. The homage to a decade of Chinese revolutionary fervor remains unexplained (and frequently unnoticed, at least judging by one of the curators' assessments at Zeitz MOCAA).[24] Following this logic, the last image might generate a kind of confusion, a vertigo produced in the wake of a range of references whose relationship to one another remains opaque. On the other hand, emphasizing the Chinese connections might, following the logic of eddying, shift the viewer's orientation as the final dancer rotates en pointe before us.

For example, the allusion to *The Red Detachment of Women* also connotes the Chinese proverb "Women hold up half the sky" (*funu neng ding ban bian tian*). The precise structure and meanings of class and gender relations remain unclear in *More Sweetly Play the Dance*. Nevertheless, Dada Masilo has earned a reputation as a choreographer and dancer whose career has emphasized strong if ill-fated female protagonists from Carmen to Juliet, so her playing the role of an armed revolutionary seems fitting. In what ways does Chinese iconography provide a means to reimagine South Africa under the protection or stewardship of women? *More Sweetly Play the Dance* refuses to elaborate a response. The question takes on greater significance when posed within Zeitz MOCAA, a South African cultural institution initially under the direction of men (first Mark Coetzee and then Azu Nwagbogu before Koyo Kouoh took over in May 2019). In any case, these issues become more pronounced in the next seascape to which I turn, Pieter-Dirk Uys's *African Times*. The name of the play suggests an epic chronicle. In fact, this theatrical event does reference certain histories of South Africa, but the narrative as a whole is far more speculative.

AFRICAN TIMES

For over four decades, from the time of South Africa's relative international isolation to its current political ties to China, Pieter-Dirk Uys has worked as a theater artist and political satirist, attracting the favorable attention of national icons such as Nelson Mandela and before that, the less favorable attention of authorities during the apartheid era. His solo shows involve his playing a number of characters, although he has also written (beginning in the late 1960s) several plays for multiple actors. As scholar April Sizemore-Barber has noted, "[Uys] is the gay Boer-Jew who makes a career out of inhabiting others' subjectivities."[25] Perhaps his own sense of familial displacement (his mother fled the Nazis in 1936 and subsequently committed suicide) has animated his commitments to fight against state violence and to create new bonds of human relation through humor. He has played many famous figures, including former prime minister P. W. Botha and Archbishop Desmond Tutu, with uncanny mimicry of, for example, Tutu's signature laugh. Of all his theatrical activity, Uys is most famous for his alter ego, Evita Bezuindenhout, self-described as "the most famous white woman in South Africa"; this persona grew from a series of weekly columns into an embodied performance in Uys's revue, *Adapt or Dye*.[26] Evita has achieved fame unto herself and continues her own website (separate from her creator's). She has

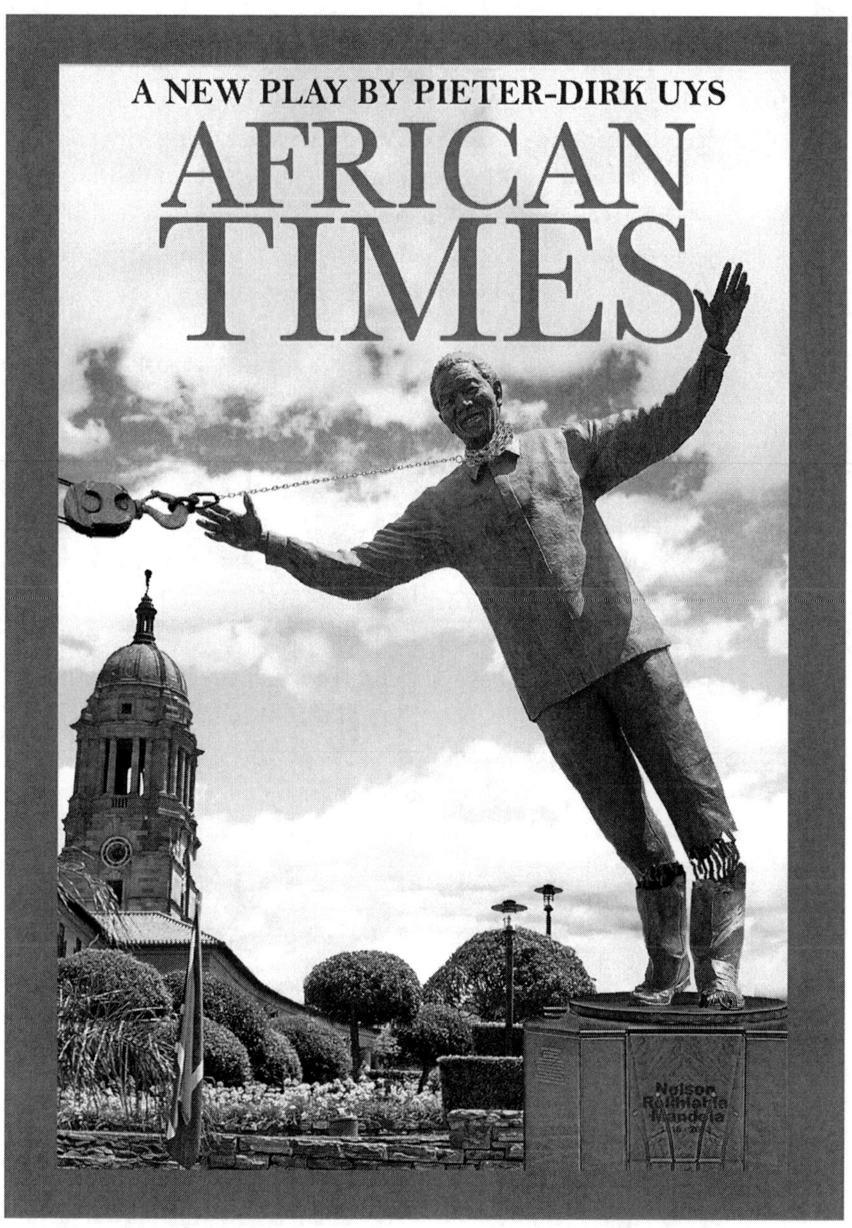

Fig. 5.3. The cover of the published version of *African Times* suggests that Nelson Mandela's envisioned structure for South Africa is falling apart. Courtesy of Pieter-Dirk Uys.

served as a vehicle of social critique well beyond the demise of apartheid, continuing to focus on the various issues that confront the new rainbow nation, including, for example, posting YouTube videos that address immigration.[27] Uys himself has also continued to engage in social justice work, with particular dedication to HIV and AIDS education; indeed, he self-funded a tour of schools from cities to townships, where he addressed issues of sexual health, especially during the period of "denialism" by former president Thabo Mbeki and his health minister, Manto Tshabalala-Msimang. The 2015 National Arts Festival (held in Grahamstown each year since 1974) celebrated Uys's seventieth birthday, with a retrospective of some of his major works as well as two premieres, including *African Times*, which is, to my knowledge, his first creative work to address Chinese–South African relations.

The opening lines of *African Times* suggest a seascape: "There's water everywhere."[28] These are the words of Sibongile, the oldest of three black sisters who reunite at their family compound, called Ubuntu, in the Western Cape. The decaying infrastructure has led to the home's islanding in a futuristic South Africa; the home, despite its name, stands as a metaphor for the condition of the nation, which has apparently been isolated (as the audience soon learns). Describing the country though this specific setting suggests that the promise of *ubuntu* has eroded.

Desmond Tutu has explained the philosophical concept of *ubuntu*, frequently expressed as a worldview and a structure of relations undergirding the new South Africa.

> My humanity is caught up, is inextricably bound up, in yours. . . . It is not, "I think, therefore I am." It says rather: I am human because I belong. I participate. I share. A person with *ubuntu* is open and available to others, affirming of others, does not feel threatened that others are able and good, for he or she has a proper self-assurance that comes from knowing that he or she belongs in a greater whole and is diminished when others are humiliated or diminished, when others are tortured or oppressed, or treated as if they were less than who they are.[29]

African Times does, in fact, explore human connectivity, but Uys's invocation of ubuntu is largely ironic. Set in a dystopian future, the play depicts a South Africa that has returned to relative isolation. Instead of the apartheid government and its critics around the world producing a state of insularity, this time the situation seems to have resulted from the failures of the rainbow nation to meet its ostensible promise.

The adult daughters of a senior statesmen in this new xenophobic South African regime have each chosen a different path in the wake of their mother's death by cancer and their own individual trials (this is, perhaps, the extent to which Uys reiterates Anton Chekhov's famous 1901 drama, *Three Sisters*). Sibongile has taken a leadership role in the ruling political party. A former schoolteacher, the middle sister Nomsa, struggles for a new direction after being raped. The youngest, Karobo, has just returned from China with her father, a South African diplomat, and his new wife, Liu Chen, an English professor from Shanghai. Almost as soon as they arrive, the unseen minister dies of a heart attack. The characters embody larger social dynamics (e.g., the emigrant or the Chinese opportunist). Liu thus serves as the stage device for exploring Chineseness in the play.

The drama opens with Sibongile in conversation with the mechanized voice of Vorster, who is part of the GM2, a high-tech security system. The dialogue occurs on an interior set, a dining room initially draped in sheets. Sibongile is in the midst of preparing for her father's return, a patriarchal restoration that never happens. The water to which she refers has resulted from an apparent leak outside, but the spectators never see anything but this one room during the two-hour duration of the play. The soaked area apparently surrounding the compound helps to construct the claustrophobic atmosphere of the drama, along with the unseen Vorster (who echoes Harold Pinter's Dumb Waiter from his eponymous 1957 play) and the television, which cycles through scenes from the triumphant past of Nelson Mandela (these elements link the play to the screen installations I discussed insofar as all of the artworks address technological mediation).

Political systems never quite come into focus, although their failure seems everywhere evident. Characters reference a "massacre" and "xenophobic attack" in KZN (Kwa-Zulu Natal, a province created in 1994, the coastline of which abuts the Indian Ocean).[30] Sibongile also worries over whether anyone has leaked news of her father's return. Vorster's ongoing warnings (announcing, in a double entendre, "subversion within the safety radius outside Ubuntu") reinforce the sense of imminent danger.[31] But no one actually identifies the source of the threat. At one point, Nomsa asks her sister about Vorster: "Isn't he a grandson to that Boer prime minister on whose watch Biko was murdered?"[32] A prominent antiapartheid activist, Steven Biko was tortured and killed by South African state police in 1977. Nomsa's query foregrounds the contradictions of living in a nation in which one's coworkers, neighbors, and employees might have links to black oppression. The failing infrastructure magnifies the unease. Maintenance requests, including security enhancements, have been continually deferred, despite repeated requests to an unspecified department. The minister's clandestine return elicits the reaction, "You mean our submarines now actually work?"[33]

Uys presents an islanded South Africa, yet one linked to the rest of the globe through underwater channels maneuverable by submarine. Mention of this form of transportation focuses attention on literal processes of eddying. Seamounts (mountains arising from the ocean floor that do not reach the surface) produce several hydraulic phenomena, from deep eddies (swirling currents that pull vessels downward) to tsunamis. Eddies more generally denote currents moving against the main one. Navigators of ocean crafts require knowledge of such aquatic occurrences to avoid sinking their ships. On a metaphoric level, the mercurial quality of maritime travel would seem to apply to the wavering political stability of Uys's South Africa. The only international link that seems to sustain the nation-state's interactions with the rest of the world is China, which again is reduced and embodied through the character of Liu.

In contrast to this very restricted yet insecure space, nostalgic allusions to a more vibrant if still contentious South Africa occur. Karobo explains her homecoming after years of absence, saying "Yes, I missed it. You know, the sea, the air, the Karoo, the wine . . . the *toyi-toyi*. Home."[34] Nomsa responds to her sibling with, "We have wonderful images of the sea-air-Karoo-wine-sun. I'll run some for you tomorrow."[35] What has happened to physical relations in this place? The new iteration of RSA leadership has retreated to the Cape Dutch homestead under the protection of armed security; economic divisions split a country formerly riven by the racial and class lines of apartheid. Potentially violent meetings have yielded to the relative safety of nonengagement, a postmodern nihilism. Nomsa's delineation of proliferating pictures without apparent substance notably excludes the embodied protest of the *toyi-toyi*. Politics in the sense of a public sphere of debate or a corporeal encounter with the other is simply impossible in Uys's African times. Indeed, the play underscores this point near its conclusion when the sisters see their doubles attending a state funeral on television. Political and social life never materializes in anything but simulacra. In this sense, theatricality literally replaces statesmanship, and South African politics in the play become actions without much apparent efficacy.

Representations of Chineseness further this scenario. Liu's first action in the play is to snap a selfie with Sibongile, whom she had never before met. This new family portrait analogizes the domestic sphere to a transnational one, for the minister has sought a relationship with Beijing following what appear to be UN sanctions. The supposedly harmonious transnational family in which Sibongile only just discovers she belongs suggests a kind of Confucian capitalism in which China will have the opportunity to remake its new South African cousin into a desired image; social structures like *guanxi* and filial piety finally produce new opportunities for the Chinese character. Indeed, in the last scene, the three sisters vacate the stage, leaving the Chinese woman Liu alone as master of the house. Such restructuring of power remains underneath the veneer of familial ties and pregnant onstage tableaux.

The material effects such a transition of power engenders never come into focus, but Liu's ties to mainland China significantly and provocatively invert the historical exchanges that saw South Africa and Taiwan (as opposed to the PRC) enter into formal diplomatic and economic relationships during and immediately following the apartheid years, as Gillian Hart has shown in her book *Disabling Globalization*. Black dispossession of land in South Africa was linked to the rise of Taiwanese industrialization *and* the movement of some three hundred Taiwanese factory owners to the eastern areas of the country in places such as Newcastle. Hart demonstrates how "sharply divergent histories of agrarian transformation" in the two states "have shaped the conditions of reproduction of labor, and of global competition."[36]

Such histories remain absent in Uys's staged vision of China. In place of substantive exploration of what new PRC–RSA connections might do, the play offers vague markers of Chineseness and engages in generalized anxieties about sinophilia leading to the loss of South African sovereignty. The audience hears Liu before she enters the stage, and what they hear is a heavily accented voice complaining of the dark and "all that gushing water outside."[37] Because both the Ubuntu compound and South Africa are effectively islanded in the play, Liu eventually likens life at Ubuntu to "life in the Forbidden City."[38] This formulation posits equivalence in terms of the perceived insularity of two places—one Chinese and the other South African—that

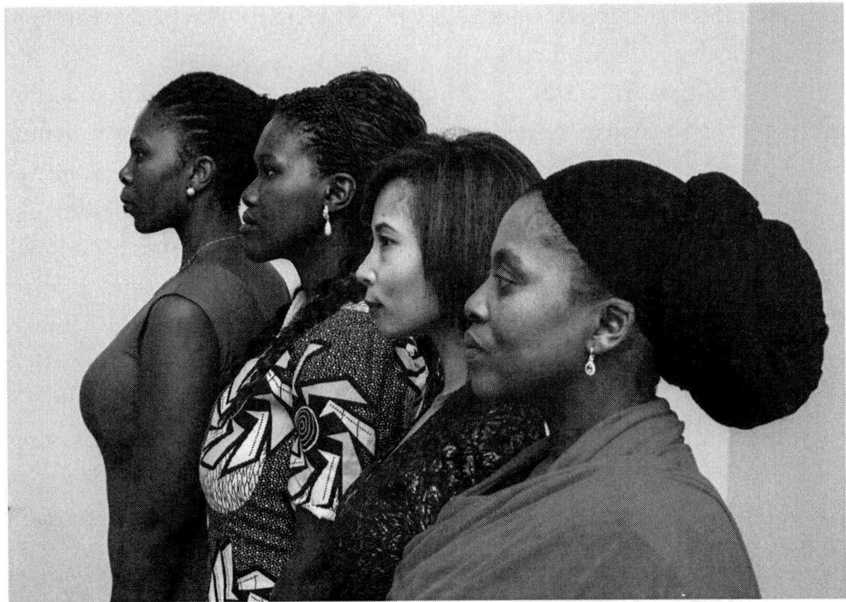

Fig. 5.4. The cast of *African Times*. In the photo, from *left* to *right*, are: Karabo Nkosi (Ntombi Makhutshi), Sibongile Nkosi-Skosana (Peggy Mongoato), Liu Chen (Sue Pyler), and Nomsa Nkosi (Zoliswa Kawe). Photo courtesy of Pieter-Dirk Uys.

are paradoxically also both spaces that serve as seats of diplomacy. Here, the extended exchange between Karabo and Liu begins to shift what a term like ubuntu means in this new South African–Chinese configuration as Karabo explains: "I am what I am because of who we all are."[39] Ultimately, the play does not find in that phrase possibilities of relation and communal being in anything other than exploitative terms. At the conclusion of the piece, Liu starts becoming a subject aware of what such a phrase might mean for her as the Chinese widow of a powerful South African state envoy.

The political dilemmas that I have briefly described within *African Times* recurred as a kind of metacommentary in the material context of the play's debut. Uys's work premiered at the National Arts Festival in Grahamstown as part of "A Season of Pieter-Dirk Uys." Uys both wrote and directed this play for the festival in 2015, a year officially designated "the Year of China in South Africa," with over two hundred events planned across the country over twelve months. Such fanfare included the festival's sponsoring of the Guandong Puppet Art Theatre's "family fare" show in conjunction with the

Chinese Embassy. In contrast, the program billed *African Times* as a "political family drama."[40] Here, it might also be useful to think back to the politics expressed through the rather jaded perspective of Karobo, including her nostalgic invocation of toyi-toyi. The National Arts Festival also included a lineage of protest theater, perhaps most notably in the Baxter Theatre's revival of Barney Simon's 1985 *Born in the RSA*. That production, directed by an original cast member, concerns several intersecting narratives in a kind of "living newspaper" dramaturgy, including the tale of a white university student turned informant. The production ends with a riveting and powerful performance of a running, chanting protest: toyi-toyi. Such juxtapositions within the festival itself render all the more apparent the evacuation of progressive politics imagined through Chinese–South African relations in *African Times*.

Uys adapted his 2015 work from his 1975 play *God's Forgotten*, a production scripted approximately half in Afrikaans and half in English. Although the plot is relatively consistent, the differences prove instructive in thinking about the changing status of South Africa and its place in a globalized economy. In this regard, several elements in *God's Forgotten* bear mentioning. The three white sisters end up as the remaining members of the Brand family and part of the ruling class in the segregated nation-state. They continually attribute the offstage violence that permeates the play to black folk, including an unspecified group of "black terrorists," whom the eldest sibling, Tosca, insists murdered the Afrikaaner statesman, despite testimony to the contrary that he died of natural causes "in the lift!"[41] The character of Liu has its origins in an American character named Gudrun Vanbeck, who is of German descent. At the end of the play, Gudrun plans to leave South Africa.

These details address the contemporary relations of power. The linguistic address speaks to the policy concerning mandatory education in Afrikaans and English passed in 1955, which partially fueled the later Soweto Riots in 1976. When the play premiered in 1975, the United States had not yet passed sanctions against the apartheid regime (which did not occur until the mid-1980s despite the UN General Assembly's call for a boycott in the early 1960s). The war to which the dialogue refers and that caused the death of Tosca's husband connoted the ongoing fighting in what was then South West Africa (present-day Namibia). The South African Border War (also known as the Namibian War of Independence and the Angolan Bush War) raged from 1966 to 1990; South Africa successfully enlisted US sympathy in an attempt to contain Soviet influence.

Smaller variations between *God's Forgotten* and *African Times* further reveal political issues of the day. Aliza (Karabo's equivalent) also expresses nostalgia for home, but no toyi-toyi is mentioned in the 1970s.[42] Aliza does refer to the lack of attention given to South Africa as a whole, referring to the "white dictatorship."[43] Sarah (Nomsa's equivalent) speaks of South Africa's insularity, noting "five years of total isolation."[44] That isolation leads to Aliza watching slides of the natural beauty of the cape, including its beaches. However, Sarah demonstrates how the ecological beauty of the sea might depend on one's perspective as she recalls, "Many years ago, there was a political prison near here surrounded by water."[45] Robben Island, of course, had been used as just such a prison from the seventeenth century through the premiere of the play to the end of apartheid. Like *African Times*, this play finally likens one's place in the South African nation-state to a theatrical role. The state funeral for the deceased diplomat occurs with actresses who perform the dual roles of family and citizen. Ultimately, *African Times* repeats with a difference the narrative of *God's Forgotten*. Black and Chinese power have supplanted, respectively, that of the Afrikaner and the American. The more recent drama pivots on a new channel across the Indian Ocean between China and South Africa.

DALeast

As my last example of South African seascapes, I turn to DALeast, a street artist born in Wuhan, who lives in Cape Town. Born in 1984, he began graffitiing with a group in China in 2004. Since that time, he has achieved an international reputation, traveling approximately half of the year to work on commissions for murals in cities around the globe. Although he tends to keep personal details out of the public domain, DALeast likely represents what Yoon Jung Park calls a "transmigrant," a term she only applied to "the remigrated Taiwanese South Africans, the industrialists who came to South Africa during apartheid under a most attractive incentive scheme and left" when conditions negatively altered profit margins.[46] However, Park conducted her research from 1999 to 2005, and China has, since that time, produced new streams of overseas laborers, an ever-swelling upwardly mobile middle class as well as a new generation of elites that have shifted and will undoubtedly continue to alter the demographics of the Chinese population in South Africa. In any case, my interest in DALeast is not that he embodies an empirical demographic trend, but that his work provides a different way to consider how Chinese circulations in South Africa might provide new perspectives on globalization.

I consider several images of his street art extant in various sections of the city. DALeast does not explicitly mark Chineseness in his work with a lexicon of easily identifiable signifiers. Instead, his work most frequently adorns the facades of public, usually urban, spaces with what look like three-dimensional cybernetic animals. His technique of painting individual lines creates the impression of intricate, layered structures of metal strands or shards that form futuristic, industrial creatures. DALeast's murals suggest something of what Jennifer Parker-Starbuck has argued in relation to *War Horse* (a British theatrical production that involved South Africa's Handspring Puppet Company). Parker-Starbuck writes that the puppet play reveals the specific history of the European front in WWII that saw "a disconnected relationship with the animal, resulting in its reappropriation by machines."[47] South Africa has markedly different historical relationships to animals from either Europe or China. A tension emerges here between an ecology that supports a touristic infrastructure based on viewing wildlife and a relationship with a new world power that is on its way to becoming the world's largest extractor of resources. DALeast's work addresses some of these tensions, albeit not directly.

The image titled *Deer Park* (2012) sits on the slopes of Table Mountain in Vredehoek (which means "corner of peace"); technically, this artwork occupies a space in the Rocklands Rd Park, a fenced lawn and children's playground that occupies the area immediately below the larger nature reserve. In 2001, Vredehoek was reported to be 82.75 percent white, with English and Afrikaans estimated as being spoken by nearly 90 percent of the residents (in contrast, the white population of Cape Town as a whole was estimated in 2011 to be about one third of the total). I mention demographic figures here only to give some context for the neighborhood in which one finds this image. Given that the art splays across an edifice on a hill, the overall effect is to create a vista that includes, on a clear day, the ocean in the distance beyond the trees. To see the work in its setting is, therefore, to encounter a seascape. The street art works in conjunction with the environment to provide less an

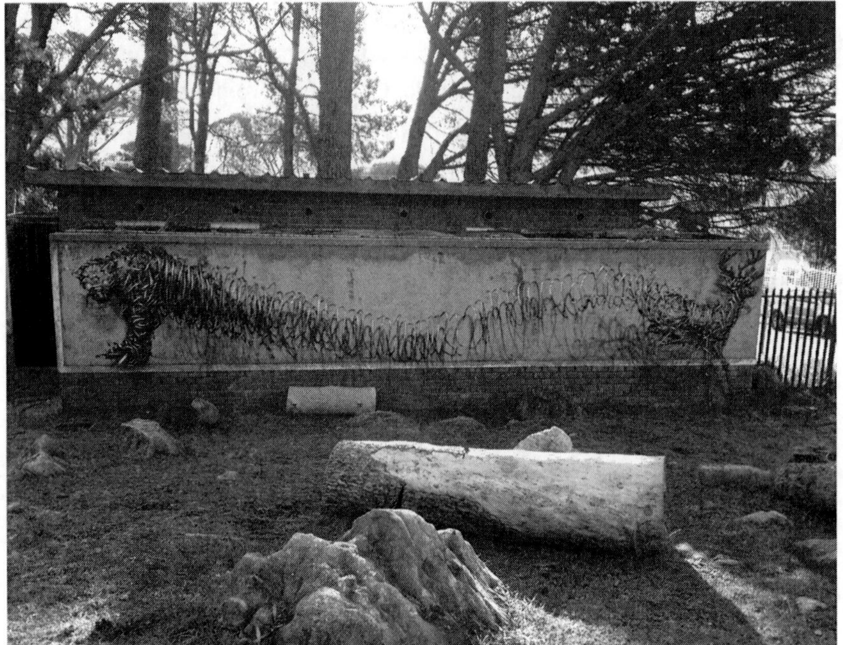

Fig. 5.5. DALeast's *Deer Park* in Vredehoek. On a clear day, the viewer
can see the sea through the trees. Photo: Marc Major.

image in public space than an image that helps to reimagine how, for whom,
and for what that space has been constructed. DALeast's work elicits a query
about who and what might have been displaced to create a scenic view over
the ocean.

Deer Park presses on the ostensible division between organic and industrial. On the edge of the state park, the painting marks the Anthropocene
in terms of human elimination of indigenous wildlife, such as the cape lion
(hunted to extinction when Europeans arrived). DALeast has attached the
feline predator to another species, perhaps a fallow deer introduced to
the region in the mid-1800s from Europe. According to at least one source,
the colonial desires to refashion the Cape into a semblance of Europe have
left a legacy of "invasive," species including fallow deer and the famously
fecund rabbits of Robben Island.[48] The unspooling connection between the
wild cat and the stag suggests something about the alteration of normative
relationships between predator and prey. It also provokes thoughts about

how one defines species and what sort of dependencies exist among them, particularly given Cape Town's ignominious history of racial segregation and the ways such divisions have persisted in various permutations through gentrification. In this oblique manner, DALeast provokes a consideration of race within this vista of arrival and departure.

Although not a seascape as such, I discuss another site of DALeast's work to elaborate some of the themes of his work and the way they elicit a continual interpreting of Cape Town as space. I discuss these murals to foreground mechanisms and thematics of mobility in a city that for decades had many laws curtailing movement. About a half hour's walk down the hill from *Deer Park, Raiden-Ex 1* (2014), another of DALeast's animals, adorns the walls of an underpass. The city has turned that otherwise neglected concrete area into the Mill Street Bridge Skate Park. Although this gentrification project also aims at youth, the demographic skews toward teens. Perhaps this transformation explains the title (which remains unseen unless one looks on the internet). "Raiden" is also the name of a *Mortal Kombat* (a popular video game) character who happens to wear a conical coolie hat. I would not push the associations here too far, save to mention that any of DALeast's intentional or inadvertent referents to Chineseness, if they exist, remain oblique. But this does not mean that DALeast does not offer a relevant commentary on globalization.

Raiden Ex-1 depicts another hybrid cat caught in motion, its paws attached to what look like spinning wheels. The image approximates an experience of velocity refracted in the movement on the street and in the park itself. Whether cars or skateboards, these modes of travel also create relationships between the organic and the engineered. Enda Duffy elaborates this assessment, writing in *The Speed Handbook* that "the vehicle as prosthesis takes over some of the powers of locomotion of the body, then demands of it new intensities of sensory perception."[49] DALeast captures something of the urban feel of traffic in his image, asking us to consider kinesthesia and, in the case of the skateboarders doing kickflips and indy grabs off the ramps, proprioception. The lion rolling along the street encourages a questioning of mammal and machine. Although Duffy does not discuss race specifically, in South Africa in particular (but also, for example, in the former segregation of buses and trains in countries like the United States), mechanical means of movement have been and to a lesser extent remain racialized. Even today, one

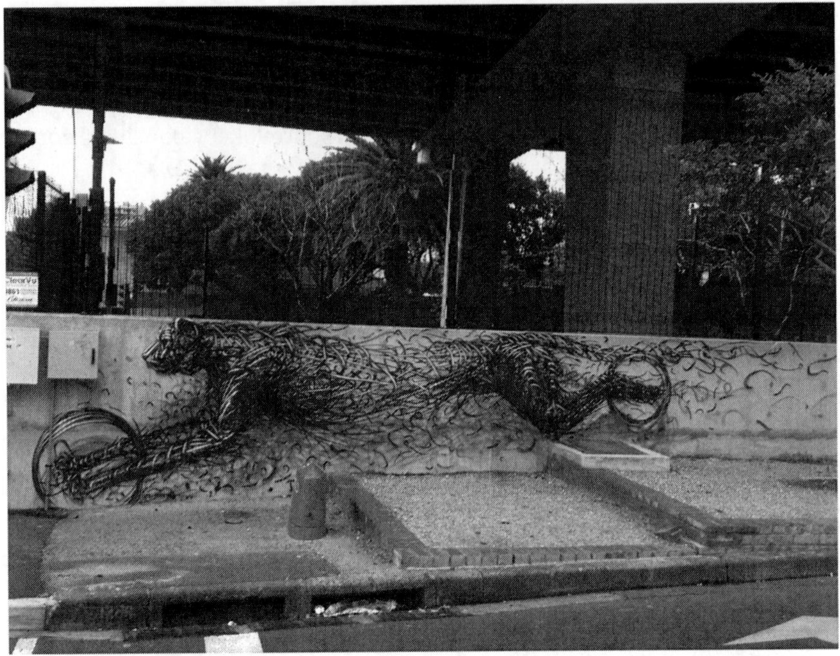

Fig. 5.6. DALeast's cyborg cat cruises alongside the skatepark parallel to traffic.
Photo: Marc Major.

can still catch someone walking down the highway to the township from the city. The cost of owning and maintaining cars, as Makhulu also notes, helps to maintain the segregation of Cape Town neighborhoods underserved (purposefully or not) by public transport. In this case, a bus station sits opposite the entrance to the skate park.

Another of DALeast's creations, a bird taking flight, covers the left-hand side of the gated entrance to the recreational space; the two images together in their particular location by the skate park and bus stop suggest different forms of mobility. Apartheid-era authorities had policed communities precisely to keep them from moving, to keep them separated. These images, then, counter such a history by showing hybrid animals in a morphing landscape that recalls Cape Town's much longer history as a port city. The murals suggest continually evolving forms through the mixture and juxtaposition of different elements; such exchanges characterize ports and lead us back to seascapes.

Following this history, we might pursue DALeast's mechanized fauna to Woodstock, a suburb just outside Cape Town proper, one that once lay adjacent to the infamous District Six. Unlike the forced relocations that occurred next door, Woodstock remained a gray area, where people of different races mixed. In a parking lot, DALeast's *Parking E* (2011) depicts perhaps a fish eagle or osprey, with wheels for talons, in the process of landing. An actual minaret attached to a nearby building shapes part of the background. This scene suggests some of the diversity in this municipality. Never a large population, the Muslim community has nevertheless been a consistent presence in the Cape from the period of the Dutch East India Company forward. A site of arrival on the edge of Table Bay, Woodstock contained one of the city's most renowned beaches before land reclamation altered the topography. The area was repurposed for industrial use. Woodstock has since become an increasingly gentrified hipster neighborhood, but it remains tied to a history of ocean currents.[50] The coat of arms continues to feature a bisected image of a shipwreck above a horse and rider, an apparent tribute to Dutch East India Company employee Wolradd Woltemade.[51] Before he and his horse perished, this legendary figure rescued several passengers of the vessel *De Jonge Thomas*, one of the many ships that met its end in the waves off the coast. *Parking E* does not comment directly on these various processes of urban development. Consistent with DALeast's other works, it offers a point of contrast, one through which to consider various kinds of mobility as well as the ways in which ostensibly natural inhabitants of the region, such as the raptor, have altered in the wake of the global traffic through the city.

Parking D, another image, decorates a wall perpendicular to *Parking E* and suggests one of South Africa's species of long-horned antelopes. Its medusa-like crest of antlers, together with its particularly wiry body, suggests mutation. DALeast's menagerie indicates industrial processes that forever alter how organic beings inhabit the world, potentially demonstrating how capitalism runs amok but also the sorts of unexpected adaptations that occur in what science and technology scholar Donna Haraway calls the Chthulucene, which is the name she gives to our era of multispecies networks.[52] Haraway sees the Chthulucene as a corrective to the discourse of the Anthropocene, which emphasizes human effects on the environment. Instead, she places more emphasis on interaction. The exhibition of these two creatures, at a site where people purposefully stop, contrasts with the

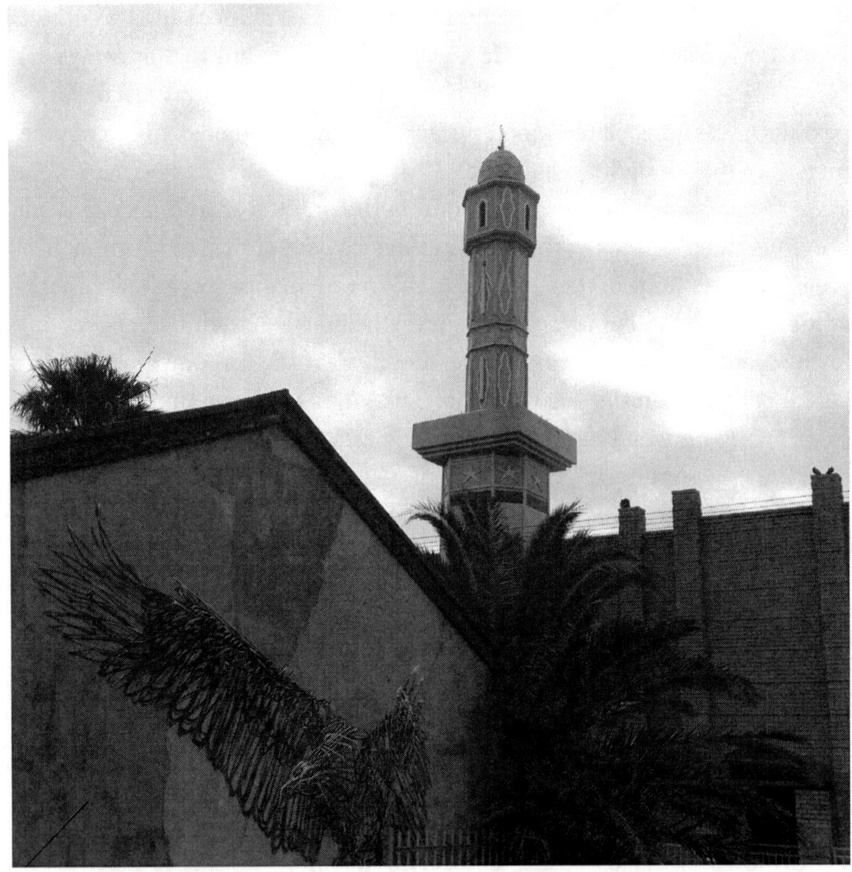

Fig. 5.7. The minaret forms the background for DAleast's *Parking E*.
Photo: Marc Major.

kind of parallel velocity established at the skate park. In general, they allow for more sustained contemplation of the works but without the constructed (in the sense of intentionally preserved) beauty of Deer Park. *Parking D* and *Parking E* designate and address city animals (despite the Woodstock's designation as a suburb). The barbed wire that forms part of the frame of the images underscores the insecurity of this kind of environment. It reminds viewers of the massive spatial control orchestrated by Cape Town and South Africa's urban planners.

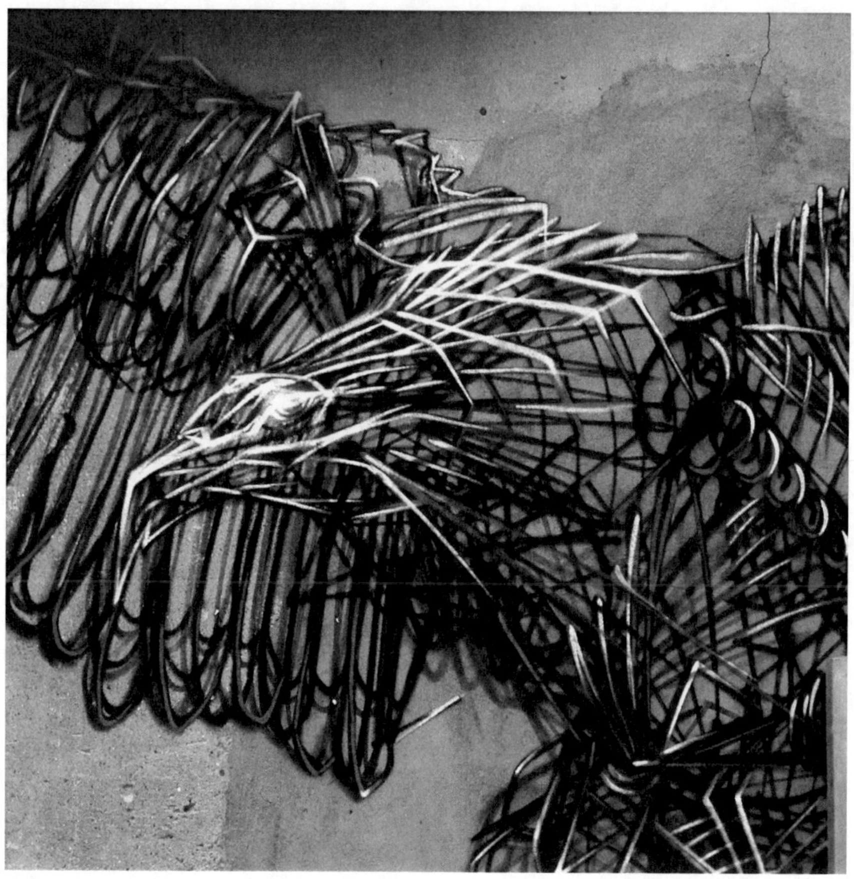

Fig. 5.8. DAleast's *Parking E* might suggest animals' adaptive capacities in the Chthulucene. Photo: Marc Major.

Representations of China in the seascapes I have discussed in this chapter operate explicitly through theatricality. One thing substitutes for another. The precarity of Chinese migrants interrupts, supplements, and potentially displaces the specific postcolonial black articulations that might characterize several exhibitions at Zeitz MOCAA, even as the black dancer in Kentridge's installation in the same museum reenacts a Chinese revolutionary. A master role player, Pieter-Dirk Uys updates the cast of an older play to account for a South Africa purportedly under black and Chinese control; those political

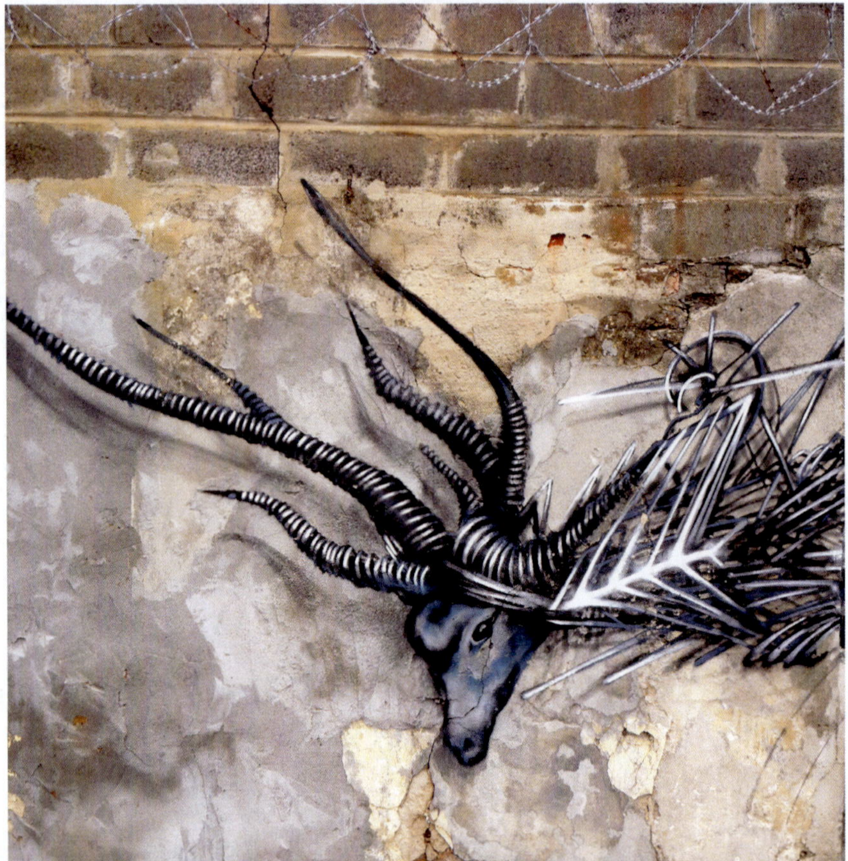

Fig. 5.9. Detail of *Parking D*. Photo: Marc Major.

voices are ostensibly performed by doubles on national television. DALeast uses intricate graffiti to visualize where the organic and mechanical have completely merged into cybernetic organisms. Such depictions project a world in transition, one in which Chineseness understood in various ways, from a force that displaces sovereignty in *African Times* to one that provides a model of armed hope in *More Sweetly Play the Dance,* alters the way we see and understand a nation-state in a relatively recent process of establishing itself as a potential beacon of democracy or as something else.

That potential for something to emerge not in spite of but through forces of globalization—particularly the political, economic, and social intersections produced in relation to Chineseness—works in part by scrambling time. Rather than a linear trajectory of one thing transforming into another, the various seascapes swirl together a number of different temporalities. These processes specifically merge the South African, Dutch, and Chinese elements in the seascapes I have described. *Eddying* is the term I use to link these processes of configuration, as it implies a kind of confusion and reorientation—in the ways that Chineseness is understood, in the convergence of Indian and Atlantic oceanic currents, in the understanding of life and death. Eddying is perhaps the most speculative logic engaged in this book; what lies on the horizon of a Chinese-inflected South Africa remains very much in an imagined future that different artists have respectively framed with apprehension or promise.

NOTES

1. Lin Songtian, "South Africa and China Are Beneficial Partners," *Pretoria News*, February 27, 2018, accessed June 9, 2018, https://www.iol.co.za /pretoria-news/south-africa-and-china-are-beneficial-partners-13508542.

2. Fatima Moose, "Trade, Tourism, and Education: China's Impact on South Africa is Growing – Part I," *The Daily Vox*, July 8 2017, accessed June 9, 2018, https://www .thedailyvox.co.za/investment-education-chinas-influence-africa-rise-fatima-moosa/.

3. Mark Fleishman, "Introduction," *Performing Migrancy and Mobility in Africa: Cape of Flows*, ed. Mark Fleishman (New York: Palgrave Macmillan, 2015), 1 and 3 respectively.

4. Anne-Maria Makhulu, *Making Freedom: Apartheid, Squatter Politics, and the Struggle for Home* (Durham: Duke University Press, 2015).

5. Loren Kruger, *Imagining the Edgy City: Writing, Performing, and Building Johannesburg* (Oxford: Oxford University Press, 2013), 10.

6. Ufrieda Ho, *Paper Sons and Daughters: Growing up Chinese in South Africa* (Athens: Ohio University Press, 2011). See also Darryl Accone, *All Under Heaven: The Story of a Chinese Family in South Africa* (Claremont, South Africa: New Africa Books, 2004), and Rachel Bright, *Chinese Labour in South Africa, 1902–1910: Race, Violence, and Global Spectacle* (London: Palgrave Macmillan, 2013).

7. https://zeitzmocaa.museum/artists/isaac-julien/.

8. James A. Hepokoski offers a thorough formal analysis of the aria in his "Genre and Content in Mid-Century Verdi: 'Addio, del passato' ('La Traviata,' Act III)," *Cambridge Opera Journal* 1, no. 3 (Nov. 1989): 249–276.

9. The piece was part of the exhibition by William Kentridge, *If We Ever Get to Heaven*, April 24–August 30, 2015. *More Sweetly Play the Dance* was also exhibited at the Marian Goodman Gallery in London (September–October of 2015) and New York (Jan. 12–Feb. 20, 2016); it was initially conceived in response to commissions for an

outdoor wall in Bad Rothefelde and a screen installation for the EYE. It was created in a studio in Johannesburg.

10. Jaap Guldemond, "More Sweetly Play the Dance," in *William Kentridge: More Sweetly Play the Dance*, eds. Marente Bloemheuval and Jaap Guldemond (Amsterdam: naio10, 2015), 7.

11. Caroline Christov-Bakargiev in conversation with William Kentridge. D. Cameron, C. Christov-Bakargiev, and J. M. Coetzee, *William Kentrdige* (New York: Phaidon Press, 1999), 8. The mechanics of Kentridge's animation process are elaborated in Lucia Saks, *Cinema in a Democratic South Africa: The Race for Representation* (Bloomington and Indianapolis: Indiana University Press, 2010), 169.

12. William Kentridge, "If We Ever Get to Heaven: Occasional Notes on *More Sweetly Play the Dance*," *William Kentridge: More Sweetly Play the Dance*, ed. Marente Bloemheuval and Jaap Guldemond (Amsterdam: naio10, 2015), 47.

13. *More Sweetly Play the Dance* press release, Marion Goodman Gallery, accessed March 29, 2017, http://mariangoodman.com/exhibition/2608/press-release.

14. *More Sweetly Play the Dance* press release, Marion Goodman Gallery.

15. Joseph Roach, *Cities of the Dead: Circum-Atlantic Performance* (New York: Columbia University Press, 1996), 251.

16. Roach, *Cities*, 4.

17. Even in texts such as Annie E. Coombes's *History After Apartheid: Visual Culture and Public Memory in a Democratic South Africa*, which explicitly moves beyond black versus white, the emphasis still falls on black and white. Other categorizations within the apartheid system, including "coloured" and "Indian," receive scant attention.

18. Kentridge, "Heaven," 47.

19. Kentridge, "Heaven," 17–18

20. Kentridge, "Heaven," 42.

21. Homi K. Bhbha, "Processional Ethics," *Artforum International* 55, no. 2 (Oct. 2016): 10, 230–237, 292.

22. See Sean Metzger, *Chinese Looks: Fashion, Performance, Race* (Bloomington and Indianapolis: Indiana University Press, 2014), chapter 4.

23. Bhabha, "Ethics."

24. I thank Sven Christian, the Adrianne Iann Assistant Curator of Books and Works on Paper at Zeitz MOCAA, for this observation.

25. April Sizemore-Barber, "A Queer Transition: Whiteness in the Prismatic, Post-Apartheid Drag Performance of Pieter-Dirk Uys and Steven Cohen," *Theatre Journal* 68 (June): 201.

26. "Evita se Perron," accessed December 19, 2019, https://evita.co.za/.

27. Her website is https://evita.co.za/darling/who-is-evita/, accessed March 27, 2017.

28. Pieter-Dirk Uys, *African Times* (Vlaeberg: Missing Ink, 2015), 9.

29. Desmond Tutu, *No Future Without Forgiveness* (New York: Random House, 1999), 31.

30. Uys, *Times*, 9 and 21.

31. Uys, *Times*, 21.

32. Uys, *Times*, 22.

33. Uys, *Times*, 14.

34. Uys, *Times*, 38.

35. Uys, *Times*, 39.

36. Gillian Hart, *Disabling Globalization: Places of Power in Post-Apartheid South Africa* (Berkeley and Los Angeles: University of California Press, 2002), 10.

37. Uys, *Times*, 30.

38. Uys, *Times*, 74.

39. Uys, *Times*, 74.

40. *Programme*, National Arts Festival, 150 and 74 respectively.

41. Pieter-Dirk Uys, *God's Forgotten. Theatre Two: New South African Drama*, ed. Stephen Gray (London: AD. Donker, 1981), 169.

42. Uys, *Forgotten*, 151.

43. Uys, *Forgotten*, 153.

44. Uys, *Forgotten*, 154.

45. Uys, *Forgotten*, 179.

46. Yoon Jung Park, *A Matter of Honour: Being Chinese in South Africa* (Lanham, MD: Rowman and Littlefield), 2008.

47. Jennifer Parker-Starbuck, "Animal Ontologies and Media Representations: Robotics, Puppets and the Real of *War Horse*," *Theatre Journal* 65, no. 3 (October 2013): 379.

48. http://www.capetowninvasives.org.za/project/animals/about, accessed March 30, 2017. On the rabbit controversy, see http://www.nytimes.com/2010/02/01/world/africa/01safrica.html, accessed March 30, 2017.

49. Enda Duffy, *The Speed Handbook: Velocity, Pleasure, Modernism* (Durham: Duke University Press, 2009), 6.

50. Such gentrification is not without controversy; see https://www.theguardian.com/cities/2014/aug/12/gentrification-woodstock-cape-town-suburb-hipster-heaven, accessed March 31, 2017.

51. The information about Woodstock is taken from Gabriel and Louis Athiros, *The Cape Odyssey 103: Featuring Woodstock South Africa's Earliest Suburb* (Tokai: Historical Media cc, 2014).

52. Donna Haraway, *Staying with the Trouble: Making Kin in the Chthulucene* (Durham: Duke University Press, 2016).

EPILOGUE

DALEAST'S CYBORGS POINT TO NEW CONFIGURATIONS IN AN age of Chinese-inflected globalization, and his depiction of fanciful fauna brings me to a set of creatures constructed by another Chinese artist living abroad: Cai Guo-Qiang. Cai's own journey connects New York City (his place of residence since the mid-1990s) to Shanghai and might again remind spectators of networks initiated and sustained among far-flung locales by early transnational corporations such as the Dutch East India Company. Cai himself manifests relationships among seascapes, globalization, and theatricality. During his days at university, he studied stage design at the Shanghai Theater Academy. He subsequently moved to Japan (1986–1995) and New York (1995–present). His personal and professional trajectories establish a kind of migratory movement, shaped in part by littoral spaces and islands, that moves from China to the Atlantic seaboard of the United States. His shows have taken place from Australia to Brazil, and his individual works have been part of exhibitions from Korea to South Africa. His fireworks for the Beijing Olympics reached an enormous audience through various screen media. Such expansiveness extends the narrative of Chinese immigration to encompass the cosmopolitan mobility achieved by a globally recognized artist. Cai's 2014 installation *The Ninth Wave* (*jiu bolang*) invited the viewer to consider the Chinese Atlantic as an analytical rubric as opposed to designating an actual place. Indeed, like all the various streams of Atlantic studies, the Chinese Atlantic is a conceptual metaphor; in this regard, Cai's artwork provided a window onto the diffusion of Chinese cultural and economic production (and destructive environmental impact) across East and West that suggests the ongoing implications of my study.

With *The Ninth Wave*, Cai created a large-scale seascape that references China's historical entanglement in European colonial empires and the legacies of such contacts and exchanges. From July 12 through July 17, 2014, a barge containing Cai's *The Ninth Wave* sailed from his hometown, Quanzhou, in Fujian Province, to Shanghai. The flatboat carried a wooden fishing vessel adorned with ninety-nine pieces shaped and decorated as different mammals to create the effect of a floating display of taxidermy. The overall piece suggested a kind of perversion of Noah's Ark, for the artist posed many of the creatures as if they were desperately clinging for life. The journey along the littoral portion of China's *dongbu* region retraced a path long important to merchants and one pivotal to the First Opium War (1839–1842), when British imperialism brought ships from Macau and Guangzhou (previously Canton) to Xiamen (previously Amoy), Ningbo, and Shanghai. The installation arrived at the Power Station of Art, on the site of what had been the Pavilion of the Future at the 2010 Shanghai World Expo, which has more recently been converted to the first state-operated contemporary art museum in China. The voyage of the barge implied a historical trajectory, capturing China's progression from a "semicolonial" kingdom to a global power.

The artist used a literal maritime passage to contextualize some of the formal and thematic concerns of his sizeable seascape; *The Ninth Wave* refers to both his fishing boat (inclusive of its cargo) and the exhibition of which it formed a central part. Cai magnified the scale of this seascape through a performance entitled "Elegy: Explosion Event" on August 8, 2014, when he released a large array of fireworks and colored smoke from the barge, transforming not only a section of Shanghai's Huangpu River but also the atmosphere above the city into a theatrical spectacle. Opalescent vapors plumed in the sky, reminding viewers of China's omnipresent air pollution. The combination of these acts and images would seem to celebrate China's progress in terms of the technological and scientific mastery of combustible chemicals even as they suggest that foreign imperialism, together with China's own development, have produced a global environmental apocalypse.

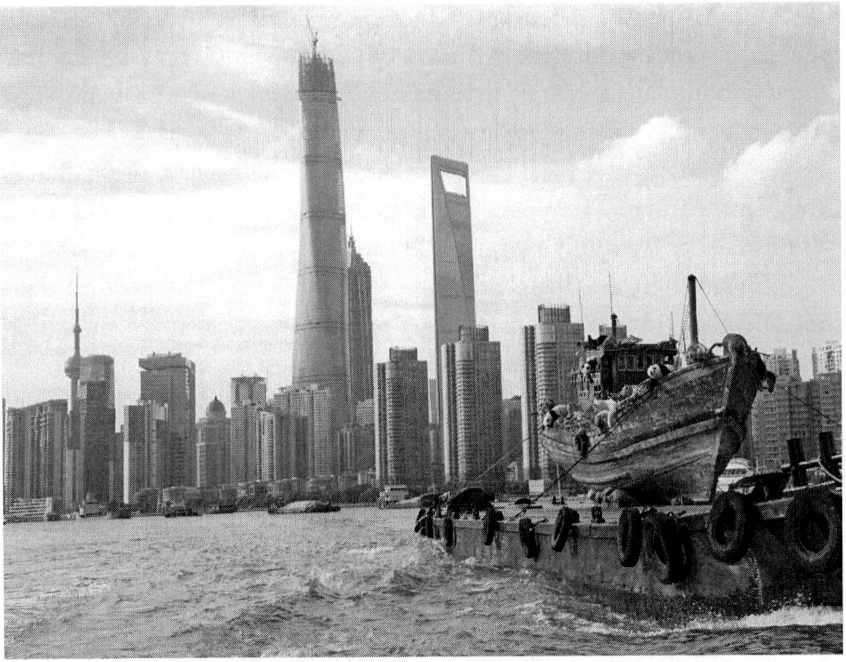

Fig. 6.1. Cai Guo-Qiang (b. 1957), *The Ninth Wave*, 2014. Installation incorporating ninety-nine life-sized replicas of animals, a wooden fishing boat, one white flag, and an electric fan. 1700 × 455 × 580 cm (669⁵⁄₁₆ × 179⅛ × 228⅜ in.). Power Station of Art, Shanghai. *The Ninth Wave* sailing on the Huangpu River by the Bund, Shanghai, 2014. Photo by Wen-Yu Cai, courtesy Cai Studio.

By constructing a wide-ranging archive of marine perspectives across vast distances and through several media, the installation offered a number of vantage points that facilitate interpretations of globalization and its antecedents. Seascapes alternately stabilize the perpetual motion of the sea and attempt to analogize this phenomenon through a number of aesthetic devices, which this book has explored. Seascapes emphasize not only what but how we see, calling attention to the desires and perceptual apparatuses that facilitate visualizing the global. From this perspective, Cai created a historically weighty construction of Chinese globalization in *The Ninth Wave*. The route between Shanghai's *pudong* and *puxi* regions (respectively, the east and west banks of the river, with towering skyscrapers on one side and colonial architecture on the other) illustrates the condition of a "re-globalizing"

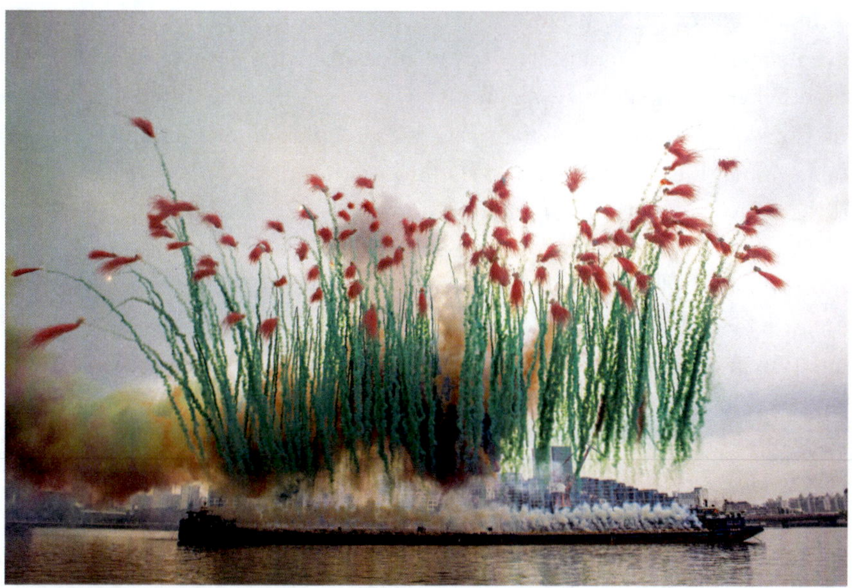

Fig. 6.2. Cai Guo-Qiang (b. 1957), *Elegy: Explosion Event for the Opening of Cai Guo-Qiang: The Ninth Wave*, 2014. Realized on the riverfront of the Power Station of Art, Shanghai, on August 8, 5:00 p.m., approximately 8 minutes. Fireworks, ephemeral. Photo by Lin Yi, courtesy Cai Studio.

metropolis.[1] The onboard menagerie of everything from camels to pandas suggested histories of transcontinental trade; the former recalled transport dating all the way back to the Silk Road, while the latter called to mind China's current nonhuman ambassadors, loaned out by the Chinese government to zoos around the world. Panda breeding offers a case study in biopolitical management that extends well beyond China's borders. In a related vein, the animals drifting down the Huangpu gestured to a biblical story about nothing less than the survival of species.

Cai's vessel sailing through Shanghai has genealogies that cross both local and transnational referents. The smoke erupting from the barge on August 8 (exactly six years after the opening of the Olympics in Beijing) visualized the cataclysmic potential of industrial development gone awry, and several Shanghai residents reportedly feared that some sort of corporate disaster had produced the multihued clouds.[2] The event conjured memories of sixteen thousand pig carcasses that surfaced in nearby Jiaxing the year before when animals fatally afflicted with porcine circovirus floated downriver.[3] Such events constitute a material history of environmental devastation. Twining together catastrophe and opportunity, Cai's work demonstrated the contradictions of globalization by fabricating an adaptation of a Judeo-Christian fable reimagined for China. Cai's appropriation of this myth reversed the direction of adaptation in which his contemporary Isaac Julien engaged in *Ten Thousand Waves* (when the latter artist invoked the goddess Mazu). Such multidirectional exchanges characterize Chinese Atlantic seascapes. *The Ninth Wave* pulls together Cai's own twenty-first century transnational circulation and the work's allusion to global greenhouse gases, together with the much older circulations of religious iconography and objects of diplomacy and commerce. These components of the exhibition mark China's relationships—however vexed—with other regions of the world now and in the past.

A GENEALOGY OF *THE NINTH WAVE*

Cai's *The Ninth Wave* explicitly or implicitly cited several antecedents, but his title directly references Ivan Aivazovsky's eponymous painting from 1850. This piece is the best known of some six thousand works by the Armenian Russian; it depicts half a dozen individuals clinging to flotsam as the largest in a series of waves (the ninth) threatens to engulf them. As a preeminent seascapist in and beyond his lifetime, Aivazovsky repeatedly chose the ports along the Crimean Peninsula on the Black Sea for his subject. His position as painter for the Russian Navy shaped his interest because, in this professional capacity, he would encounter both training exercises and actual conflict. Several of Aivazovsky's canvases document and imagine the Crimean War (1853–1856), a conflict immortalized to generations of English speakers through Alfred Lord Tennyson's "Charge of the Light Brigade" (1854) and references to Florence Nightingale. This conflict, the impact of which can still be felt in geopolitical divisions, suggests the sorts of transnational encounters nascent within the seascape and from which globalization emerges as much, for example, as do Aivazovsky's own travels from Russia to the United States.

The Ninth Wave further interrogated European imperialism's relationship to globalization. To float down the Huangpu River and gaze at its west bank is to confront colonial construction in the form of the architecture of the Bund. According to local lore, a sign at the northern end of this stretch (the entrance to Huangpu Park) read, "No dogs or Chinese allowed." Cai's piece similarly raised questions about humans and their relationship to animals as well as the very definition of humanity itself (remembering that Cai's ark contains no people). Mel Chen has used the term *animacies* in order to consider sentience and liveness. Chen develops animacy as "an often racialized and sexualized means of conceptual and affective mediation between human and inhuman, animate and inanimate."[4] Chen's scholarship applied to Cai pushes a reading of the artist's concerns with environmental degradation and the ways in which animal-like representations substitute for people in Cai's *The Ninth Wave*. Indeed, the literal infrastructure of the Bund leads, in Cai's work, to apparent human destruction and the survival of a few other species. The precise relationship of these mammals to homo sapiens remains unclear. Nevertheless, following Chen's notion of animacies, we might understand Cai's work as a provocation that queries what forms of life we deem expendable or salvageable in this current moment of ecological crisis within formerly colonized (or at least semicolonized) places.

These concerns with Cai's creatures on the ark might further be unpacked if we understand them as (not quite) taxidermy. Cai's team constructed the bodies out of wool fitted onto Styrofoam. A naturally occurring fiber, the material cover in this case had been painted and reshaped. Performance scholar Jennifer Parker-Starbuck has written that, although "a dead or lifeless arrangement (taxis) of skin (derma) seems the furthest thing from the liveliness/liveness of theatre and theatrical languages," such immobile objects nevertheless perform.[5] Cai's fabricated wildlife connotes in this vein, as proper taxidermy does, divisions between life and death, animation and stasis, the synthetic and the organic. Parker-Starbuck ultimately argues for taxidermy as a form of temporal mediation. "Perhaps taxidermic forms might begin, through their ability to conjure movement through stillness . . . to slip in and out of time(s) in order to throw them [humans and animals] into a more critical ongoing relationship with the present and the future."[6] Cai's menagerie, posed between the architectural extravagance of *pudong* and the colonial veneer of *puxi*, suggests how these infrastructures have affected and continue to impact the lives of human and nonhuman species. The pseudo-mammalian freight gestures to deep histories of traffic in which the question of the human repeatedly surfaces.

We might also understand Cai's work as materializing the Chthulucene insofar as the images illustrate evolving relations between the organic and the mechanical.[7] From Donna Haraway's perspective, we might see Cai in the same frame as DALeast; both artists reveal interactions among species and the ecologies they shape and in which they are embedded. Such interactivity produces the emergence of contradictions and surprising adaptations by humans and nonhumans alike. The second half of this book has tried to articulate the importance of the seascape in showing a transformation of the human as one part of an evolving ecology that involves people and technology as well as other organisms and elements that shape our planetary environment.

Cai's 2014 exhibition was shaped by and also produced movement. By August, the exhibition had already attracted twenty thousand visitors, making it the most successful show in the museum's relatively short history (it opened in 2012). The "ark" from Cai's *The Ninth Wave* stood in the center of the large atrium space that serves as the museum's entrance; its sheer size forced spectators to walk around the installation, which could also be viewed from the floors above. The piece required this sort of peripatetic spectatorship for visitors to see the full structure of the ark; it entailed a corporeal engagement and willful action on the part of a museumgoer. The dynamic between observer and artwork created a form of theatrical experience rendered all the more complex by the crowds within the museum (Shanghai is, after all, one of the most populous cities in the world).

Theatricality can engage other aspects of the sensorium in addition to visuality, proprioception, and kinesthesia. One could, for example, smell a noxious order wafting down one of the corridors on the first floor. This passageway led to Cai's related installation, *Silent Ink,* in which twenty thousand liters of black ink had been pumped into an artificial lake carved out of the gallery floor. A steady shower of obsidian-colored liquid rained from the ceiling, creating ripples across the surface. Surrounding the amoeba-shaped pool, a concrete walkway was lined with industrial detritus: rebar, broken concrete, and insulation. The sound of the small black waterfall and the overwhelming smell assaulted the visitor. This kind of physical engagement reveals another facet of theatricality produced through this manufactured Chinese seascape.[8] The sensual experience of moving through a particular space that immerses the museumgoer in industrial waste exposed the

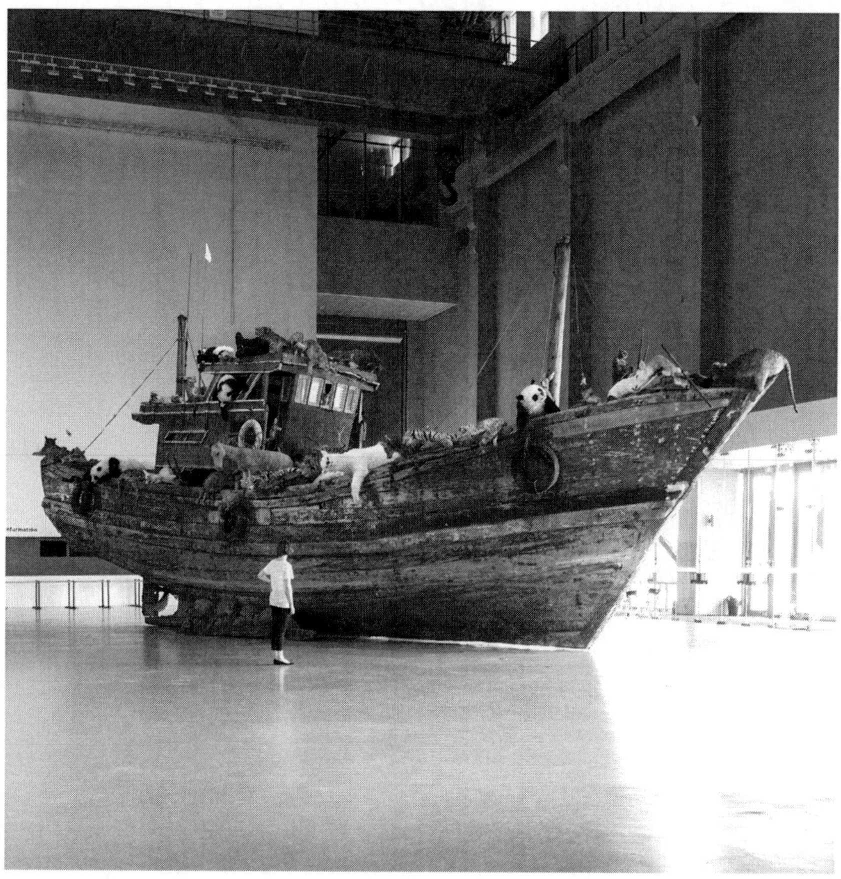

Fig. 6.3. Cai Guo-Qiang (b. 1957), *The Ninth Wave*, 2014. Installation incorporating ninety-nine life-sized replicas of animals, a wooden fishing boat, one white flag, and an electric fan. 1700 × 455 × 580 cm (669⁵/₁₆ × 179⅛ × 228⅜ in.). Power Station of Art, Shanghai. Installation view at the Power Station of Art, Shanghai, 2014. Photo by Zhang Feiyu, courtesy Cai Studio.

lopsided distribution of resources that privileges spectacle over, for example, a collective action to clean up the streets of Shanghai. The spectator's pleasure (even if paradoxically derived from the representation of environmental horror) was an affect produced by the staged event of a massive ink well. The physiological effect of inhaling whatever particles lingered in the air compounded the sensation.

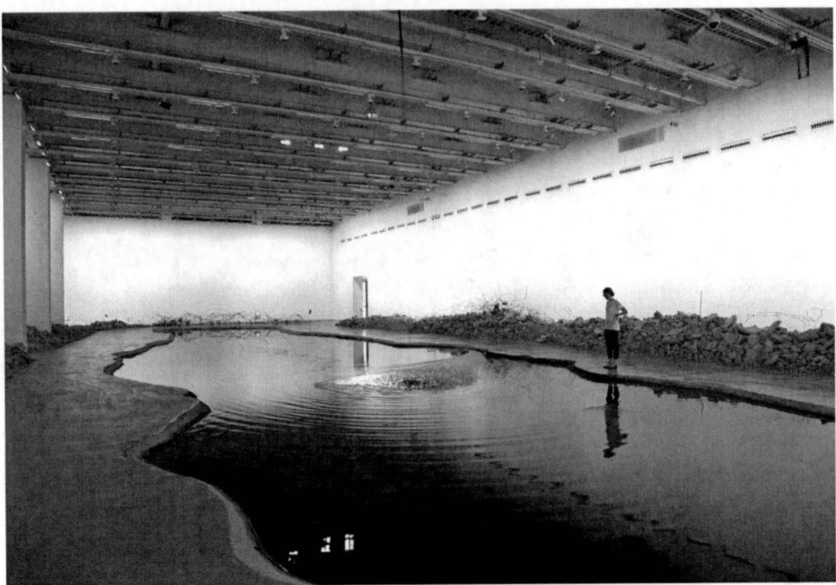

Fig. 6.4. Cai Guo-Qiang (b. 1957), *Silent Ink*, 2014. Concrete fragments, steel bars, insulation, water pump, pond: 20,000 liters of black ink. Pond: 250 square meters. Collection of the artist. Installation view at the Power Station of Art, Shanghai, 2014. Photo by Wen-You Cai, courtesy Cai Studio.

Cai's exhibition demanded that a spectator actively engage the artistic worlds he imagined in terms of both the creation of an experience and the narration of historical contexts. On its second floor, the Power Station of Art displayed a huge 400 x 2700 cm panorama of Shanghai's most iconic seascape: the Bund. Cai created the effects of transition and decay through one of his signature aesthetics. After working with volunteers to stencil images of the Bund's famous architecture along with an assortment of real (water buffalo, tigers, monkeys, deer, waterfowl, fish) and fantastic (phoenixes, humanoid giants) creatures around and on top of the buildings, Cai applied gunpowder to the drawing and then lit it, leaving behind a residue from the chemical process on the paper. The surface appears distressed; the tiny explosions leave parts of the image blacked out or otherwise obscured.

This artistic technique also references Chinese historical innovations. Gunpowder emerged in China during the ninth century, and its written

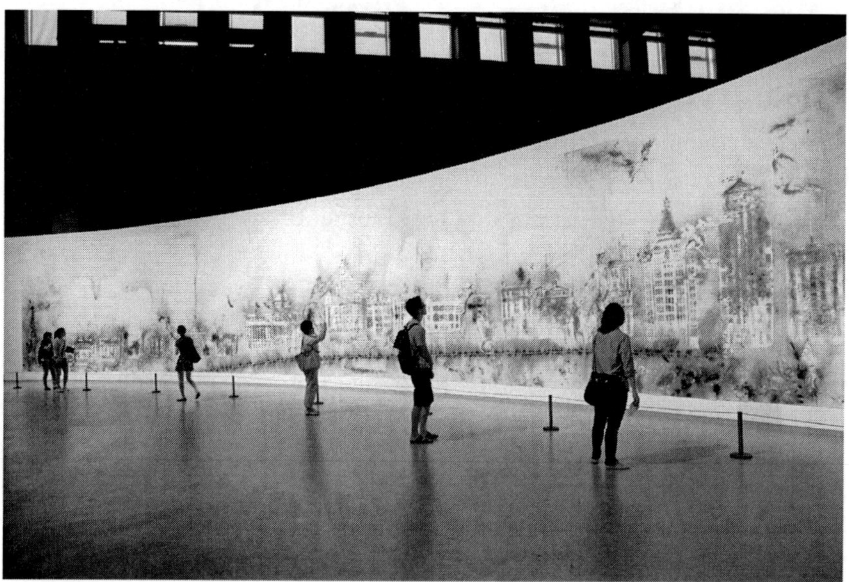

Fig. 6.5. Cai Guo-Qiang (b. 1957), *The Bund Without Us*, 2014. Gunpowder on paper. 400 × 2700 cm (157½ × 1063 in.). Bao Long Art Museum, Qingdao. Installation view at the Power Station of Art, Shanghai, 2014. Photo by Wen-You Cai, courtesy Cai Studio.

recipes appeared as early as the Song Dynasty (960–1279). Cai's use of gunpowder points to the annexations of Chinese territory by Western powers in the nineteenth century, since his chosen subject is the waterfront boulevard where banks and other elements of the colonial infrastructure developed. Cai underscores this temporal reference by including homages to late Qing Dynasty painters such as Wu Changshuo and Xu Gu. But the visions of cats and ducks provided by these artists have been radically recontextualized.[9]

Provocatively titled *The Bund Without Us*, the piece envisions an ambiguous, perhaps dystopian, future absent of people in which various other creatures dominate the city. Nevertheless, the work engages human action. The sheer size compels viewers to walk parallel to the horizontal axis of the artwork in order to discern the details. In this instance of Cai's work, theatricality might be used to describe the labor and pleasure of live bodies as they engage the remains of a performance (the lighting of the gunpowder). Depending on the distance one stands from the artwork (again, this piece could be viewed from a higher floor at a different angle), the spectator watches others scrutinize the image. These bodies become part of the image itself; despite the artwork's title, *The Bund Without Us* enables the projection of present human spectators into the future depicted. In this regard, it functions like his taxidermic creatures on the ark in facilitating a consideration of human and animal relations now and at other times.

The effect, where the space of exhibition incorporates the spectator into the implicit world evoked through the art, occurs in several of Cai's signature pieces, as well as several of the installations I have described in earlier chapters. In another room, Cai displayed *Head On*, a commission by Deutsche Bank (one of the world's largest foreign exchange dealers) that depicts ninety-nine life-size replicas of wolves, the majority of which were suspended in an arc through the air only to crash into a glass wall. The work has been exhibited all over the globe, including venues such as the Guggenheim Museum in New York (2008) and the Deutsche Guggenheim, where the show opened in 2006. Critics often read it as a commentary on a human tendency to follow the pack and a meditation on the difficulties of crossing cultural barriers (the glass surface is often understood as a reference to the Berlin Wall). Here, I am less interested in its allegorical import than in the way that the exhibit theatricalizes space. People engage the exhibit in different ways. Some stare through the transparent surface at the contorted bodies of the wolves that have careened into the glass; others stand underneath the stream of lupine sculptures (painted sheepskin stuffed with hay and metal wires with marbles for eyes) or crouch to take a selfie with one of the strays that seems to have wandered away from the pack. The dynamic space constructed for the viewer is clearly indebted to flows of transnational capital, given the Guggenheim's support of this project. The wolves might also suggest the costs of consumption, and the installation's display in Shanghai calls attention to the fact that the Deutsche Guggenheim announced its closure in 2012. Following these associations, the piece offers a means to reflect on museum space and its imbrication with various forms of financial circulations; it also encourages the museumgoer to consider one's own imbrication with such systems. Theatricality here indicates the tensions between human agents as actors and the mediated world in which they live. Following Weber's notions of a totalizing framework, the piece demands that spectators consider how we are structured by forces outside of our control.

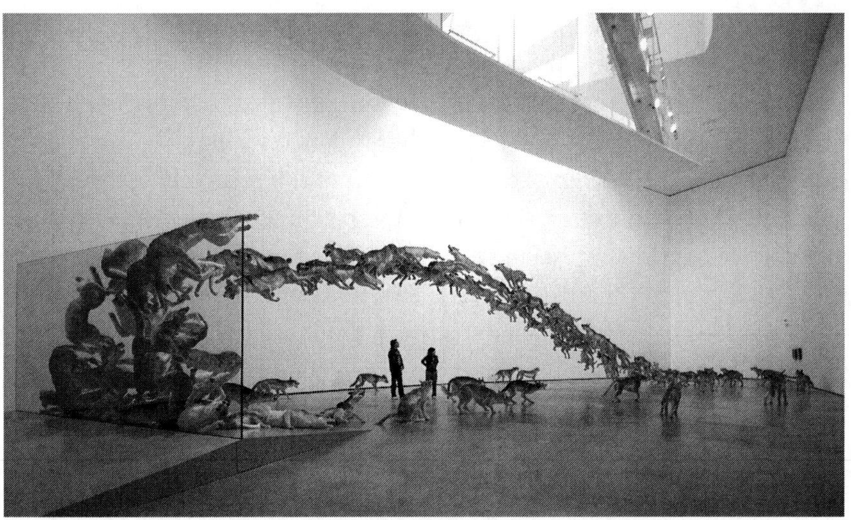

Fig. 6.6. Cai Guo-Qiang (b. 1957), *Head On*, 2006. Ninety-nine life-sized replicas of wolves and glass wall. Wolves: gauze, resin, and hide. Dimensions variable. Deutsche Bank Collection. Installation view at the Guggenheim Museum Bilbao, 2009. © FMBG Guggenheim Bilbao Museoa, 2009. Photo: Erika Barahona-Ede.

Mediation is, indeed, the final reflection offered through Cai's museum show, and this immersion in technology further ties globalization to theatricality. Weaving toward the final spaces of the exhibition, visitors entered a wide gallery space on the walls on which hung large screens. Films of several performance events looped continuously. The flat, rectangular surfaces of the screens captured Cai's explosion events from a number of sites in several countries over a span of more than two decades. These pyrotechnic displays included *Century with Mushroom Clouds: Project for the Twentieth Century* (1996), in which small puffs of smoke rise after a solitary figure activates a handheld explosive device. Performed for the camera at such locations as the Nevada Test Site and various vantage points overlooking Manhattan, these activities highlight human agency and precarity in relation to nuclear power. But the relative size and sounds of these clouds paled in comparison to the more flamboyant flashes of light from Cai's attention-grabbing pieces such as *Projects for Extraterrestrials* or his work on the 2008 Olympics. This room of the gallery immersed the spectator in screens, which represent events of different scales, from small explosions to those that fill the sky. The images suggest the ways people increasingly access information about the world that lies beyond their immediate reach.

Cai's screens play specifically with notions of scale.[10] Moving one's head toward a particular sparkle of light might result in tracking an ignited line of explosives across the surface of a building or over a relatively vast swath of land. The explosions, often shot from multiple angles, including bird's-eye views, force continual shifts in perception, despite the fact that the screens themselves do not change. Nevertheless, as Giuliana Bruno has argued, the properties of screens include "surface luminosity and textural hapticity."[11] The projections of light on these panels illuminate the viewer, creating repeatable surface encounters in contrast to the actual explosion event, which is always singular—some of the materials consumed in the act of ignition and others transformed into the smoky afterlife of the performance. Theatricality in this vein describes some of the ways in which performance expires and remains. It emphasizes both gain, in terms of a multiplication of viewing opportunities, and loss, in terms of a distancing from live events. Such dynamics characterize globalization.

The various facets of Cai's exhibition encourage one to think through and theorize seascapes in relation to globalization and theatricality. Cai's exhibition at the Power Station of Art signifies Chineseness using a wide array of technologies, including mobile objects such as boats containing pandas and stationary ones such as screens that create surface encounters by displaying technologies like fireworks. These encounters are facilitated by and also generate flows of capital and people; in this regard, and following spatial theorist Henri Lefebvre, Cai assists us in seeing space as dynamic. The confrontations of artworks and spectator-participants produce affective responses and sensory engagements. In other words, a local phenomenological experience provides access points to actual or approximated global processes (an encounter with the work of a globally successful artist or with a re-creation of toxic fumes that raises awareness about industrialization and the destruction of environmental resources).

Both Cai and DALeast address the Chthulucene—marking the destructive potential of a Chinese age, to be sure, but also the new possibilities for relation among humans and among humans and nonhumans as new industrial ontologies emerge from the increasing mechanization of life. Migrants themselves, both artists point to a new class of global circulating elites who have been given space to express the contradictions of globalization. How-ever, neither body of work would seem to be exclusively about China as such. Instead, the artists occasionally affix Chineseness, often quite indirectly, to other sorts of cultural currents, especially the movement of industrial products and the subsequent transformations of all organic beings. In this manner, they would seem to search for new forms of relation between sub-ject and object, sentient being and inanimate thing, often in relation but not reducible to genealogies of personhood.

Cai's exhibition, with which I have ended this book, foregrounds and also helps to fashion mythic and historical narratives that suggest globalization. Through a kind of writerly immersion into the details of the exhibition, I hope to have recreated the sense of being awash in a sea, a sensation that I analogize to globalization itself. This writerly gambit here and throughout this book produces disorientation constitutive of the affective dimension of globalization itself—and, of course, the churning of the ocean. Globalization submerges us in a set of evolving processes for which concrete conclusions may be of less value than a method of asking ongoing questions.

Seascapes enable us to see the shifting status of the human as we relate to and take shape through certain kinds of spatial dynamics. I have described some of these modes of visualization through selected overlapping logics—reeling, incorporating, flowing, ebbing, and eddying—that might help to parse, disambiguate, or hydrolyze the global. These logics frame ever-moving conditions. From this view, the Chinese Atlantic as an analytic that emphasizes the aquatic is necessarily incomplete, as all seascapes are. Nevertheless, submersion into this paradigm generates new ways of imagin-ing and even sensing the large-scale processes that constitute the world in which we live.

NOTES

1. Jeffrey H. Wasserstrom uses this term to describe the various ways in which Shanghai has connected China to different parts of the world at different moments of history. See his *Global Shanghai, 1850–2010: A History in Fragments* (New York: Routledge, 2009). Shanghai's early constructions of modernism and cosmopolitanism through literature, cinema, and everyday life have been well documented. See Gail Hershatter, *Dangerous Pleasures: Prostitution and Modernity in Twentieth-Century Shanghai* (Berkeley and Los Angeles: University of California Press, 1997); Leo Ou-Fan Lee, *Shanghai Modern; The Flowering of a New Urban Culture in China 1930–1945*

(Cambridge: Harvard University Press, 1999); and Zhang Zhen, *An Amorous History of the Silver Screen: Shanghai Cinema, 1896–1937* (Chicago: University of Chicago Press, 2005).

2. Becky Davis, "Q. and A.: Cai Guo-Qiang on Art, the Death of Nature and China's Modern Reality," *New York Times,* Sept. 3, 2014, http://sinosphere.blogs.nytimes.com /2014/09/03/q-and-a-cai-guo-qiang-on-art-the-death-of-nature-and-chinas-modern -reality/?ref=topics&_r=0.

3. Frank Langfitt, "China's Pollution Crisis Inspires an Unsettling Art Exhibit," NPR, August 23, 2014, http://www.npr.org/blogs/parallels/2014/08/21/342189261/chinas -pollution -crisis -inspires -an -unsettling -art -exhibit. See also Nicola Davison, "Rivers of Blood: The Dead Pigs Rotting in China's Water Supply," *The Guardian,* March 29, 2013, http://www.theguardian.com/world/2013/mar/29/dead -pigs -china -water -supply.

4. Mel Chen, *Animacies: Biopolitics, Racial Mattering, and Queer Affect* (Durham: Duke University Press, 2012), 10.

5. Jennifer Parker-Starbuck, "Animal Pasts and Presents: Taxidermied Time Travelers," in *Performing Animality: Animals in Performance Practices,* eds. Lourdes Orozco and Jennifer Parker-Starbuck (New York: Palgrave Macmillan, 2015), 150.

6. Parker-Starbuck, *Animality,* 153.

7. Donna Haraway, *Staying with the Trouble: Making Kin in the Chthulucene* (Durham: Duke University Press, 2016).

8. There are many possible references for such a lake, but, for one, see Tim Maughan, "The Dystopian Lake Filled by the World's Tech Lust," BBC April 2, 2015, http://www .bbc.com/future/story/20150402 -the -worst -place -on -earth.

9. *Cai Guo-Qiang, The Ninth Wave* (Shanghai: Power Station of Art, 2014).

10. Cohen and Frazier historicize this term, arguing that it became a matter of strategic importance during the Cold War. Deborah Cohen and Lessie Jo Frazier, "Scale: Exploring the 'Global '68,'" in *Framing the Global: Entry Points for Research,* ed. Hilary E. Kahn (Bloomington and Indianapolis: Indiana University Press, 2014).

11. Giuliano Bruno, *Surface: Matters of Aesthetics, Materiality, and Media* (Chicago: University of Chicago Press, 2014), 6.

SEAN METZGER is Professor in the School of Theater, Film and Television at the University of California at Los Angeles. He is author of *Chinese Looks: Fashion, Performance, Race* (IUP 2014) and coeditor of *Awkward Stages: Plays about Growing up Gay, Embodying Asian-American Sexualities,* and *Futures of Chinese Cinema: Technologies and Temporalities in Chinese Screen Cultures.*

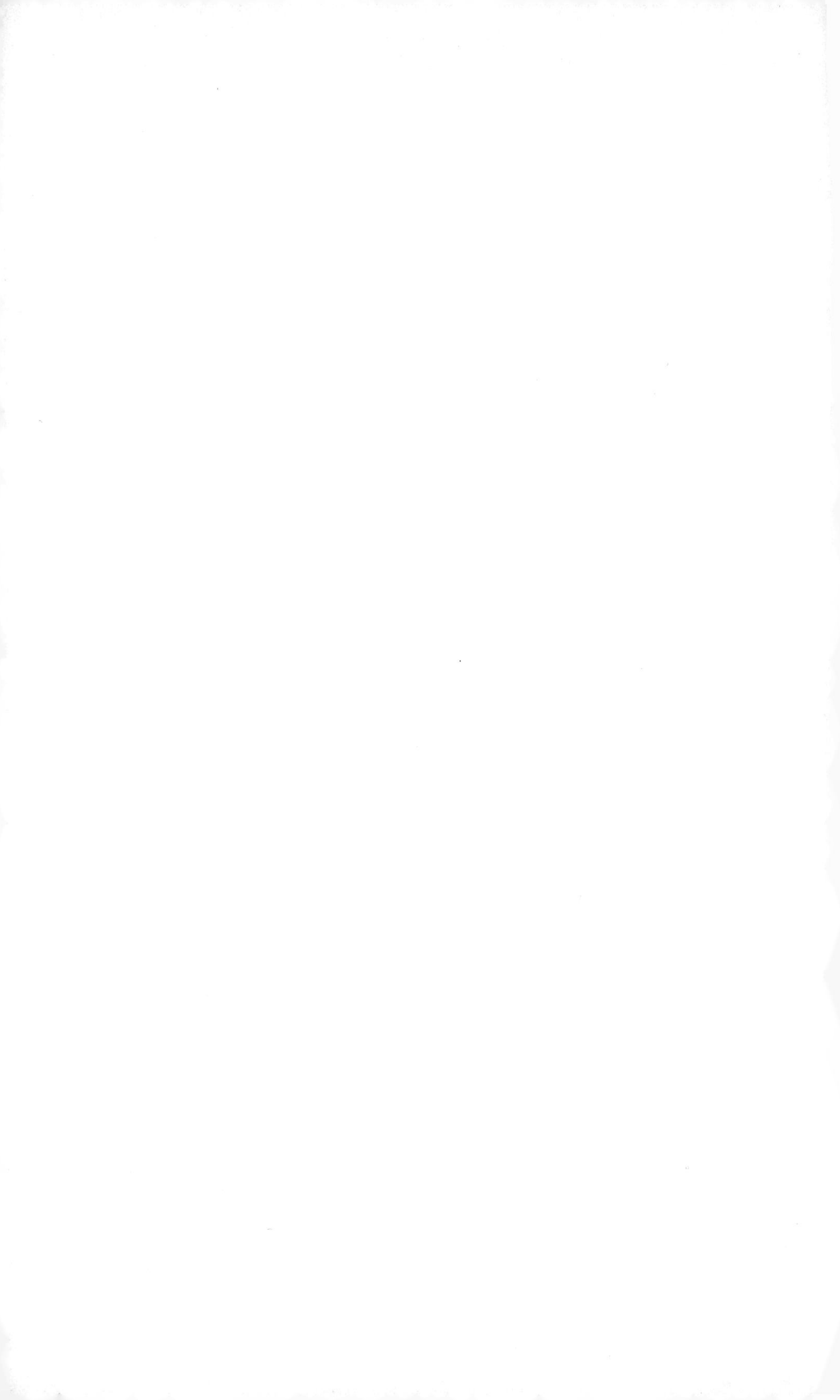